Advance Praise

"*Empathy in Action* is the essential guidebook to creating the workplace of the future. Building a more human and profitable business starts with empathy."

—ARIANNA HUFFINGTON, Founder and CEO, Thrive Global

"My number one principle in business is customer obsession. Truly understanding and anticipating your customers' needs (empathy) is not only at the heart of delivering exceptional customer experiences but is also how leaders can stay a step ahead of the blind spots that can derail even the best of companies. Tony has been at the helm of one industry transition after another, from the internet to videotelephony to video gaming apps and now, Contact Center as a Service. He has the credibility and experience to start a broader business conversation about delivering better customer experiences through empathy."

—JOHN CHAMBERS, Chairman Emeritus, Cisco and CEO, JC2 Ventures

"*Empathy in Action* touches on the new paradigm shift where consumers have certain expectations from the brands that they interact with. Loyalty is not a given—each interaction a consumer has with a company can 'reset' loyalty as competition is so fierce. This book explores how it all starts with employee satisfaction, which directly correlates with customer satisfaction. If companies want to stay relevant in this new world, these dynamics must be explored and implemented."

—ANDREA CHIN, Executive Director Global Consumer Care - IT at The Estée Lauder Companies Inc.

"Regardless of industry, the fundamental foundation for all successful businesses is exceptional customer service. This book examines why customer experience has fallen short in the past and sparks your imagination about a new world of superior, empathetic customer experiences."

—JOHN DONAHOE, President and CEO, Nike

"'Experience' happens when leaders guide their organization to behaviors and habits that earn admiration and sustainable growth. Use this book as a practical guidebook to achieve these outcomes."

—JEANNE BLISS, Best-selling author of *Chief Customer Officer 2.0*

"As we permanently shift to a digitally connected world that shapes every aspect of how we live, learn, worship, play, and work, this book provides tremendous insight into the opportunity for leaders to blend empathy and experiences in a way that leads to better business outcomes. My friend Tony has always been passionate about the consumer experience. *Empathy in Action* invites us to challenge the status quo and drive breakthrough innovation and success through a customer- and employee-centered approach."

—PAT GELSINGER, CEO, Intel

"In this fast-changing digital economy, winning enterprises are putting a laser focus on providing a world-class, end-to-end customer experience. I gained new perspectives on the power of empathy in anticipating and delivering on customer expectations. I recommend this book for anyone looking to innovate customer experience."

—SHANTANU NARAYEN, Chairman, President, and CEO, Adobe Inc.

"If you want to truly be customer-centric, then put yourself into the hands of these two CX masters, Bates and Petouhoff. From accounting for experiences on your balance sheet to spelling out how you must lead differently, *Empathy in Action* delivers a systematic, intentional approach to transform your organization. Keep this book close by because you'll be referencing it frequently!"

—CHARLENE LI, *New York Times* best-selling author of *The Disruption Mindset* and Founder, Altimeter

"If you care about your customer and employees, I recommend *Empathy in Action* for your whole organization. It's a guide for reexamining our approaches to customer and employee experience that has the potential for those daring enough to shift paradigms to transform business as we know it."

—SANDY CARTER, VP, AWS WWPS Partners and Programs

"For a decade or more, we have been talking about customer centrism and customer experience. Last year, during the pandemic, we began to hear about the importance of business empathy in realizing a great customer experience. But very little had been done about what that actually means when it's put into action. But now industry dynamo Natalie Petouhoff and Genesys CEO Tony Bates take empathy and give it substance. Not only do they help define how to see and feel the shoes the customer is in, but also what it takes to walk in those shoes. If you want to truly understand what empathy means in business, how to apply it, and how to measure how successful you have been, then this is a must-have book. So, if you feel anything for your customers, order this book and start reading it, even if you are still in your own shoes when you do. Because, trust me, by the time you are done, you will be living the book's title—*Empathy in Action*."

—PAUL GREENBERG, Best-selling author of
CRM at the Speed of Light (4 Editions)

"In an age where almost every interaction we have is through a lens of technology, too many nameless, faceless corporations have set aside the human connection for the bottom-line efficiency of technology. The secret to loyal customers isn't in technology or efficiency; it is in creating that empathetic connection at scale. In this amazing book *Empathy in Action*, Tony and Natalie have laid out a road map for leaders to lead from the front and reestablish that critical, empathetic human touch. A must-have for any leader's library."

—ALAN WEBBER, Program VP, Customer Experience Strategies, IDC.com

"Whether you are a start-up or an intrapreneur inside a company, this book is your key to become obsessed with your customers and your employees. The authors' four empathy pillars—listen, understand + predict, act, and learn—are the key to what drives innovation and disruption. I can't wait for my students and clients to dive into this book."

—JAN RYAN, Professor & Executive Director of Entrepreneurship &
Innovation at University of Texas and Partner at Capital Factory, Inc

"Empathy as a leverage tool toward employees' and customers' loyalty and company growth. *Empathy in Action* closes the gap between theory and what occurs to your customer and employee experience when you add empathy to the formula. Unlike many other books expressing the author's 'opinion,' you have a book based on facts, outstanding research, exceptional proofed results, and great ideas that will help your company evolve. We are still far from closing all experience blind spots, but this book will certainly bring you many steps closer. I highly recommend this book if you want to insert empathy in your organization effectively! A practical reading that will assist your organization to gain real market differentiation and advantage."

—RICARDO SALTZ GULKO, Cofounder of European Customer
Experience Organization

"Few people are as qualified to dissect and discuss the importance of empathy in business and culture as Dr. Natalie Petouhoff. Her deep expertise in understanding the wants, needs, and psychology of both customers and employees gives her unique insights into how better understanding leads to better business results. *Empathy in Action* will no doubt be a must-read for business leaders, the C-Suite, and even the "E-suite"—those seeking to obtain deeper levels of empathy—to better serve customers, employees, and citizens."

—**DAVID ARMANO**, Founder, Armano Design Group,
Forbes contributor, and former Edelman executive

"Companies are missing the massive opportunity to transform their transactional relationships with customers into bonds that are formed and informed by their experiences. In all my research and writing, it is clear that businesses with a traditional approach to customer service have only a matter of time before they're replaced by a vendor that truly understands and wants to help their customer. This book offers readers the rationale behind adopting a customer-centric business model and the unexpected blind spots to avoid."

—**ADRIAN SWINSCOE**, Advisor, best-selling author, and *Forbes* contributor

EMPATHY
IN ACTION

IDEAPRESS
PUBLISHING

WASHINGTON, D.C.

EMPATHY IN ACTION

HOW TO DELIVER GREAT CUSTOMER EXPERIENCES AT SCALE

TONY BATES AND
DR. NATALIE PETOUHOFF

IDEAPRESS
PUBLISHING

Ideapress Publishing | www.ideapresspublishing.com

Cover Design: Jeff Miller, Faceout
Interior Design: Jessica Angerstein
Illustrations: Shreya Jain

Cataloging-in-Publication Data is on file with the Library of Congress.

ISBN: 978-1-64687-043-1

2 3 4 5 6 7 8 9 10

We dedicate this book to Tony's mum, Val,
and Natalie's mom, Donna.

CONTENTS

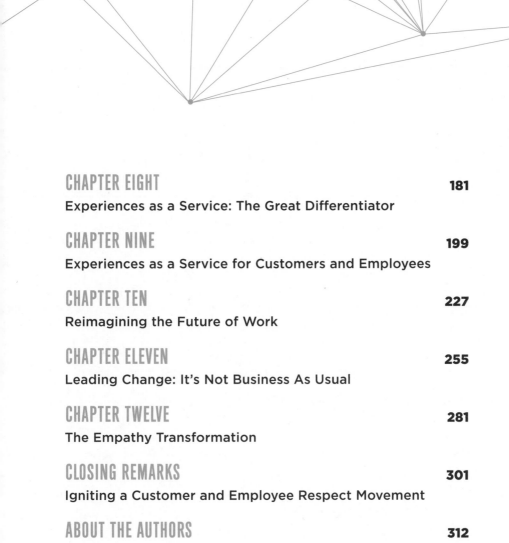

" Daring leaders who
live into their values
are never silent
about hard things.

—Brené Brown

STARTING AN INDUSTRY CONVERSATION: HOW TECHNOLOGY ENABLES A MORE EMPATHETIC WORLD

Tony's Journey

The most important mentors in my life are my mother and my wife.

Val's (my mum) "superpower" is unconditional love, and the most valuable life lesson she taught me was to "never judge anyone unless you've walked a mile in their shoes." Cori's (my wife) superpower is her never-ending ability to reach out and help others. She's a consummate "giver." Like all givers, she's highly empathetic, routinely putting others' needs above her own.

The deep wisdom and open-hearted approach to life that these women exemplify guides much of my own approach to being a CEO. When I stop and look at the bigger picture, I see a world that desperately needs more empathy. Empathy is powerful, and it holds the power to fuel better businesses, better lives, and a better society. It's not a synonym for nice. Empathy goes much deeper than that—ultimately, I've learned that it's really about respect.

Empathy is a conscious act. It's a commitment you make to understand a person in the context of their own life and experiences and then to treat them accordingly. After an empathetic interaction, the recipient feels heard, understood, and respected. But it's been missing in the business world.

Over the course of my life and career, I've become focused on the idea of technology as a tool for promoting empathy in our daily lives. Many ideas have arisen from this one simple concept, with one question leading to another. After several decades of experience as a leader and intrepreneur, I've finally arrived at the core question that inspired this book: What if empathy became as important a design factor in new products and services as functionality, efficiency, or profit?

I believe empathy is the next frontier in technology. With this book, my coauthor, Natalie, and I hope to spark a broad, industry-spanning conversation about how technology can create and enable a more empathetic world. It all begins with business owners' and industry leaders' policies and priorities, but—most importantly, as you'll see—the needs of customers and employees they serve.

I've witnessed firsthand the astounding technological evolution of the past 30-plus years. Our current era is one that's been forged by boundless imagination. As Albert Einstein said, "Imagination is everything. It is the preview of life's coming attractions." That's been my experience with technology. It is, simply put, the way our collective imagination takes form.

My career began in the mid-1980s when a group of interconnected computers run by the US Department of Defense formed as the precursor to the internet of today. This network was called ARPANET (Advanced Research Projects Agency Network).

ARPANET proliferated by connecting computers at dozens of universities across the United States, including UC Berkeley, Stanford, and MIT. In my first job as a network operator at the University of London Computer Centre (ULCC), we imagined the impossible: What if those ARPANET gateways could connect these colleges to European universities all the way across the Atlantic Ocean? We did just that, running the ARPANET gateway pioneered out of the work of Peter Kirstein at University College London.

Later, we connected NASA and the NSF net over a tiny 512K connection from the United Kingdom to the United States. Ironically, we called it the "fat-pipe project." Finally, we were able to transition the United Kingdom from its own proprietary networking standards to a common standard enabling computers to communicate on a network using the Transmission Control Protocol/Internet Protocol, or the internet as we know it today.

By the time I moved to Northern Virginia in 1994 to work at MCI, I was helping build the largest internet network in the world. At the time, the World Wide Web and browser had been recently invented, showing new ways to access information and communicate.

These early career experiences were not inconsequential; they were foundational to the ubiquitous global internet we use today—and they also provided a blueprint for my career, which has been shaped by a passion for technology and the extraordinary mentors who were able to transcend current thinking and teach me to envision incredible new realities.

My early mentors were John Seymour at the University of London Computer Centre, and the late Peter Kirstein at the University College London. And, later, Graeme Fraser taught me to think big; Mike Volpi taught me about the power of communication; John Chambers taught me about vision; John Donahoe taught me about mission and purpose; Randy Pond taught me about humility; Steve Ballmer taught me about scale and the power of data; and Pierre Lamond taught me that experience matters and you must be ensconced in the fundamentals of your product and business.

The bulk of my career, more than 14 years, was spent at Cisco during the internet boom. Cisco's vision was "changing the way we work, live, play and learn"—and that's exactly what we delivered to the world.[1] When I joined Cisco in 1996, 20 million American adults had access to the internet—a population about the size of New York.[2] By the time I left Cisco in 2010, there were two billion internet users worldwide[3] and 255 million websites.[4]

Today, just a short time later, almost 4.66 billion people are active internet users—almost 60 percent of the world's population.[5] Change is accelerating beyond anything we could have imagined.

During this period, I was also working on integrating Scientific Atlanta. This 50-year-old company provided digital set-top boxes for the home and was one of the most significant acquisitions in Cisco's history. I gained an appreciation for the enormous complexity required in integrating and harmonizing systems to support live video streaming. I also learned that if you want to imagine the future, you must look beyond the comfortable reality of today. In this case, the market capturing my attention, video-over-the-internet, was also disrupting the market that had served me so well: building and selling internet routers to telecom service providers.

Around this time, my interests shifted from hardware routing for service providers and enterprises to bringing video-over-the-internet into consumers' homes. I was on the YouTube board and could see that the lines between business and consumer, which had been separate worlds, were blurring. I saw video-as-a-platform as a means of human expression and had my first inklings of imagining personalized experiences and moments connected via technology.

Eventually, my passion for video and the customers' experience led me to accept a leadership role at Skype in 2010. My vision for Skype was to create a virtual town square, a virtual piazza, a gathering place. I loved the product and was enamored with the consumer brand; great customer experience stories are so much more compelling than a company name. Skype ushered in a new reality of online video conferencing for personal and professional use.

Often, unforeseen global market conditions can change business in the blink of an eye. During the global COVID-19 pandemic, where would we have been without tools like Skype, Zoom, and Microsoft Teams for our work, our families, and our communities as a whole? These have become our "new normal."

I didn't learn from success alone, however. In spite of Skype's success during the early 2000s, we had made one glaring mistake: we were late to mobile. In 2010, the number of cell phones sold worldwide was about 300 million.[6] By 2012, that number had more than doubled to 680 million.[7]

Later, while I was president of GoPro, the now-famous maker of action cameras, mobile apps, and video-editing software, I witnessed another missed opportunity. While the success of the moment was exhilarating—we were growing like gangbusters from $1.34 billion in 2014 to $1.6 billion one year later—we didn't seize the bigger picture: evolving from a product company to a platform company.[8] This cost GoPro in the long run.

These mistakes represent important lessons and they highlight a topic we discuss at length in this book: the danger of blind spots.

Currently, I am chairman and CEO of Genesys®. When I joined in May 2019, Genesys checked every box for me. It's a global company with a great customer base. The size, at about $1.5 billion in revenue with 5,000 employees, was perfect. Small enough that you can introduce a vision, create change, and be impactful—perhaps even double the business—but large enough that you can implement the corporate leadership required to scale. It was also ripe for transformation as a market leader offering on-premise contact center solutions in a world quickly moving to the cloud. Genesys also provided a once-in-a-lifetime chance to apply all I've learned about transcending current thinking and innovating ahead of my competitors.

The key to both was a concept I'd seen modeled throughout my life: the innovation we and so many others needed was empathy.

This was the true lightbulb moment that propelled me toward a radical new future, and it is the reason this book was written.

A recent global study of 5,000 adults found that customer service, while seen as more efficient than in the past, is widely experienced as impersonal by those who engage with it.[9] While a majority (71 percent) believe that customer service has become more personalized, nearly half (48 percent) still note a distinct lack of compassion in the way they experience it.[10]

What would a better, more empathetic reality look like? How would our industries improve if people truly felt they were being treated with compassion and empathy throughout their customer service interactions?

As I started my new Genesys journey and my burgeoning focus on empathy as strategy, I was introduced to Dr. Natalie Petouhoff, a thought leader, a brilliant researcher, and a published author in the customer experience space. The timing was perfect. She was intrigued by the same questions running through my own mind.

I think you know where those questions led us—after all, you're reading the answer right now. By the end of our journey together, I hope you'll be ready to answer a whole new set of questions for yourself and your businesses.

Natalie's Journey

Like Tony, I had a mother who formed the heart and center of our family. She made everything special—and she made sure we all knew just how much and how deeply she loved us.

I learned a great deal from witnessing her passion as a teacher. She fought hard to educate others and, by doing so, guided them toward a better standard of living. Thanks to her unconditional love and guidance, I grew up truly believing I could make a difference in people's lives and that anything was possible.

As an ode to that boundless faith in the power of human belief, I carry a famous quote by Eleanor Roosevelt in my wallet. On July 4, 1957, the First Lady wrote: "The future belongs to those who believe in the beauty of their dreams."

My mother had beautiful dreams, and she taught me to dream the same way.

We lost my mother when I was 14. I was able to carry on her legacy by helping to raise my three siblings, all of whom became amazing adults that continue to make the world a better place through their unique accomplishments.

As the daughter of a dedicated teacher, a strong education was always a priority for me. After completing a course of study at the University of Michigan, I was awarded a fellowship by General Motors. This support allowed me to pursue a PhD at UCLA in material science and engineering. Learning about the complex workings of the world around me transformed my entire worldview.

Pursuing my PhD thesis in high-energy particle physics was one of many endeavors in critical thinking. My education taught me to ask why things are the way they are and to wonder if there was a better way to make them happen. As part of my thesis, I looked at the materials used to make spaceflight possible.

On a deeper level, I was learning more than the lessons of the moment—I was learning to look at root causes and solve problems in new ways.

Despite the drama of launch sequences and the incredible image of astronauts walking among the stars, spaceflight is one of the most dangerous parts of a crew's return to Earth. For a long time, many of the materials used to withstand the high temperatures encountered on reentry were too brittle. Under such intense pressure, they often cracked and peeled, leaving the exposed vehicle in danger of burning up.

Throughout my research process, I examined how technology could be used to transform these materials and how they might be combined in new ways to deliver on the promise of a safe return home for astronauts and their crews. I had to reimagine the creation of those materials, rearranging the molecules atom by atom. On a physical level, this was accomplished using cutting-edge technology such as high-energy particle accelerators. By transforming materials in novel ways—often through the use of Earth's most powerful machines—a vehicle's alloy surface could withstand extreme temperatures and remain flexible, allowing it to withstand reentry forces and bring our passengers home.

My experiences gave me an entirely new lens through which to view the world.

As I embarked on my own "flight" into the working world, I used similar critical-thinking skills to reimagine the problems I was tasked with solving. These were the largest challenges faced by the biggest organizations, including industry leaders like General Motors and General Electric.

Time and time again, my work was a process of looking at the way things were and asking, "Does this make sense?" "Are there any other, better ways to deliver on these same promises?"

As it turns out, asking these questions aloud can be very hard. I often found people doing what they were told without question, let alone answering any of the questions living between the lines. It's always easier to fly below the radar. I saw that this was true even if the things people were doing made little sense for customers, employees, or companies as a whole.

One of my first forays into the customer experience field came when GM asked me to evaluate whether we should continue the use of two-sided galvanizing to prevent corrosion of car and truck bodies. This is a process that coats the metal in superheated zinc to form a chemical "shield" that protects it from corrosion. The financial department was looking at cost-cutting strategies. As engineers, we worried that reducing the corrosion protection would damage our brand if our cars had large holes in the sides. After the corrosion testing came back and showed that the car doors would rust more without double galvanizing, I asked what the leadership's decision was going to be. I assumed that they would come to the same conclusion I had: despite the cost, double galvanizing was necessary to ensure our vehicles' quality in the long-term.

GM's team responded that they were choosing to go with one-sided galvanizing instead of the double-sided method I had suggested. For me, the obvious choice has always been to produce a better product and a better customer experience.

I asked them, "Aren't you concerned about the customer's experience with our products?" Their reply? "You're an engineer! Not a marketer. Why are you so concerned with what the customer thinks?" Unfortunately, this wouldn't be the last time I was faced with shifting paradigms in cultures to help others see the situation from the customer's point of view.

In my work at Hughes Electronics, I straddled working as an engineer on the radar systems used to guide pilots (our customers) on their missions, and leading internal programs for employees. I designed their integrated product development employee teaming initiative where all disciplines from various departments—marketing, sales, engineering, finance—came together for the first time to work as one team. This multidisciplinary approach for Hughes increased their ability to deliver projects on time, within budget and scope, with a customer-centric approach. I also created the employee development program, allowing a synergistic focus of employee's personal and professional goals. By creating a separate employee development process that focused on What's in It for Me? (WIIFM), it zeroed in on their passions, desire to learn, and grow, their productivity and quality of their work improved by 30 percent.

As I progressed in my career as a management consultant, I led the transformation of both customer and employee experiences through the implementation of new strategies and the latest technologies. Organizational change management became one of the most important aspects of any technology transformation project—without it, the hearts and minds of the employees aligning on people-centric, large transformation projects had a failure rate of 70 percent.[11] With it, companies found themselves leapfrogging ahead of those that were stuck and unwilling to disrupt themselves.

As a customer experience industry analyst at Forrester, I not only advised brands in the latest trends in customer and employee experience, but also analyzed technical capabilities of vendors who provided the related technology, including Salesforce, Oracle, Microsoft, and SAP.

As the global digital strategist at Weber Shandwick, coming of age at the advent of the digital tech revolution, I learned the value of brand reputation and how vital it can be to an organization's financial strength. I watched as customers gained more and more power as they routinely posted online reviews with brutal honesty—for better or worse—where companies' bottom lines were concerned.

My work at Salesforce (one of the first vendors to empower companies with Software-as-a-Service) provided further sights into how technology companies develop and create the tools organizations use to deliver on the promise of customer and employee experience.

For me, these experiences reinforced the need for companies to rethink their basic strategies and the technologies they rely on from a customer and employee perspective, as opposed to a company-only one.

My decision to join Genesys was founded on the personal goal of working with a company committed to changing the status quo for customer and employee experiences. The guidance I and my colleagues provide every day proves a customer/employee-centric focus is not only better for a business' customers and employees, but also for the company as a whole.

My customer-centric focus has earned me the honor of many industry and media awards, including a spot on Forbes' "Top 100 Most Influential Women in the World" list, and "Top 50 Customer Experience Professionals."

All of this makes me wonder: Why are these experience-first models still neglected by so many organizations? Part of it was their financial models, and part of it was that it's only now, for the first time in history, we actually have the technology to make experience-first strategies possible.

And at the same time, it's not technology alone, but how we design the technology so when people interact with it, it creates a better outcome for individuals and their organizations. If there's one thing I've learned, it's this: our most incredible technological advances are nothing more and nothing less than a pure expression of what *we* think is most important in the world. In short, we are living in a time when empathy and technology can become a single, unifying force for success.

Start there, and you'll have taken the first step into a whole new world. And with our experience and passion for the technology fueling these changes, I hope that Tony and I can be the first to welcome you to the age of Empathy in Action™.

Our Journey

Through the experiences we've shared above, Natalie and I discovered a shared vision and purpose and set out to write this book. We hope to do nothing short of sparking a business movement prioritizing empathy as the customer and employee experience industry's central focus.

For more than a year, we've collaborated, one chapter at a time. Dr. Petouhoff's gifts for ideation and synthesizing our ideas resulted in frameworks which have brought our shared philosophy to life in a language any practitioner would understand.

As we were exploring the transformation of experiences, we noted that traditional experiences are measured by using business-centric metrics of efficiency and effectiveness, where cost-cutting is the main objective, represented by this formula:

$$\text{Business-Centric Experiences Focus} = \text{Cost Cutting} = \text{Efficiency} + \text{Effectiveness}$$

The true epiphany was when we white-boarded what we'd eventually name the Empathy in Action Equation. When a company looks at experiences through the lens of its customers and employees, (i.e., the definition of empathy is to put yourself in another's shoes) everything about the experience changes, from the metrics we use to measure it to the experiences themselves. Efficiency and effectiveness now become customer-employee loyalty creating metrics instead of cost-cutting measures, with empathy becoming an exponential force multiplier.

$$\underbrace{\begin{array}{c}\text{Customer/Employee-Centric} \\ \text{Experiences} \\ \text{Focus = Loyalty}\end{array} = \left(\text{Efficiency x Effectiveness}\right)^{\text{Empathy}}}$$

THE EMPATHY IN ACTION™ EQUATION

The old ways are dying. Organizations that continue to put all of their time and resources driven by traditional metrics focused solely into short-term, company-focused efficiency and effectiveness without utilizing empathy as their driving force will fail to survive in this new, incredibly interconnected era.

No matter the industry, empathy can and will be an unparalleled exponent that garners trust, and trust creates loyalty. True loyalty leaders will employ a paradigm that puts people where they belong: at the core of who you are and what your organization does.

The good news? You don't have to make these changes alone. Today's technologies have matured to a point where we can use tools like AI to contextualize company and third-party data in a holistic configuration—one that delivers empathic customer and employee experiences consistently, no matter which part of your organization they are interacting with.

It's time to revolutionize the way we work. Ours is a future centered around empathy—as the authors of this book, we envision a reality where the who informs the what of the work we do, the strategies we implement, and the priorities we champion. We're ready to ask the right questions and to wonder at the possibility of a world in which a company's prosperity is indistinguishably linked to the lived experiences of those who fuel it: employees and the customers they serve.

In a world connected like never before, there's no going back to the narrow focus of the past. The age of empathy is here, and it is opening doors we never knew existed. The only question that remains is this: Are you and your business ready to embrace and lead the changes to come?

We hope that, by the end of this book, your answer will be a resounding, confident YES and you will join us in that conversation.

" Continuing to do the
same thing while
expecting or wanting
different results is
the definition of
insanity.

—Albert Einstein

Chapter One

TECHNOLOGY: EVOLUTION, EXPERIENCES, AND EMPATHY

The Empathetic Business: What It Means to Put People First

For years, leading experts such as Tom Peters, Don Peppers, Martha Rogers, Peter Drucker, Joe Pine, James Gilmore, Fred Reichheld, Amy C. Edmondson, Simon Sinek, and others have made a point to emphasize the importance of customer experience (CX) and employee experience (EX). It's not hard to understand why—but how often do organizations really heed the experts' advice?

Many companies think they provide great customer and employee experiences, but most customers and employees wouldn't agree.[1] Research paints a picture of why this paradox is so common—while 71 percent of companies cite overall customer experience as their top strategic performance measure, only 13 percent of those same organizations self-rate their customer experience delivery as scoring a 9 out of 10 or better.[2]

The majority of companies are still operating under the long-held belief that putting their focus on business-centric goals will make them market leaders, thereby driving their own unprecedented business growth. In this narrow equation, amazing, categorically human experiences aren't nearly as important as the revenue they provide.

While the shift toward customer and employee centricity still hasn't happened in many companies, business success is nonetheless dependent on the revenue generated by those customers, and that revenue is indisputably generated by the employees who work to serve them. With this in mind, we sought to understand how shifting from a business-centric (B-centric) focus to a customer/employee-centric (C&E-centric) focus could affect businesses' success. Like many others, we believe that the way customers and employees are treated influences a company's overall success. What we learned from our research was just how significant that effect truly is.

In targeted studies, researchers found that companies who demonstrably make customer/employee centricity their focus see a 92 percent increase in customer loyalty, an 84 percent uplift in revenue, and a 79 percent margin in costs saved.[3]

In such cases, the numbers speak for themselves. So where are businesses going wrong? And if customer and employee experiences are so important, why haven't they truly become the driving force behind the decisions businesses are making?

We explored these questions at length, and we'll share what we found in the coming chapters. These discoveries are the missing pieces of the puzzle that makes implementing empathy so frustrating. And we'll explore innovative, empathic approaches to business that generate more profit and, at the same time, consistently create more positive customer and employee experiences.

Of course, it pays (in this case, literally) to start with some basic definitions.

What's Empathy Got to Do with It?

The word "empathy" has many interpretations. Many confuse empathy with sympathy, and though related, the words have very different meanings. Sympathy involves an understanding based on your own perspective: it can be a feeling of pity or compassion when you see someone in a difficult situation.

Empathy involves putting yourself in another person's shoes and understanding why they may feel a particular way. With that understanding, you can put empathy into action by taking steps to help that person based on their perspective—not your own.

Daniel Goleman, author of *Emotional Intelligence*,[4] lays out three definitions of empathy:

- Cognitive Empathy: The ability to understand another's perspective
- Emotional Empathy: The ability to physically feel what another person feels
- Empathic Concern: The ability to sense what others need from you

We want to be clear—this book is not about creating a "Kumbaya Factory," in fact, we've adapted Goleman's cognitive definition of empathy. Our aim is to outline a business-focused definition of empathy with a three-way lens to view the world. This adapted definition describes empathy as

The act of a company putting themselves in the shoes of their customers and employees to reorient the way they make decisions and conduct business, resulting in amazing customer/employee-centric experiences.

The premise is that for companies to really grow and disrupt their industries, they need to look at how they do business and focus on an empathetic perspective (Figure 1.1). We explore how moving from a business-centric paradigm to a customer/employee-centric approach transforms the roles of people, process, strategy, finance, and leadership—as well as the use of exponential technologies to deliver exceptional customer and employee experiences. Why exponential technologies? They can uniquely drive accelerated rates of change with groundbreaking capabilities unlike any other type of technology we've experienced before.

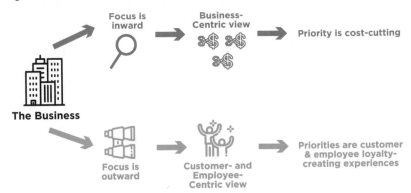

Figure 1.1 A business' focus determines its priorities.

We're at a technological tipping point where we can meet the criteria of customers, employees, and companies for the first time in history. Using the late professor Clayton Christensen's jobs-to-be-done theory,[5] we found that when exponential technologies are deployed, companies can redefine the meaning behind business-centric metrics like efficiency and effectiveness, transform the experiences they deliver, and connect how customer/employee-centric experiences deliver better financial results for the company.

We've labeled the process of creating customer/employee-centric business models the Empathy in Action Flywheel™. Throughout the rest of this book, we explore the essential elements of this process—specifically, customer/employee-centric business strategies (Chapters 2, 3, and 8), relevant financial metrics (Chapter 4), empathetic leadership (Chapters 11 and 12), trust-based organizational models and cultures (Chapters 7 and 10), and empathetic technology (Chapters 5, 6, and 9). When these elements are synchronized, leaders have the opportunity to transform the business landscape in a truly world-changing way.

By combining expert theories and principles—drawn from sources as diverse as history, neuroscience, psychology, management theory, and the evolution of technology—we've used hindsight and the resulting insight to create a powerful new perspective to aid the foresight of business leaders. Use this book as a guiding lens and consider all the principles and methodologies as tools to paint the full picture of your organization's future.

Humanity's Superpower: How Technology Shapes Lives and Business

While we are rarely conscious of just how big a role technology has played in shaping our shared reality, it is a fact that's been present since the beginning of human evolution (Figure 1.2). Though some innovations are small and others are significant beyond our imagination, each one brings something new and valuable to our world.

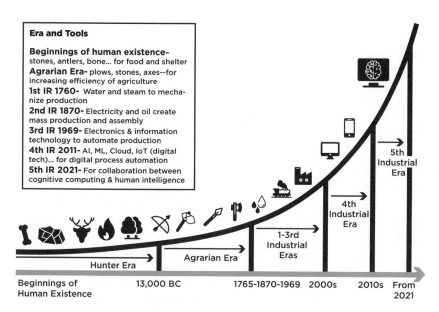

Era and Tools

Beginnings of human existence- stones, antlers, bone... for food and shelter

Agrarian Era- plows, stones, axes--for increasing efficiency of agriculture

1st IR 1760- Water and steam to mechanize production

2nd IR 1870- Electricity and oil create mass production and assembly

3rd IR 1969- Electronics & information technology to automate production

4th IR 2011- AI, ML, Cloud, IoT (digital tech)... for digital process automation

5th IR 2021- For collaboration between cognitive computing & human intelligence

Hunter Era

Agrarian Era

1-3rd Industrial Eras

4th Industrial Era

5th Industrial Era

Beginnings of Human Existence

13,000 BC

1765-1870-1969 2000s 2010s From 2021

Figure 1.2 As technology evolves, it shapes our societies.
Source: Explain That Stuff: Technology Time Line[6]

From the Stone Age to the Bronze Age, through the Iron Age and Industrial Revolutions, our technological advances enabled us to transform from nomadic hunters into agrarian city-builders, then into industrial powerhouses and, finally, into the information-based societies of today. Over the span of millennia, we found ways to do more in less time, and through each innovation, we found ourselves evolving to the next level of capability, the next revolutionary shift, and the next adaptation. No other animal on Earth can invent the way we do. Technology, more than anything else, is what drives human ingenuity.

In fact, experts inextricably connect the various phases in our species' evolution with the dominant engineering materials, tools, and technology of that period. They choose to label our history based on this feature, over and beyond our linguistic prowess, our complex social interactions, or our economic achievements.

To see why, we need to travel back in time and look at how everything we know—from where we lived to how we worked, what our homes and communities looked like, to the social structures and the support that governed us—shifted in response to the predominant technology of each era (Figure 1.3). Some of the most dramatic changes occurred when we shifted from agrarian societies to the First and Second Industrial Revolutions (the ages of steam and electricity).

The combination of the combustion steam engine and electricity to power farms, city grids, and factories created some of the most powerful and impactful technological advancements in history. Before the first two revolutions, most families around the world worked as subsistence farmers, and a few artisans worked as blacksmiths or jewelers, creating handcrafted goods to sell or relying on wealthy patrons to purchase their labor.

This changed around the eighteenth century. With the advent of efficient, tireless steam-powered engines, wealthy people began buying small farms, turning the land into patchwork, large-scale agricultural operations.[7] This change in technology meant fewer jobs for farmers, so many of them migrated to cities. The lifestyle they had known for centuries changed in a matter of decades. Their homes, their communities, and their day-to-day work underwent a substantial change.

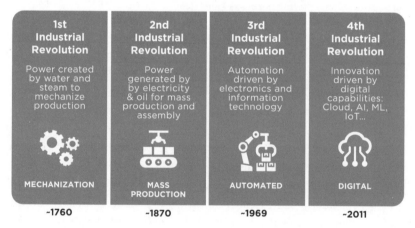

1st Industrial Revolution	2nd Industrial Revolution	3rd Industrial Revolution	4th Industrial Revolution
Power created by water and steam to mechanize production	Power generated by by electricity & oil for mass production and assembly	Automation driven by electronics and information technology	Innovation driven by digital capabilities: Cloud, AI, ML, IoT...
MECHANIZATION	MASS PRODUCTION	AUTOMATED	DIGITAL
~1760	~1870	~1969	~2011

Figure 1.3 Four industrial revolutions that have driven changes in our lives. Source: Desoutter Tools and Wikipedia.org[8]

In America alone, 11 million people migrated from rural to urban areas looking for work between 1870 and 1920. Technology had replaced them in fields and orchards. Around the same time, an additional 25 million immigrants, mostly from Europe, came to the United States and moved directly into the nation's cities.[9] Tenement housing sprung up to accommodate this large migration of people, but ultimately, the infrastructure of the nation was wholly unprepared.

It's hard to imagine what it must have been like to go from living in the open-air countryside to dwelling in dirty, unsafe, and hastily constructed houses—houses without indoor plumbing and which left tens of thousands vulnerable to rapidly spreading illnesses and terrible disasters like the infamous fires that claimed hundreds of lives in Chicago, New York, and San Francisco.[10]

The human cost of the Western Industrial Revolutions provides a stark example of what can happen when the human elements of life are neglected in favor of profit-centric business models. The uninhibited, business-centric use of steam and electrical power in factories led to mass production and economies of scale, creating a newly minted middle class.[11] There was clearly potential for pure, positive change, if only businesses chose to use foresight rather than act with insulated zealousness, without regard to the effect on employees who made it possible.

Unfortunately, the daily reality for many people was cramped factories singularly focused on business-centric efficiency, and workers were thoughtlessly exposed to many risks—including terrible injuries from machinery, lung problems due to poor ventilation, and exposure to toxic solvents and heavy metals. This came with 10- to 14-hour workdays, six days a week.[12] In their eagerness for business-centric notions of "progress," companies polluted rivers, oceans, and lakes, and the air was turned black as toxic waste bellowed from unregulated factories. In many places, it was unsafe to drink, swim, or at times, even breathe.

But for all these negative effects on society, we ought to remember the positive ones, too. Namely, the sharp increase in wealth for the middle and upper class and medical developments. Discoveries such as Edward Jenner's invention of the smallpox vaccine and Louis Pasteur's discovery of bacteria improved health care, and people began to live longer. There were glimmers of a better world on the horizon—we just needed the right people to pursue the opportunities they represented.

Eventually, they did. Workers formed labor unions, receiving higher wages and better working conditions through collaborative effort. As a result of their activism, these neglected laborers finally began to see the benefits of the first two industrial revolutions as well. Inventions like the spinning jenny meant textiles like clothing and bedding were available in greater variety, and factory innovations like the assembly line meant goods such as cars and refrigerators became accessible—making daily life much easier for the masses.

Many years after the Second Industrial Revolution, the effects of that era's technology continue to shape our lives and culture. Natalie remembers the brownstone she grew up in, located in the industrial hub of New York City. The entire family lived in that home—aunts, uncles, grandparents, and cousins. But when her father was offered a position to build one of the largest automotive assembly plants in the world deep in rural Kentucky, her parents moved her and her siblings there.

She no longer had the family support structure of grandparents and aunts and uncles within one dwelling, and she had to adapt. Natalie's family was not alone in this type of migration. As new rural factories opened throughout the world, hundreds of thousands of families moved to work in them. This created unprecedented business opportunities focused on serving these new communities. We saw the creation of a vast network of freeways, huge shopping malls, and large, organized suburban housing developments. This formed the heart of what many Americans still view as the "American Dream." That dream, in its best form, combined the technological innovations of the era with a passion for making life better—and many businesses wanted to do this for as many people as possible.

It was not all sunshine and roses, of course. As we explore the cultural and societal impacts of technological change in later chapters, we'll also look at examples of where companies missed the mark.

Ultimately, your ability to succeed for the long-term and truly reach people on a deeper level comes down to three things.

The Innovation Trifecta: Hindsight, Insight, and Foresight

We've covered the basic concept of technological evolution, but now we need to take it further. After all, technology has evolved far beyond factory machines and steam-powered tractors. As we move deeper into the information age, entrepreneurs are poised to shape the future of business, culture, and lived experience like never before. To determine whether using a customer/employee-centric view could truly change the business landscape at the level of prior revolutions, we first looked at the role empathy, trust, and loyalty now play in our businesses and our lives.

Why is it so important to look at technology through the lens of empathy, trust, and loyalty? Until now, technology's potential has generally been applied with a focus on company-only, cost-cutting efficiency and effectiveness. In this paradigm, there is little to no emphasis on customer or employee centricity, often to the detriment of the overall customer and employee experience.

In basic terms, this is the primary reason so many companies and businesses find themselves stagnating, with high turnover, widespread burnout, and a lack of anything resembling a consistent, loyal, or trusting customer base.

To put it bluntly, most companies have a problem with blind spots.

What Are Business Blind Spots?

As we studied the many ways in which technological evolution creates new business opportunities, we also observed how the criteria for business success rarely evolves at the same rate. Instead, priorities often remain stuck in the realm of our business-centric past. To honor the creators of the Johari Window (Joseph Luft and Harry Ingram[13]), we call these outdated operating mindsets and stale paradigms business blind spots.

Business blind spots, even when they emerge from the best of intentions, can severely inhibit a company's ability to succeed. This is especially true in our exponentially driven, intensely connected digital world. To bring these blind spots to life and help you, well, spot them, we've given them feature boxes in each chapter.

> **Blind Spot**
>
> A blind spot is something that you don't know you don't know. Shining a light on them puts them squarely in your line of sight; once visible, they are an opportunity to rethink the way companies are run.

By looking at business strategy from customers' and employees' point of view, it quickly becomes obvious what companies must change—or, if neglected, what will cause them to get left behind by savvy competitors. The purpose of implementing these changes is to ultimately lead to the kind of customer and employee trust required to acquire their loyalty . . . and to then drive significantly higher revenues and improve margins for the business as a whole—all things that Wall Street, investors, and other stakeholders want, too.

Taking inspiration from the work of renowned entrepreneur and philosopher Werner Erhard,[14] we define a business blind spot as something "you don't know that you don't know" about the way you operate your business. True to term, companies typically don't realize they even have blind spots—or that they need to devote serious work to finding and fixing them.

At first glance, some may not seem like a blind spot at all until we unravel how it could be obstructing success, that is. In other cases, you may recognize a blind spot in your own business but find yourself unsure of how to resolve it.

We provide answers for you in this book, but you'll need an open mind and a willingness to consider some major changes to your current strategy to make them work. After all, as the late, great Albert Einstein said, "Continuing to do the same thing while expecting or wanting different results is the definition of insanity."[15] That quote perfectly sums up the core of our next principle: the status quo trap.

What's the status quo trap? Well, it's pretty self-explanatory and also extremely common; you can blame that largely on human nature. As a basic rule, we like routines. For some reason, we also don't like to admit we like routines when it comes to the realm of business and innovation. The result is that we often fall into day-to-day habits that soon don't even feel like habits—after a while, they're "just the way things are done." Until we address that, we can't make much progress on our road to clarity. Sure, you can make changes without recognizing your deeper routines, but will they be the right changes?

Probably not.

Our research found that, when leaders do make changes, business growth often doesn't follow as expected. Why? They hadn't taken the time to recognize a blind spot; therefore, they missed the opportunity to turn it into a competitive advantage. When blind spots remain out of sight in this way, they present hidden obstacles that trip up businesses and prevent them from delivering the intended result.

Our goal is to give you a way to put blind spots squarely in your line of sight. Once you learn to see them, these revealed business blind spots become opportunities to rethink the way you run your business. From there, the road to disruptive innovation becomes a lot clearer.

Experiences Can't Be Afterthoughts: Where Blind Spots Like to Hide

Customers and employees are directly connected to a brand's reputation, constituent loyalty, and financial success. This has never been more true than it is today.

In the *Harvard Business Review* article "Loyalty Economy," researcher Rob Markey shows how companies that lead in customer loyalty grow revenue at a rate 2.5 times faster than their industry peers, and they deliver two to five times the shareholder returns over a 10-year timescale.[16]

The accelerated rate of change in the capabilities of exponential technology is driving a sense of urgency, and this is centered around the need for companies to adopt exponential business models, which we cover in the following chapters. Along with new business models, we need more collaboratively focused mindsets toward finance

> **Blind Spot**
>
> Loyalty leaders are more successful than their peers because they design their businesses to be customer- and employee-centric, putting people before profit.

and corporate leadership and practical methodologies to implement these new concepts. For the first time in history, we have an unparalleled arsenal of tools and strategies that, if used well, have the potential to transform our business landscape forever.

One of the biggest blind spots standing in the way of a business' ability to use these tools is a simple lack of insight. In many cases, companies fail to formally recognize, or have lost touch with, what brings value to a business. Spoiler alert: it's a lot deeper than cool gadgets or a useful service.

It can be difficult to break out of the paradigms most businesses have been operating under, i.e., that their purpose is merely to create products and services. But think of it this way: What if you didn't have any customers? Would you still have a business? Simple logic will tell you that no customers means no business—regardless of your internal strategies or well-written standard operating procedures.

From this point of view, it's obvious the purpose of a business is to serve people, namely, customers and the employees that assist them. So why aren't more businesses C&E-centric (customer/employee-centric)?

Looking back at our insights regarding technology's capacity to foster widespread human change, we found another, more surprising question hiding behind this basic business blind spot: Why don't businesses use technology to advance customer and employee experiences from the customer-employee point of view?

> ### Blind Spot
>
> How a firm is evaluated on Wall Street or by investors has little to do with the very people (employees and customers) who provide the revenue to make business possible.

In his book, *Management: Tasks, Responsibilities, Practices,* Peter Drucker states that the purpose of a business is to create and keep customers.[17] While companies often value their customers and employees on a basic level, their priorities are rarely aligned accordingly. They fail to prioritize making the customer-employee experience the very best it can be.

In part, this is due to the common habit of operating under old paradigms and with unconscious biases about the financial contribution-versus-cost of customer/employee centricity, which is mirrored by the pressure businesses face to produce quick Wall Street or investor profits.

Thus far, the need to demonstrate financial strength has actually seemed antithetical to being C&E-centric. This has resulted in business practices that compromise product quality or customer/employee experiences in favor of short-term financial gains, thereby shortchanging the very people who make the business possible in the first place (yep, you've got it: customers and employees).

Unfortunately, the way a firm is evaluated on Wall Street or by other investors is rarely aligned with the real, flesh-and-blood people (employees) who drive the business and those who provide the cash flow to sustain and grow it (customers). Maybe this sounds obvious to you, but despite how clear-cut the problem seems when we look at it from a distance, up close, it tends to be much harder to see.

Accounting For Accountability: The Limitations of Wall Street's Principles

Many of the practices behind the current trend of shortchanging customers and employees stem from the 1890s and the blind spots that arose at the beginning of our modern financial accounting system, and the major technological innovations that made them possible.

Titans of this era—big names like Pierre Du Pont, Walter Chrysler, J.P. Morgan Jr., Henry Ford, and William Boeing—created some of the most ingenious inventions and products of their time. They were so innovative, in fact, we often forget the less savory aspects of how they built their empires and the stockholder value that accompanied them.

The bottom line is that these titans were all about the bottom line. For employees, the working conditions were often horrendous, and they were treated with little to no respect.[18] Far from the assembly line, Wall Street investors looked on from their skyscrapers and expected companies to put profit first and all other considerations second. At this time, the vast majority of the US population was poorly educated, poorly paid, and until the 1930s, lacked union representation. An employee or the average customer (with little disposable income) was viewed by industrial and financial titans as expendable, and often, with downright contempt.

Even in the 1970s, an essay by Milton Friedman published in the *New York Times* stated that the only responsibility of corporations was to maximize shareholder value at all costs, regardless of the consequences for customers and employees.[19]

Business-centric brands jumped on these ideas, continuing to treat employees and customers as replaceable.

This is hardly the attitude most of us are hoping to model for possible customers or talented potential employees. So why are so many businesses still reliant on the strategies and paradigms based on that attitude?

As the profit-at-all-costs mentality remained entrenched, ever-dynamic market conditions did not. As quality plummeted and consumers flocked to Japanese and European brands known for their quality, innovation, and reliability, American companies faced disastrous consequences. And yet, despite the fact that many companies lost an enormous market share to these competitors, many of them still didn't make a huge shift toward customer or employee centricity. In decades past, there was enough time to turn a ship around. Today, in an exponentially driven world, the time line has been dramatically shortened, and we'll show how that works. Remember what Einstein said about refusing to change? It's more than a catchy quote. For businesses, it's life or death.

> ### Blind Spot
>
> Businesses are vulnerable to their competition when they misunderstand the degree to which exponential technologies have shifted every aspect of life.

Without new attitudes, strategies, and empathetic technologies, a C&E-centric approach seems like a risky strategy in a world still operating from a B-centric, investor-fueled mindset.

Is it, though? Some of the best minds in the world are beginning to question assumptions about what a business' purpose truly is. In August 2020, the Business Roundtable—which represents over 180 of the world's largest firms—overturned a 22-year-old policy statement that defined a corporation's principal purpose as maximizing shareholder return.

Representatives unanimously decided that companies should not only serve their shareholders, but also deliver value to their customers, invest in employees, deal fairly with suppliers, and support the communities in which they operate.[20] The Business Roundtable is essentially saying a company's focus affects what they prioritize and a business' short- and long-term results. With so many executives supporting the prioritization of customer and employee experience on grounds equal to creating shareholder value, it's clear that we need to account for these experiences in a tangible way.

On the heels of this new business philosophy, against the backdrop of technology that is evolving faster and altering the business world more rapidly than ever, and with unparalleled customer and employee expectations thanks to the advent of online reviews, the verdict has become deafening: B-centric businesses and their Wall Street-oriented investors run the serious risk of being completely left out of an emerging global megatrend.

> **Blind Spot**
>
> Not incorporating an empathic view into customer/employee experiences reduces their trust and loyalty, directly affecting the financial success of a business.

Deliberating with Diligence: The Intentional Creation of Customer Value

In the *HBR* article "Are You Undervaluing Your Customers?" Rob Markey lists four broad leadership strategies, all focused on customer loyalty and customer lifetime value as the best way to drive superior corporate performance and to begin accounting for customer-based corporate valuations (CBCV).[21]

- Managing for customer value
- Combining design-thinking with new, loyalty-earning technologies
- Organizing around customer-employee needs
- Leading for loyalty

It's time for leaders to take note and use a design-thinking approach, which is defined as problem-solving with empathy as the first step. No matter what you're creating, a design-thinking approach allows you to develop a better product or experience by really putting yourself in customers' and employees' shoes to understand what they want and need. You can do this in many ways, but one of the best methods is to simply read online reviews and, most importantly, ask customers and employees directly. Some determined leaders even go undercover, engaging in "secret shopper" or "secret employee" experiences like in the TV show *Undercover Boss*[22] to develop an accurate understanding of the experiences they are delivering. An important thing to remember is this: empathy is like a muscle. Some of us have a naturally high level of empathy, but most people need to really work and think creatively in order to develop this conscious skill. It's better to ask than assume.

Companies need a way to optimize experiences from the customer/ employee point of view and a good example is the holistic, survey-based method we'll look at in Chapter 4 called the Experience Index™. Starting with empathy redirects the way leaders choose strategies, processes, and technology, allowing them to orchestrate business operations to not only focus on the customer and employee, but to actually arise from their mirrored experiences. By engaging the whole business ecosystem in this process—from customer-facing operations to back-office employees, partners and alliances, board members, and investors—and by doing so with an empathic point of view, a brand can transform itself and establish business and shareholder values that are intrinsically people-centric.

After gaining this empathetic insight, companies need a definitive way to optimize experiences from this people-centric point of view. Part of that is looking at your business processes as well as investing in C&E-centric exponential technologies. The accelerated rate of change in technology's capabilities is driving the sense of urgency for companies to adopt exponential business models and new mindsets for finance, strategy, and leadership. These models and mindsets are the keys to delivering VIP, personalized experiences, crucial to galvanizing loyalty at scale and delivering groundbreaking business value.

By aggregating all customer and employee experiences, technologies like AI (artificial intelligence) and ML (machine learning) can analyze billions of interactions and find patterns to improve the experiences. Businesses can then tailor their strategies to the lived experiences of the people they serve.

Balancing Beyond the Sheet: Where Customer Value Metrics Are Lacking

One reason customer experience isn't given the appropriate strategic, operational, and financial focus it deserves is that most income statements or balance sheets don't provide visibility into the tangible value of a company's customers or employees. Revenue is counted, but its direct relationship to customer or employee experience isn't. Not understanding the connection is part of what is hurting companies and they don't even see it—yet.

Unless customer value is part of their balance sheet, leaders will be tempted to continue operating, measuring, and reporting using old B-centric metrics and standards. And investors will continue to rely on B-centric accounting principles that focus solely on physical and financial assets. Without a standard, consistent, and widely accepted system to measure and report customer value, Wall Street and other investors have an incomplete picture to compare a company's short- and long-term value with that of its peers.

> **Blind Spot**
>
> Without financial accounting standards that include reliable, auditable customer/employee relationship metrics, it's difficult to enter the new era of customer/employee capitalism.

For businesses to succeed in an economy where option-laden customers and employees are quick to change their loyalty based on singular experiences, new ways to account for customer and employee value are essential. Even with the few customer-experience-to-value reporting standards or requirements currently used, business leaders should begin finding ways to track customer/employee loyalty-creating metrics as they do key assets like buildings, inventory, equipment, and marketable securities. In this way, it can become the norm.

It is difficult to enter the age of customer/employee-based capitalism or build C&E-centric businesses until the tools we use to deliver and measure their experiences include reliable, auditable, and actionable standards. This book serves as a call to action for business leaders, along with Wall Street and investors, to bring the business community together to create C&E-centric standards and develop the tools to implement and measure them.

Innovative Understanding: Bringing B2B and B2C Technology for the Age of Empathy

Technology is intrinsically linked to the employee/customer experience. It enables delivery of those experiences at scale, and it is responsible for the many connections needed to bring different stakeholders together on shared ground.

But current customer/employee experience technology is still stuck in a B-centric efficiency and effectiveness paradigm, and much of its potential is, therefore, completely missed. This equation represents the old, B-centric experience approach:

> **Blind Spot**
>
> Solely focusing on business-centric technology and business-centric efficiency and effectiveness jeopardizes the customer/employee experience and the long-term success of a business.

The Old Paradigm

Business-Centric Experiences Focus = Cost Cutting = Efficiency + Effectiveness

Where:

Efficiency   is based on cost-cutting efficiency

Effectiveness   is based on cost-cutting effectiveness

Business-centric efficiency measures whether time or resources are being wasted. Business-centric effectiveness measures whether the company has accomplished a goal: higher brand awareness, reach, or sales conversions. Relying solely on B-centric efficiency and effectiveness metrics as business drivers provides the intellectual quotient necessary for short-term success, but it severely neglects the emotional quotient that provides the visceral quality of the experience inspiring long-term loyalty in value-creators. A lack of customer/employee-focused strategies, technologies,

> **Blind Spot**
>
> Old paradigm CX and EX puts a business at risk because it is too business-centric, leaving the customer/employee experience as an afterthought, negatively affecting loyalty, revenue, and margins.

measurements, and outcomes is a severe setback for a business in any industry or sector.

Traditionally, efficiency and effectiveness weren't viewed through the lens of empathy (the customer/employee POV). And while efficiency and effectiveness are undoubtedly essential to business, we found that evaluating both metrics through the customer/employee POV revealed how so many businesses have eroded the relationship with the mainstay of their company—people. To reverse the disastrous results of such erosion, we must develop a strategy tool kit that transforms efficiency and effectiveness from traditional cost-saving measures to metrics of loyalty-generation. "The two E's" must become more than thrifty metrics. They need to emerge as the core of your employees' and customers' brand experience.

Linear Technology's Limits

When a business isn't creating experiences that drive trust and loyalty, it is most often operating from an obsolete paradigm of business centricity with old, linear technologies at its core. In part, this is because companies continue to use antiquated technology. It's impossible to deliver exceptional experiences and build trust, inspire loyalty, or deliver the brand's promise when relying on ineffective or outdated tools.

> **Blind Spot**
>
> Technology shapes customer/employee experiences; those experiences collectively shape the brand's reputation and financial success.

As an example of the part empathy plays in this, take someone who wants to reset a password. They don't want to wait in a long phone queue to talk to an agent. They want to change their password now. The technology to provide this solution is already out there, so why wouldn't you invest in it?

Businesses need to design and deliver frictionless experiences from the customer's point of view. In this instance, it might mean using an intelligent AI chatbot to reset the password in a matter of seconds, rather than the minutes or even hours it would take when a customer reaches out to an overworked service department.

Though some companies are creating this as a one-off experience, it's not enough. We prescribe the intentional, dedicated design of holistic experiences that consistently deliver empathy, no matter what the customer is trying to accomplish. At the same time, these solutions reduce the cognitive burden and level of effort required of the employee, making the quality and potential of their work life much better.

Worldwide Influence: The Larger Context of Empathy

There is a much broader narrative surrounding trust/empathy as it takes place in the wider world—not just through customer/ employee experiences. By reimagining how to deliver empathy to stakeholders, we also asked: "How can corporations do their part to make the world a better place while operating for a profit? How can companies move from being business-centric to empathy-centric in everything they do?"

This book is an extended call to action compelling each of us—from new employees to experienced leaders—to think about the juxtaposition of technology with empathy in our societies, our businesses, and in our personal lives. We need to seriously examine the future of how companies, technology, and humanity will connect, and in doing so, we will get a clear picture of why empathy-based companies offer a more sustainable and financially lucrative business strategy.

As leaders, we coauthors have begun this transformation. Natalie and I know that this kind of radical change is a journey—but pursuing it is not only the smart thing to do, it's also the right thing to do. This kind of empathic change will distinguish, differentiate, and strengthen us in an increasingly dynamic and ever more agile marketplace. Making these changes will allow us to recruit intelligent, motivated, and fulfilled employees, which represent the key to any business' success, and it will allow us to attract and keep some of the world's best customers.

There's a synergistic effect garnered by running your company with empathy as the guiding principle. The strengthened bonds among employees, customers, and the company brand create a "magic glue" that makes a considerable difference in how outcomes are achieved— and whether they are achieved (or even thought of) at all. The resulting environment is both a better place to work and a better partner to do business with.

Employees spend a great deal of time at work, often more than they spend with their own families. Work culture plays a big part in our lives while simultaneously shaping the wider culture around us; we are all consumers as well as employees. We all buy things. We've all had some horrible customer experiences, some good ones, and unfortunately, statistically speaking, very few amazing ones. While we may not think about it consciously, customer and employee experiences affect everyone, every day.

Empathy: The Force-Multiplier Flywheel

In his works "The Age of Customer Capitalism"[23] and *When More Is Not Better: Overcoming America's Obsession with Economic Efficiency*,[24] economist and thought leader Roger Martin lays out a plan for the new "age of customer capitalism." He envisions a world in which companies put customers first not only on principle, but also as a means to create greater value for their shareholders.

His arguments highlight why the blind pursuit of shareholder value erodes the customer-focused lifetime value of a business, demonstrated through case studies involving companies too focused on efficiency and managing investor earning expectations to provide the customer and employee experiences to sustain either. Despite the well-publicized and highly respected nature of his research, few have acted on Martin's assertions—perhaps out of fear of harming short-term earnings or negatively affecting investors' perspectives of the brand. And because technologies, operational capabilities, and corporate financial measurement systems remain B-centric, customer and employee experiences continue to be compromised, thereby limiting companies and preventing them from attaining the type of exponential growth empathetic practices make possible.

Business-centric points of view stunt business growth and block innovation. They put customer loyalty and employee trust at risk. With that in mind, we took a look at the tools available and asked companies, "Are you missing the force-multiplier flywheel?" (Figure 1.4). The balance this tool represents is only possible when the North Star triad of empathy, trust, and loyalty is combined and orchestrated to deliver the best possible customer-employee experiences consistently, and at scale.

We'll return to this diagram and explain each part of it as a reference point; each chapter unfolds new pieces of a plan to gain the momentum necessary to deliver empathy-based disruption to your industry. The bottom line? Empathy must be incorporated into how leaders make decisions, how managers treat their people, how software/hardware gets designed, and how we rewrite the technology employees/customers use to deliver/receive experiences. As we'll show, it's nonnegotiable—and it becomes more so every single day.

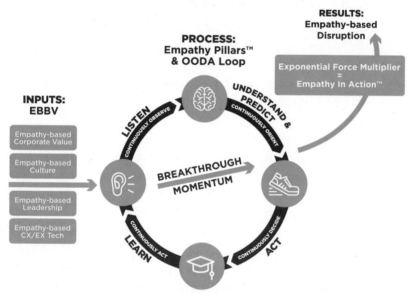

Figure 1.4 Empathy is the force multiplier in business using EBBV, the Empathy Pillars, and the OODA Loop process.

Taking the Wheel: How Empathy Drives Innovation

IDEO is an award-winning global design firm that takes a human-centered, design-based approach to helping organizations innovate and grow by changing the customer/employee experience. By taking note of companies like IDEO, we can begin to understand where the opportunity for real innovation and disruption in the CX/EX (customer experience/employee experience) exists.

As a founding principle of our own work, we embrace IDEO's view that empathy and innovation are unequivocally correlated:

Design empathy is an approach that draws upon people's real-world experiences to address modern challenges. As companies allow a deep emotional understanding of people's needs to inspire them—and transform their work, their teams, and even their organization at large it unlocks the creative capacity for innovation.[25]

Companies like IDEO help businesses focus on the CX/EX at all levels, from the on-the-ground, in-store experience to the unboxing of a newly purchased product at home, and then into the experience of service delivery. Whether customers or employees remain loyal is directly related to how these experiences feel to them. After all, we all share a basic human need to feel heard, acknowledged, and understood. Companies who ignore this—either intentionally or unintentionally—are crippling themselves.

> **Blind Spot**
>
> Empathy, i.e., putting yourself in your customer/employee's shoes, is the main driver for innovation, disruption, and financial success.

The Primacy of the Personal: Technology and Our Lives

After looking at exponential technology's advances, the ways in which they can be designed and deployed, and their tangible effects on how people feel before, during, and after an experience, we saw these principles form a pattern of necessity time and time again:

- **The Empathy Factor**—You must understand what experiences should look like through the lens of your customers and employees (engaging with the ideal)
- **The Trust Factor**—You must empower your business to deliver employee-centric experiences and build employee trust so they truly feel you have their back, and are then motivated and enabled to provide outstanding personalized customer experiences regardless of whether the ideal was fully met (engaging with the personal)
- **The Loyalty Factor**—You must consistently deliver customer/employee-centric experiences which unwaveringly build trust to the point that they garner both customer and employee lifetime loyalty and lead to extraordinary business outcomes (engaging long-term)

Reinforcing Bridges: Putting Meaning Behind CX/EX Empathy, Trust, and Loyalty

To reinforce empathy as a true business construct, rather than warm but ultimately empty lip service, it's necessary for us to define the scope of what Empathy in Action actually means as a deliverable.

Delivering empathy doesn't mean being "nice" or learning to express sympathy via HR training videos. It's not merely a mindset plastered on motivational posters in the break room, either; it's nothing less than the way you do what you do.

To deliver Empathy in Action, you must actively throw out the old, B-centric way of looking at efficiency and effectiveness. Instead of only pointing your compass toward the business-centric, cost-cutting efforts that often put customer/employee experience at risk, companies need to head in the direction of efficiency and effectiveness that generates trust and loyalty.

To define the Empathy in Action principle itself, we begin with some simple questions each time we work with a company or organization:

- Did the company consistently put themselves "in the shoes" of their customers and employees when designing and delivering all experiences?

If so,

- Did the customer get what they needed without a lot of extra effort or wasted time?
- Did the employee have everything they needed to best meet the customer's needs without extra effort or time wasted on their part?
- Did the employee feel motivated while serving the customer?

If the answer to all these questions is yes, it is the beginning of Empathy in Action. Loyalty-creating customer experiences fulfill three criteria, they . . .

1. Have a VIP, one-to-one, concierge quality
2. Are contextually relevant and real-time
3. Provide a personalized experience at scale (You can't get to exponential growth if only certain parts of your customer base are treated like VIPs.)

Working from this perspective, we developed 10 CX action statements that guide the design of people-centric experiences and illuminate the technology needed to deliver on personal, trust-building promises:

1. Help me even before I know there's a problem.
2. Show you know me before you even meet me.
3. Empathize with my situation.
4. Demonstrate that you know the road I traveled to get here.
5. Listen, understand, and predict what I need, then act accordingly.
6. Don't ask me to repeat myself.
7. Present me with answers I want as well as the ones I didn't know I needed.
8. Address my issue and stay with me until it's fixed.
9. Check in with me to make sure it all worked out; learn from my experience.
10. Above all, keep my data safe.

These statements aren't fluff. They are exactly what customers have asked for (often literally and word for word in surveys and assessments) and express what customer-employee experts have recommended companies aim toward for years. But for this to happen, a company must have active ways to listen to, understand, and predict a customer's intent, and then not only act on it but also learn from all resultant interactions at scale.

Additionally, it requires that companies empower employees with the right information, tools, and action plans to serve the customer. This greatly enhances the employee's work experience, the result being that both experiences continuously and synergistically improve.

Empathy as Exponent: Embracing the New CX/EX Equation

As we analyzed previous industrial revolutions—in which B-centric definitions of efficiency and effectiveness drove innovation and our civilization forward while neglecting the human elements necessary to sustain that momentum—we had an epiphany.

The antiquated, focus of the past is sorely missing something in today's interconnected world. Experiences delivered by outdated technologies mostly focus on cost-saving, often compromising or negatively impacting customer/employee experiences.

In an era of ever-increasing customer and employee expectations,[26] the experience equation must transform from:

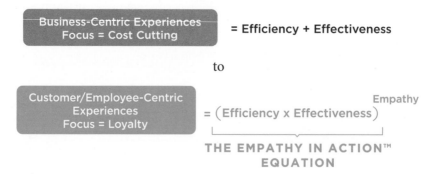

to

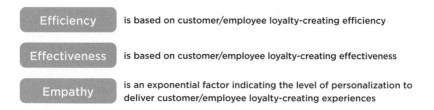

$$\text{THE EMPATHY IN ACTION}^{\text{TM}}\ \text{EQUATION}$$

Where:

Efficiency is based on customer/employee loyalty-creating efficiency

Effectiveness is based on customer/employee loyalty-creating effectiveness

Empathy is an exponential factor indicating the level of personalization to deliver customer/employee loyalty-creating experiences

We call this the Empathy in Action Equation.

How does this new C&E-centric equation work? Table 1.1 provides some comparisons. Instead of looking at the goals solely from the business-focused, cost-saving POV, a customer/employee-centric view takes into consideration broader factors that engage customers and employees, and thus inspire more loyalty toward the company.

These extraordinary customer/employee experiences result in accomplishing what the company wanted in the first place—lower costs (lower employee turnover and reduced training costs, lower customer acquisition costs), increased employee productivity, astounding customer experiences which gain higher levels of market share, volume, and repeat business, and from all of these factors, a long-term jump in baseline revenue and margin.

Table 1.1 Comparison of B-centric vs. C&E-centric efficiency and effectiveness.

	Business-Centric: Cost-Cutting	Customer/Employee-Centric: Loyalty-Creating
Efficiency	• Company time wasted	• Employee cognitive burden lessened • Customer effort reduced

Effectiveness	• Company goal reached: awareness; sales conversion	• Employee goals reached
		  • Easy to help customers
		  • Enjoy their work
		  • Choose a flexible schedule
		• Customer goals reached
		  • Short, fast, easy interactions
		  • Right answers the first time
		  • Reliable, consistent interactions

How can companies provide these exponentially (and measurably) better, real-time, contextually relevant, personalized experiences? We'll explore different answers to that question more in the upcoming chapters, but for now, you should simply know that empathy is the exponential factor that, when embedded, becomes the force-multiplier flywheel. This is because Empathy in Action isn't a product or task list, but rather an innately holistic process, that positively affects a business' culture, the experiences it offers, and the financial contributions of these improved experiences to the business' overall success.

All of this is just the beginning of a whole new world for corporations willing to invest in—and benefit from—an empathy-based, force-multiplying business model.

Your first step, however, is to stand up and state your intentions in the first place. This book explains how to go about this transformation and serves as your playbook.

Taking a Stand for the Future's Past: What Does Your Lens Look Like?

One of the best ways to build a better future is to consistently ask "What kind of past do you want to be from?"

The future of technology and our world are not a series of accidental mishaps, nor are they coincidences we are helpless to control. It's possible to consciously, intentionally tilt the odds toward a fantastic future by understanding the past as it relates to what eventually becomes "the future." At some point, the world of today was the world of the future, and it was built by those who had the foresight to bring it about.

To tap into this influential mindset, look to the past and reflect on what strategies and technologies worked for our predecessors, what didn't, and why. To change the future, you must remember that people create it. Even in pop culture images of the machine-ruled futuretopia, it's people who build, strategize, and program that technology. It's up to us who make or use technology to be more deliberate about our choices in coming industrial revolutions—and beyond. There will always be more unknowns than known, and you should never forget that there is always a new frontier waiting to be discovered. More than anything, it's this perspective that separates average minds from revolutionary ones.

Someday, when we look back on the past, what stories would we be honored to tell? What legacies do we want to leave behind? What would it look like to be part of a brighter future, and how can we realize this vision through the development and deployment of better experiences today?

Technology is an extension of who we are. We can imbue it with our hopes and dreams for a future full of humanity—we just need to understand what (and who) we are optimizing for and why we are doing it in the first place. The outcome for companies investing in personal transformation will be based on the reality of customers who solely patronize companies that provide them with better experiences, and employees who are more discerning than any other labor force in history.

Businesses need to figure out whether they are delivering on this vision and, if not, determine where the gaps are and take steps to fill them. We'll show you how exactly how to find those gaps and fill them in our closing remarks.

The World Is a Conversation, So Talk Like You Mean It

The authors of *The Cluetrain Manifesto* wrote: "Markets are conversations."[27] One condition for getting the most out of this book is an open mind; to join a conversation about the new standards of customer/employee experiences not only as a listener, but also as an active participant. This book is meant to stimulate new conversations long after you've turned the last page, and to change not only the perception but also the reality of how all companies deliver customer/employee experiences.

Imagine a revolution that takes entire industries from a cost-centered to a loyalty-centered approach toward business. For that to happen, everyone must be willing to participate in this evolving conversation, because we have only just begun to see the possibilities. We need the insight of all industries and sectors to fully embrace the potential of empathy-based business.

If you join us in the dialogue, you must do so on an ongoing basis. This conversation will forever be evolving. If you don't stay current, you will be responsible for your company's choice to fall behind those that are forging new paths. Consider this an opportunity to reenergize your professional career, to think differently, and to advance your brand as spearheading change. We hope this book lights a fire within you as it has in us.

TAKEAWAYS

- Technology has affected all aspects of life throughout history, and has consistently determined business outcomes for companies.
- Older, business-centric business models are not focused on the value of employee or customer trust, and can't garner the same level of loyalty as customer/employee-centric models.
- It's time for companies to explore ways to create more business value by providing—and prioritizing—customer/employee-focused experiences.

TONY'S
LEADERSHIP CORNER

Blind Spot: Making decisions based 100 percent on intuition

Intuition is my superpower.

I grew up from humble beginnings just outside of London. I dropped out of college in my first year. I taught myself how to code on the London Tube while commuting to my first job at the University of London Computer Centre. While I don't have the fancy upbringing and college degree, I do have the ability to read people across all spectrums. Growing up, I was able to resonate with lots of different kids, whether they were tough, smart, cool, or shy; I was friends with all of them. And in my career, I've always been surprised by people who say their biggest challenge is navigating politics in organizations. It's always been fairly easy for me to navigate by reading people and situations and knowing when to push or not.

I've also always been a bit of a rabble-rouser, maybe because I didn't grow up with the expectations and constraints that come with a more rigid upbringing. I've followed my gut and been willing to risk it all for my convictions. I left the UK and headed first to Amsterdam, and then followed my dreams to succeed in high tech in Silicon Valley. I felt a visceral sense for each new wave: the internet, the power of communication technology, then connected consumer devices, and now experiences for the customer experience market.

Unfortunately, my intuition has failed me at least twice. In both cases, I was taken with a charismatic leader and an exciting company vision without doing enough due diligence on the company's culture. It's very difficult to evaluate culture until you're on the inside, but you can certainly look for clues and talk to people to hear their firsthand experiences. The best way to avoid the blind spot of naive optimism is to trust your gut—and back it up with data!

" Disruptive innovation is a term referring to a technology and its application which significantly affects [or changes] the way a market or industry works.

—Professor Clay Christensen

Chapter Two

THE FIFTH INDUSTRIAL REVOLUTION: PERSONALIZATION

In the first chapter, we explored how technological advances have impacted the way we do business, how we live our lives, and the structure of society. History has shown that, while the evolution of technology and its effects form a repeating and consistent pattern, the time frame between major technological revolutions is shortening. This is because technology's capabilities are advancing exponentially rather than on a linear trajectory.

Today's unprecedented rate of technological innovation is a key driver behind the need for leaders to rethink their business strategies by incorporating dynamic, exponential technologies in novel ways. Companies that respond to change by pivoting, iterating, and adapting to these new technologies see a similar exponential change in their business' growth rate. Laggards are left further and further behind.

Tracing the Up-Curve: Technological Acceleration through the Ages

While the Stone Age is reckoned in millions of years, subsequent ages are counted in mere tens of millennia. By juxtaposing these spans of time with the industrial revolutions, we see new technological capabilities changing within decades. When you look at the broader pattern, an exponential rate of change is revealed.

Zeroing in even further to focus on recent history, we see a similar pattern (Figure 2.1):

- The First Industrial Revolution happened in the eighteenth century.
- The Second Industrial Revolution occurred almost two centuries later.
- The Third Industrial Revolution happened only a half-century later.
- The Fourth Industrial Revolution happened three decades later.

The time frame is shortening because technology's capabilities are increasing by factors that continue to grow, thereby providing a matching, exponential shift in the business landscape.

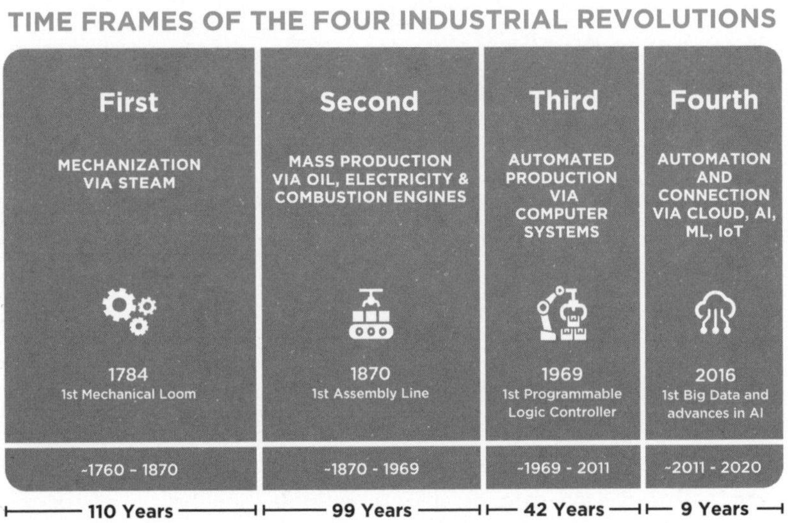

TIME FRAMES OF THE FOUR INDUSTRIAL REVOLUTIONS

First	Second	Third	Fourth
MECHANIZATION VIA STEAM	MASS PRODUCTION VIA OIL, ELECTRICITY & COMBUSTION ENGINES	AUTOMATED PRODUCTION VIA COMPUTER SYSTEMS	AUTOMATION AND CONNECTION VIA CLOUD, AI, ML, IoT
1784 1st Mechanical Loom	1870 1st Assembly Line	1969 1st Programmable Logic Controller	2016 1st Big Data and advances in AI
~1760 - 1870	~1870 - 1969	~1969 - 2011	~2011 - 2020
110 Years	99 Years	42 Years	9 Years

Figure 2.1 The time to the next innovation is advancing nonlinearly in each industrial revolution.
Source: Institute of Entrepreneurship[1]

Powering Change: Understanding the Significance of the Industrial Revolutions

To understand the significance of what we call an industrial revolution, there are two components we must put into perspective:

- The creation of new technologies with highly advanced capabilities
- How the new capabilities completely transform the old way

The First Industrial Revolution drove mechanization and was fueled by the invention of the steam engine, which replaced economies based on agriculture and handicrafts with ones based on large-scale industry, mechanized manufacturing, and the industrial factory system. New machines, transformed power sources, and novel ways of organizing work made existing industries more productive and efficient.

The Second Industrial Revolution utilized electricity and related advances to create the concept we now know as mass production. Innovations in manufacturing and production technology enabled the widespread adoption of telegraph and railroad networks, gas and water supply pipelines, and city sewage systems.

Rapid advances in the production of steel, chemicals, and power helped fuel the unprecedented efficiency of this mass production model. The expansion of rail and telegraph lines allowed the movement of people, goods, and ideas to expand and accelerate on a scale never seen before, resulting in new waves of globalization. Trains, automobiles, and aircraft made it faster and easier to travel. Ideas and news spread quicker than ever before via telegraphs, mass-printed newspapers, and affordable radios.

The Third Industrial Revolution saw the emergence of computers, digital technology, and associated applications. Innovations included semiconductors, mainframe computing, personal computing, and the internet, which all culminated in the Digital Revolution.

We have now passed the Fourth Industrial Revolution, driven by four main technological developments: high-speed mobile internet, AI (artificial intelligence), resulting advances in automation, the use of big data analytics, and cloud technology. The resulting real-time, continuous connectivity in business and our personal lives further fueled this digital change engine.

The results experienced by companies have been radical. Because technology can now communicate in real time, brands have the opportunity to deliver on the promise of real-time organization, i.e., to respond to customer needs and demands instantaneously. The same advances also allow them to transform their business models from selling a product to providing a managed service (SaaS is a prime example of this).

We've entered the Fifth Industrial Revolution, defined by the realization that "for profit" and "for benefit" are not conflicting business models, permitting us to put our focus on humanity and personalization through deep, multi-level cooperation among people, technology, and businesses (Table 2.1).

Table 2.1 Introducing the Fifth Industrial Revolution.

1st Industrial Revolution	2nd Industrial Revolution	3rd Industrial Revolution	4th Industrial Revolution	5th Industrial Revolution
Power created by water and steam to mechanize production	Power generated by electricity & oil for mass production and assembly	Automation driven by electronics and information technology	Innovation driven by digital capabilities: Cloud, AI, ML, IoT...	Deep multi-level collaboration between people, machines and awareness
MECHANIZATION	MASS PRODUCTION	AUTOMATED	DIGITAL	PERSONALIZATION
~1760	~1870	~1969	~2011	~2021

Wired for Revolution: Digital Disruption Defined

In our new business paradigm, innovation and success no longer depend on the old model of business-focused efficiency and effectiveness. According to Singularity University (SU), when two or more exponential technologies are combined to solve a previously unsolvable challenge, the possibility of developing a solution similarly increases exponentially.

Exponential technologies include ML (machine learning) and AI; AI-enabled, data-enhanced chatbots and agents; mobile business applications; fully digital customer experience management platforms; XaaS (X-as-a-Service offerings); IoT (Internet of Things); cloud and hybrid cloud offerings; and more[2] (Table 2.2). Many of these technologies are enabling radical advances in the personalization of customer and employee experiences.

Table 2.2 Emerging and exponential technologies.
Source: Deloitte[3] and Singularity University[4]

Strategic	Tactical
AI and Machine Learning	Mobile Business Applications
Big Data & Data Science	AI-Chat and Voice Bots
IoT	AI-enabled Employees
Social Business Tools	On-demand, X-as-a-Service
Open APIs	Containerization
Digital Customer Experience Applications and Platforms	Contextual Computing
Mobile Business Apps	Adaptive Security Architectures
Sharing Economy Business Applications	Virtual and Augmented Reality
Team Collaboration Software and Platforms	3D Printing
Integrated Workplace Applications	Low-code Platforms
Cloud Technology	Context-aware Computing
Digital Learning Applications	Wearable Technology
Microservice Architectures	Mobile Payments
Hybrid and Multi-Cloud Technology	Real-time Data Processing and Applications
Blockchain	Cryptocurrencies
Prescriptive Analytics	Bioprinting
Nanotechnology	Autonomous Vehicles

There are many definitions of digital disruption. Taking our cue from SU, we gain insight by comparing the first three industrial revolutions (which were based on linear technology) to the fourth and fifth industrial revolutions (which are based on exponential technologies).

Because the first three eras were based on linear technology, companies still using this technology have linear growth rates. Inversely, because the fourth and fifth are based on exponential technologies, companies using these technologies have the potential for exponential growth rates in all industries.

Digital disruption lies in the space between linear business growth rates and exponential business growth rates. Because the business growth rate is so quick under the exponential model, competitors are abruptly left behind. The result is a company that can completely "disrupt" their industry (Figure 2.2).

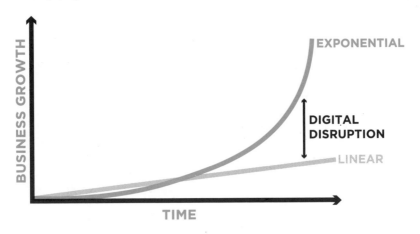

Figure 2.2 Exponential vs. linear business growth.

Urgency, Inc: Using Exponential Tech to Transform Your Business

Klaus Schwab, founder and executive chairman of the World Economic Forum, describes technological revolutions as defined by the emergence of:

. . . new technologies and novel ways of perceiving the world [that] trigger a profound change in economic and social structures.[5]

Businesses that combine the powerful capabilities of exponential technologies to create new offerings and cultivate empathetic CX/EX are delivering unprecedented digital disruption and business growth to their respective industries, for example:

- Telephone: (IP Telephony: Vonage, Skype)
- Hotel: (Airbnb, FlipKey, HomeAway, Roomorama)
- Taxi/cab: (Uber, Lyft, Curb, Free Now, Didi, Grab, Cabify)
- Classified Advertising: (Craigslist, Angie's List, eBay, OLX)
- Records and Music: Downloadable music: (iTunes, Napster, The Filter)
- Books and Publishing: (iBooks, Kindle, Audible)
- Search Engines and Advertising: (Google, Bing, Baidu)
- Financial/Transactional: (PayPal, E*TRADE, Bitcoin, Venmo, Zelle, Vertcoin, Znap)
- Personal Communications and Networking: (Facebook, Twitter, WhatsApp, Slack)
- Business and Communications: (Quip, Gmail, Skype, Zoom, Teams)
- Electronic Commerce: (Amazon, Alibaba)

Even seemingly forward-looking companies like DEC Corporation, Tower Records, Circuit City, Minolta, Thomas Cook, and Wang Laboratories were swept away in their prime thanks to business disruption's speed and scale. Market share monsters such as FAO Schwartz were bought out, with only its flagship New York store eventually reopening. Toys "R" Us, which was purchased after bankruptcy, only opened two stores for the 2019 holiday season. Further examples abound.

Now we are seeing companies that once stood on their own being relegated to pop-ups in other retailers' stores. Competitors who have reinvented their business models, their offerings, and their CX/EX priorities are displacing companies that remain stuck in the old ways.

Our concern lies with the companies still using linear technologies while trying to compete in an exponential world, and which are, as a result, losing market share (or disappearing altogether)—to the benefit of competitors with the foresight to adopt exponential technologies and strategies. One statistic is particularly illuminating: at the time of this writing, over half of the Fortune 500 companies listed in 2000 have disappeared.[6]

Data shows that businesses that focus on mastering digital disruption have an increase in profitability of 9 percent and a revenue generation rate 26 percent higher than when they started.[7] With technology transforming faster in the twenty-first century than at any other point in time, new technologies are primed to continue altering the customer and employee experience—which determines how we work, live, play, and learn—and transforming the business landscape as a whole.

Data and the work of countless experts show that focusing on customers and employees is necessary for businesses to succeed, but the question is how to make that colossal jump. By synthesizing the best sages' work, we've taken this idea of customer/employee centricity and brought it to a whole new dimension—an actionable playbook for navigating the exponential era and creating lasting bonds with your customers and employees, preparing your company for the Empathy Era.

Digital disruption can happen to any company, and it's a certainty if it is not paying sufficient attention to the rapidly changing, broader world around it. Those with too narrow or just the wrong focus are doomed.

In the book *The Disruption Mindset: Why Some Organizations Transform While Others Fail*, Charlene Li notes:

> *Companies need to develop a disruptive mindset that permeates every aspect of the organization and focuses on three elements: a strategy designed to meet the needs of future customers, leadership that creates a movement to drive and sustain transformation, and a culture that thrives on disruptive change.[8]*

Case Study: How Blind Spots Look in the Real World

One of the prime examples of a past disruptive innovation is the internet. Its adoption significantly altered the way companies did business, and it negatively affected companies unwilling to adapt to it.

Currently, disruptive innovation is happening on a more subjective level, resulting from exponential improvements in organizational design and the similarly exponential technologies that make them possible. Companies can take advantage of exponential technology to provide more than products or solutions: now, they can provide experiences as a service.

One advantage the companies listed on the right side of Table 2.3 have is access to a lot of data, and they make it more useful—and applicable—using AI and ML. These technologies can then take this enriched data and use it to transform existing customer, partner, and channel relationships through carefully cultivated experience management resulting in disruptive business models.

Table 2.3 Digital disruption requires a change in business models and the incorporation of new technologies.

Industry	Traditional Business Models	Digital Disruption of Business Models
Transportation	Yellow Cab	Lyft, UBER
Books	Borders	Amazon.com
Movies	Blockbuster	Netflix, Hulu
Music	SamGoody	iTunes, Spotify
Photography	Kodak	iPhone, Android Smartphones & Social

Just like those who were first to adopt the internet when it appeared on the scene, companies now adopting new C&E-centric people-first strategies—and utilizing exponential technologies to do so—have the same massive opportunity to displace established competitors.

Exponential Technologies: Revving the Engines of Change

Peter Diamandis, founder and executive chairman of X-Prize says:

People need to understand how exponential technologies are impacting the business landscape. They need to do some future-casting and look at how all industries are evolving and being completely transformed.[9]

Bold, written by Peter Diamandis and Steven Kotler (best-selling author and executive director of the Flow Research Collective, specializing in the science behind ultimate human performance), details how technology's capabilities have accelerated faster in the twenty-first century than at any other point in time. Computers, computational intelligence (AI/ML), and data compilation tools are all primed to continue altering all aspects of our lives—and to directly affect CX/EX in unprecedented ways.

With these hyper-paced changes come equally paced shifts in a company's responsibilities, the impact of their choices, and the significance of their decisions. This isn't limited to the way businesses deliver CX/EX; by nature, it also influences how customers choose which companies to do business with, and how employees choose which organizations to work for. Never before have customers and employees had so many options—and access to them so freely—especially online at any given time. Exponential shifts affect more than the number of competitors you face. They also drastically impact how visible, accessible, and present those competitors are to your market base.

> **Blind Spot**
>
> Most businesses don't feel a sense of urgency to change the old CX/EX paradigm because they don't realize the exponential effects of technology and change.

It's more vital than ever for companies to look at their offerings and the experiences behind them from a customer's or employee's point of view.

"EVERYTHING FROM THIS 1991 RADIO SHACK AD
I NOW DO WITH MY PHONE"

Figure 2.3 Source: Steve Cichon[10]

The Exponential Technology in Our Daily Lives

To give the concept of exponential technology more context, let's look at a device now deeply ingrained in our daily lives: the smartphone. This ubiquitous tool of modern life perfectly illustrates how exponential technology has transformed not only our definition and experience of what a phone is, but also our most essential ways of doing business.

As the telephone evolved into the smartphone, billions of dollars' worth of applications—previously separate products or services—were swiftly replaced and integrated into this one, seemingly omnipotent device. The smartphone eventually replaced digital watches, cameras, video players, music players, desktop video conferencing tools, digital voice recorders, the encyclopedia, and more.[11] As a result of this consolidation—all centered on one single, revolutionary device—hundreds of once-thriving businesses no longer exist.

This is what happens to companies that don't incorporate exponential technology into how they do business—and the pace at which they must do so is only accelerating as the Digital Era continues its breakneck trajectory (Figure 2.3).

Rewriting the Playbook: Digital Disruption Is Real and It's Here to Stay

We are now at an exponential technology precipice; like the advent of steam combustion machinery, our new technological revolution can affect society for better or for worse depending on the principles we cultivate while engaging with it. And while the advances we made in technology throughout history spurred major changes in the way products and services are developed and sold, it took great leadership to transform that technology into something useful for practical applications and businesses. This remains true today.

With experiences being the main reason people choose between companies today, leaders must learn to see how exponential technology can be used in CX/EX on a tangible level. More broadly, they must gain an understanding of how it creates more empathy, develops trusting relationships, and gives rise to long-term customer and employee loyalty.

Companies also need to understand what can happen if they don't act now. By definition, most of us are already "behind" because the pace of technology is now exponential. And since changes in previous industrial revolutions happened slowly, we are not necessarily equipped to process exponential growth. Often, we assess the pattern of change in the past to predict how much change we can expect going forward. As a result, we tend to assume a constant rate of change, and based on this assumption, we end up operating linearly rather than exponentially.

This has become a severe disadvantage and it represents the single greatest hurdle to growth and innovation in the world today.

Exponential technology not only represents the opportunity for businesses to empathize, pivot, and iterate in ways they've never done before—it is that opportunity. The longer a company waits to adapt, the more desperate their eventual scramble will be to stay competitive. Companies already shifting gears to improve CX/EX business practices have a marked advantage.

For businesses, there's only one rule of change that really matters: adapt or die.

Self-Assessments and Scoring: Confronting the Digital Disruption Blind Spot

Every company has blind spots. Opening our eyes to our own business blind spots was transformative. We saw that flaws that had held us back were hiding right under our noses, and the deeper we dug, the more obvious it became that there is no safe harbor from the pace of exponential change. We share observations from our own company and others in hopes that they will provide a new perspective to enrich your business.

Just as there was a time when people clung to the shared notion that the earth was the center of the universe, too many of today's executives cling to the B-centric view that current market share will continually, reliably guarantee future market share, and that brand dominance will always fuel brand loyalty. It is a deceptively narrow-minded view disguised as optimism, and it's important that you realize its potential to do harm to your real-market outcomes.

Similar to how the old earth-centric paradigms were replaced with Galileo and Copernicus' sun-centric models, it's time to toss and replace these B-centric models with paradigms that are based on our current, clearly observable reality. Without cultivating a new mindset and prioritizing an understanding of the value disruptive strategies represent, businesses will miss the opportunity to survive in the increasingly near future.

Those not only anticipating but planning on digital disruption—which tend to be those we label "people-centric"—will remain and survive to compete for the loyalty and value of future customers and employees.

The Ostrich Effect: "We Don't Have Any Blind Spots"

While digital disruption continues to impact all companies at an increasing rate, most don't realize—or want to admit—that they have blind spots. This is akin to an ostrich burying its head in the sand to avoid impending danger.

If you think you don't have a blind spot, you most likely have one or many. When we hear things like, "We've always done it this way and it's worked fine!" or "Not invented here . . . " (subtext: we won't adopt the best methods if they "belong" to someone else . . .) from a company's leadership, or when our conversation starts with all the reasons a new strategy or methodology won't work, we know there's a lurking blind spot that's about to snare them (Figure 2.4). No one wants to be caught by surprise, so let's look at some warning signs that signal what we call YDKWYDK—"You don't know what you don't know."

No company on earth is totally free of blind spots. But that's not the point, here. It's not about having blind spots, which is a given. It's about providing a practical and cultural framework that allows you to find them before they hurt your outcomes.

Successful companies create a culture of psychological safety where people can bring up blind spots freely without derailing their careers. Companies that celebrate their employees' and customers' honesty embrace a culture where being curious, asking questions, questioning things (not from fear, but to truly understand them), and suggesting different ways to do things is not only accepted, but preferred. This kind of culture is at the heart of innovation and disruption, and is the impetus that allows them to grow. Such companies are far better prepared for blind spots than those that punish people for speaking up.

Figure 2.4 Symptoms of a business with a blind spot.
Source: Creative Commons[12]

Your Defensible Space Is Holding You Back: Learn to See Past It

One blind spot we frequently encounter is the overreliance on what a business perceives as its "defensible space"— meaning the product or service it is most known for. This is a tricky hurdle that can feel like good business when you're

> **Blind Spot**
>
> Failing to constantly challenge your defensible space puts your business at risk.

deeply entrenched in a B-centric paradigm. The end result is anything but good business, however: if left unchecked, this overreliance quickly becomes stagnation. Instead of evolving and disrupting your business, you keep doing the same things in the same way and lose sight of the bigger picture unfolding beyond the boardroom. One example of a company that successfully avoided this trap is the aviation company Rolls-Royce. Traditionally, Rolls-Royce manufactured jet engines. Their defensible space was not only the physical product—the engines themselves—but also the ability to make and operate them effectively.

New production tools changed the game, however. Leaders at Rolls-Royce realized that technology was leveling the engine production field, turning it into a commodity-focused business. So, they moved beyond their defensible space by offering airlines the opportunity to buy their product (the engines) on an "As-a-Service" basis.

Instead of an airline investing the capital to buy the physical asset (the jet engine), paying for a maintenance contract, and then being stuck with the engine once it's reached its usability limit, Rolls-Royce developed a new business model called "power by the hour." Rolls-Royce moved from just selling jet engines to providing companies with an all-inclusive price for each hour the engine is used in flight.[13] In this way, they were able not only to adapt to the technological advances of their era, but also to set themselves apart as disruptive players in the new iteration of their field.

Case Study: Kodak's Blind Spots

One of recent history's cautionary tales regarding disruptive change is the example of Kodak, a company that sat at the very top of the camera and film industry for decades. As documented in the book *Bold*, Kodak was a $28 billion company at one time.[14] Now, they're worth a fraction of that, and much of their market share has been seized by other, newer companies. So, what happened?

In 1878, a bank teller named George Eastman wanted to take a vacation and document the trip with photographs. Unfortunately, trying to pack and travel with the cameras of the day was a horrendous experience. The camera itself was as big as a microwave oven, and the tripod and bottles of chemicals used to develop pictures were heavy. Dragging that much equipment out just to capture an image was a huge hassle. Except for the rare, dedicated hobbyist, most people wouldn't even bother to try.

Seized by a desire to solve this problem, George never went on his vacation. Instead, he began experimenting with the idea of a small, portable camera, and a set of lightweight equipment to go with it. He was so dedicated to the pursuit of creating a great customer experience that he would fall asleep by the kitchen stove, his mind still focused on developing better chemicals and an easier photography experience for the average consumer. His focus paid off—in 1884 George invented rolled film. A few years later, in 1888, he created the portable camera we know and came to love.

But that was just the beginning of Kodak's story.

From Market Master to Near-Disaster: Kodak and the Job to Be Done

Respected Harvard Business School Professor Clay Christensen wrote a book called *Competing Against Luck* that became a favorite among business experts all over the country. Dr. Christensen uses a key phrase in the book to discern what a company needs to do to stay competitive. He simply asked, "What is the job to be done?"

The way a company answers this question is revealing. Kodak's George Eastman put himself in the customer's shoes; he empathized with them and prioritized their experiences, which were also his own. He didn't want people to experience the difficulties he had in capturing vacation memories. The job to be done? Provide a better customer experience by making photography easier for the everyday person.

As a result of inventing rolled film, the cameras for the film, the improved chemical processes to develop the photos, and specialized paper to print them at scale, Kodak's business strategy and marketing slogan became, "You press the button, we do the rest." Eastman's philosophy of customer centricity launched the brand into an era of enormous success.

By putting themselves in their customer's shoes, Kodak was able to innovate on an exponential level. They produced and marketed a product that truly took care of the customer's problems, and by processing the film and printing the pictures for them, the company further enhanced the experience for millions of people.

What do you think Kodak's assumptions were regarding who they served and what they produced at this point in their evolution? They thought their defensible space was selling cameras, film, processing chemicals, and specialized photographic paper. Everything relied on the concept of film photography. But if you've ever used a digital camera or taken a selfie with your phone, you can probably guess where this story is headed.

It's easy to see why being hyperaware of the overall marketplace and advancing technology is the key to surviving and thriving in the emerging future—because Kodak's amazing, innovative success didn't last. They let the market catch up to them, and then they were too far behind to stop it from blowing right by them.

Imagine now it's 1973. A young electrical engineer named Steven Sasson (a graduate of Rensselaer Polytechnic Institute) is asked to experiment with a charged-couple device on behalf of Kodak, who wants to see if the small, chip-sized devices could be used for imaging the same way film was. In 1975, Sasson invented the world's first "digital" camera (Figure 2.5). It:

- Weighed eight pounds
- Recorded black-and-white images onto a cassette tape
- Had a resolution of .01 megapixels (10,000 pixels)
- Took 23 seconds to capture an image

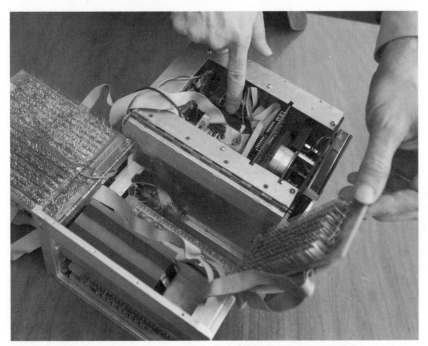

Figure 2.5 Steven Sasson with the world's first "digital" camera at Kodak.
Source: Getty

While it was not ideal (or anywhere close, by today's standards), it was a major development and a significant innovation compared to where Eastman started in 1884. When Sasson told his bosses about the camera, he expected them to say, "You, clever devil, how did you do that?"

Instead they asked, "Why would anyone want to look at their pictures on an electronic screen?" Beneath that dismissal was another question, and one that represented a hidden fear: "When will this digital camera idea pose a threat to our chemical and paper business, if at all?"

To understand the digital disruption blind spot, let's look again at what Kodak thought its business model was. In reality, Kodak wasn't just making photography equipment—they were providing a better customer experience. Photography is just a medium of expression, and the deeper concept it expresses is our desire to preserve and share our memories with our future selves and others.

At first, the company understood this. The "Kodak Moment" became a byword for a photo-worthy, shareable moment, and countless memories were captured using their cameras and equipment (Figure 2.6). Kodak had put themselves in their customers' shoes and understood they wanted to make memories last.

Sasson had tapped into this philosophy and thought, "What device could create this experience better than a digital camera?" He saw the potential of this device from the customer's point of view, and as someone who enjoyed photography himself, he connected with the idea on a deeper level.

Blind Spot

By not looking beyond your current products or services, you can't understand the business you are in, and it means missing new business opportunities.

But to Sasson's surprise, Kodak buried the digital camera idea because they thought it would undercut their chemical and paper sales, making the business compete with itself and "give up" its perceived defensible space. Kodak's first blind spot was therefore a stubborn, defensive mindset about their true purpose as a company.

Figure 2.6 Kodak marketing showed how it was in the business of preserving memories.
Source: Alamy

The Danger of Ignoring Exponential Technology's Effect on Business Models

Exponential technologies are defined by quickly advancing capabilities and simultaneously decreasing costs. This should make them very attractive to integrate into new products, services, and experiences, but as with any major change, there are always those who vacillate too long before adopting them.

Kodak's next blind spot was continuing to use chemicals and paper (linear technologies) while simultaneously refusing to explore exponential technology. There are laws that describe the rapid increase in exponential technology's capabilities. For integrated computer circuit boards, it's Moore's Law.[15] In 1965, Gordon E. Moore predicted an annual doubling of the number of components that would fit on an integrated computer circuit. Developers and designers took this as a challenge and it became a self-fulfilling prophecy.

The result was an electronics industry which delivered significantly more processing power in lighter and smaller computing devices, and for the same or less cost, every two years. In practical terms, Moore's Law meant that for a computer chip with 2,000 transistors, the costs would dramatically decline. For context:

- In 1970 it would cost $1,000
- In 1990 it would cost $250
- In 1994 it would cost $0.97
- Today it would cost less than $0.02[16]

Moore's Law meant that chip-based electronic devices had exponentially more, new innovative capabilities at similarly exponential decreases in cost.

When Sasson first demonstrated the digital camera, Kodak didn't explore the potential of Moore's Law to predict how low resolution, 0.01 megapixel images would become the high-resolution images that would soon make digital photography practical.

The result was a market that soon made Kodak practically obsolete. We've seen how exponential changes in technology's capabilities dramatically affect how we work, live, learn, and play. The next step? Simple: it's time to see the writing on the wall and let go of old, business-centric paradigms that lock you in to a narrow defensible space. Put yourself in your customers' shoes. Although they may not realize it on a conscious level, what they are purchasing from you isn't a product or a service; it's an experience. You must take advantage of exponential technologies to create better experiences and, as a result, new business opportunities for your brand.

Flash Forward to 1976: A Cautionary Tale

In 1976, Kodak controlled 85 percent of the camera and photography market. But Kodak was blinded by their own perceptions and they were too caught up in past success to realize the future that was rapidly approaching.

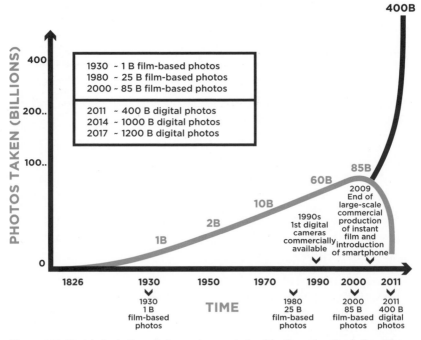

Figure 2.7 Kodak lost the photography market with the advent of the iPhone. Source: How to See the World,[17] Keypoint Intelligence/InfoTrends,[18] Multimediaman[19]

If they had focused on the competitive landscape of their present era, which included companies using exponential technologies to deliver customer experiences, they might have been the first to develop the digital camera and benefit from its innovative design. Instead, Kodak's market share disappeared one year after the introduction of the first iPhone—a digital device taking advantage of exponential technologies (Figure 2.7).

Kodak's mistakes are a cautionary tale for us all. Instead of using the digital camera to corner the market, the market cornered them.

Kodak learned about exponential change the hard way. Consistent and accelerating improvements to digital technology transformed computing capabilities to the point that a smartphone became a thousand times faster—and a million times cheaper—than a supercomputer of the 1970s (Figure 2.8).

Now, imagine being in Kodak's shoes. If you looked through their narrowly focused lens, you wouldn't even know what hit you when the market of today shifted. In our current era, exponential changes can literally happen overnight.

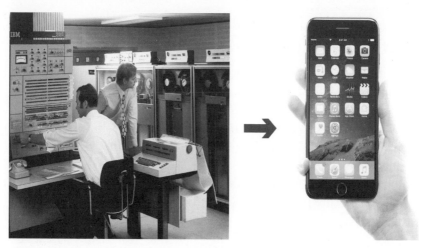

Figure 2.8 Through exponential technology, a computer from the 1970s has the same computing power as today's smartphone.
Source: Alamy

Kodak didn't foresee how disruptive exponential technology would be to the dominant business model of their industry—they were too concerned with their linear products' market shares to remember that their true purpose was to preserve and share memories, digitally or otherwise. Nor did they realize how the exponential changes happening to technology would affect their customers' rapidly rising expectations. As a result, they didn't disrupt their business model and transform Kodak's customer experience into their service. But smartphone companies, app designers, and a start-up called Instagram did see what was happening around them, and they adapted by creating Memories-as-a-Service for their customer base.

> **Blind Spot**
>
> Ignoring the "job to be done" from the customer's perspective means you aren't delivering contextually relevant experiences, putting your business at risk to those that do.

Kodak's example foreshadows the importance of applying exponential strategies and technologies to transform your business long before your competitors have the chance to outpace you.

Marathons and Sprints: Exponential Businesses Beat Their Competition

How did a $28 billion market cap company (Kodak) with 160,000 employees in 1996 fail to take advantage of the digital camera? To understand the forces that played a part in this massive oversight, let's compare two companies. One demonstrates a linear business growth model (Kodak), and one provides a prime example of exponential business growth (Instagram).

Flash forward to 2012. Kodak had to file Chapter 11 bankruptcy and downsized to only 17,000 employees. Instagram, on the other hand, had a $1 billion market cap and just 13 employees.

How did Instagram manage this incredible feat? Once again, the answer is a matter of company centricity versus customer experience.

What often happens to well-established companies that lack an innovative, disruption-based mindset is eventual defeat by a creative competitor aiming to do what they do better, faster, and with the customer firmly in mind. That's precisely what happened to Kodak.

Instagram, other social platforms, and digital camera/phone companies used exponential digital technologies to reinvent the customer experience of capturing and sharing memories. The "Kodak Moment" became an empty tagline and was soon lost to the practical, tangible advantages of the competition.

When a business is singularly focused on merely improving or changing the existing products and services they offer—rather than opening their minds to the possibility of reinvention—they are operating under a linear growth model.

> **Blind Spot**
>
> With technology changing at an exponential rate, most companies don't realize they are being left in the dark; consider how many products are incorporated into one device (smartphone), which made many businesses obsolete.

By choosing to take advantage of exponential technology instead, Instagram created unique software and an application rooted in an exponential business growth model. From their inception onward, they were clearly focused on empathically oriented customer experiences, which, in turn, saw the company grow at an exponential rate.

While Kodak tried to stave off the inevitable pace of change, Instagram deployed experiences by looking through the lens of consumers with digital strategies and exponential technologies such as the smartphone.

With an exponential business strategy and technology, Instagram put Kodak out of the business of making and sharing memories.

Learning in the Present before Becoming the Past: We Live in Exponential Times

Consider some of the revolutionary technological developments of the past 100 years. As technology advanced, the time it took to reach an audience of 50 million shifted exponentially.[20] For context, here is how long it took for each decade's major applications to achieve that reach:

- Radio – 38 years
- TV – 13 years
- Internet – 4 years
- iPod – 3 years

- Facebook – 2 years
- Pokémon Go – 19 days

As of this printing, Google had over 1.2 trillion billion searches per year; it was just 21 billion 20 years ago.[21] There were 500 million networked devices in 2003;[22] there are more than 27.1 billion in 2021.[23] Amazon had 15,000 robots working in their warehouses in 2014;[24] they had over 200,000 robots working warehouses in 2020.[25]

This growth rate and corresponding user adoption pattern applies to the customer experience as well. To future-proof your organization, you must start learning about exponential technologies and strategies as they apply to the customer and employee experience. Companies are so focused on what they are currently doing that they fail to create the necessary habit of scanning the external landscape for technological advances and shifts in paradigms, or to effectively explore how the competition is innovating. It is no longer an option to be highly aware, educated, and agile to change—it's a necessity.

If that model isn't currently part of your corporate DNA, it's essential you partner with organizations that enable you to explore how to change that mindset and adapt before it's too late.

TAKEAWAYS

- As companies transform the customer and employee experience, they are essentially embarking on a digital transformation.
- Because exponential technologies are transforming so rapidly, they can become a blind spot if a company's culture is not ready to embrace them and change.
- Recovering from a blind spot is exponentially more complex with every passing day.

TONY'S LEADERSHIP CORNER

Blind Spot: Underestimating the power of culture

We tend to underestimate the impact of culture. I first learned this lesson when Cisco acquired Scientific Atlanta for $7 billion in 2005. At that time, Cisco was a $24 billion revenue company with a market cap of $115 billion and 38,000 employees. Cisco had acquired nearly 100 companies and was well known for its proven replicable success in seamlessly integrating acquired companies.

Scientific Atlanta, a company with $2 billion in revenue and 10,000 employees, was a leading maker of products that let cable companies offer high-speed internet service to consumers. Prior to the purchase, Scientific Atlanta had been a Fortune 500 company and was one of the top 25 largest corporations in Georgia. It was considered "the patriarch of Atlanta's technology industry" for nearly six decades.

This seemed to be a perfect match: both market-leading public companies would be exponentially expanding their footprint through this acquisition. Plus, there was a cultural fit with both then-CEOs; Cisco's John Chambers and Scientific Atlanta's Jim McDonald were both raised in the South.

Chambers gave McDonald a seat on Cisco's board and agreed to let Scientific Atlanta run independently once acquired. Cisco took the same integration approach as it had done before and spent virtually no time to understand Scientific Atlanta's culture. It wasn't long before there were problems. They were in different worlds and were not aligned on the vision, technology road map, or how to work together. My then-Chief Development Officer Charlie Giancarlo asked me to take on Scientific Atlanta. I used to fly to Atlanta for the week and, when driving to the airport on Friday, I could feel the employees metaphorically waving to me as if to say,

"Goodbye, go home now." I invited Jim, the CEO, to dinner and asked, "Help me understand the trip wires between Scientific Atlanta and Cisco." Jim was very forthcoming and helped me get a better sense of the company, its culture, and its core values. Empathy came into play as I took the time to listen and understand the magic of Scientific Atlanta. Taking that time to learn was also a gift to me personally because it was my introduction to the consumer market. I became totally enamored with the consumer and it changed the trajectory of my career.

As I learned about Scientific Atlanta's culture, I realized that you cannot be successful if you misunderstand your culture. Harmonization, not integration, is an approach that can bring the team in. We went on to form the connected home video business that, over time, resulted in 290 million set-top boxes installed in more than 100 countries.

The importance of respecting existing culture came up again when I joined Skype as CEO in 2010. I held my first all-employee meeting in Estonia, which is where the engineering lifeblood of Skype is located, and was truly beaten up. The feeling I picked up was "Here's another new leader from Silicon Valley who's going to tell us what to do." I was pummeled with questions by engineers: "Do you even use Skype? Since when? What's your username? Do you cloud or peer-to-peer? Are you a top-line or bottom-line person?" It was very polarizing.

I wondered how I was going to endear myself to this team. So I took the original founding engineers to lunch and had an open conversation. They let me know: "Don't tell us what to do. Give us the problem to solve." It's essential to tap into the cultural underbelly of an organization. You can't be deaf. You have to listen. You must keep your ear to the rail so you are really connected to what's happening with the culture before you put your signature on it.

" The day before
a breakthrough,
people will say "it's"
just a crazy idea.

—Peter Diamandis

HISTRY FORESHADOWS CX PROBLEMS

No matter the era, there have always been warning signs that precede major issues with customer or employee experience problems. Whether it is deteriorating organizational cultures, unsustainable growth models, or blatant inequality, situations never become crises overnight.

Our technologies have the potential to become incredible assets or drivers of negative change depending on us—but as the humans behind that technology, perhaps we don't pay enough attention to the signs, and perhaps we are reluctant to truly think through the consequences of our actions when they feel comfortable, exciting, or prosperous. When you're caught up in the world of misplaced ideals, it's often difficult to be truly present in the real world that's still spinning around you.

If we are present, maybe we are shortsighted. Maybe we seek investor or shareholder results more than we respect the experience of the customer or employee. Perhaps we don't consider the totality of the consequences of what we create. As human beings, we all share a tendency to view the world wholly through our own perspective—especially when we are financially invested in something.

Whether intentional or not, competition requires that old mindsets retire. If you step back and look at things from a distance, you'll quickly realize that this has always been the case. While seeming well thought out, a solely self-serving vision doesn't allow you to gain the foresight you need to succeed in the long term.

People's actions build the future. No matter what kind, technology can't do anything by itself. It can't achieve anything we haven't designed, built, or programmed it to do. So, it's never been the technology that goes astray on its own. It is the people behind the technology and how it's developed and applied.

When we are present and focused on the job at hand—serving customers and employees—we can infuse technology with the very best parts of humanity. But to do that we need to ask ourselves "What decisions do I need to make today to create a future better than the past, where the quality—not the quantity or efficiency—of my customers' and employees' experiences take priority?"

The quality of our lives, businesses, and social systems are all based on our values. We must hold ourselves accountable for creating systems founded on human empathy and integrity, and we must strive to drive trust and respect among and between each other. If we don't, we run the risk of driving customer and employee experiences toward even worse blind spots; an outcome with consequences greater than we can envision now, and which can only be avoided if we choose to open our eyes to a new way of doing business.

If You Aren't Paying, You're the Product

At face value the "freemium" model seems like a reasonable business model. Customers get a "free" service or application in exchange for their attention, data, or mindshare. If you step back and look at things from a broader perspective, however, you can spot potential issues quite quickly.

Without the right intentions behind it, the freemium model can result in unintended consequences. One of the more common—and unfortunate—ones can be summed up by the statement, "If you are not paying for the product, you are the product." Like all of the mistakes and poor outcomes we've discussed, this one didn't happen overnight.

One of the signs indicating that something wasn't quite right from the customer experience standpoint was the fact that this statement was widely expressed by influential modern artists such as Richard Serra and Carlota Fay Schoolman even back in 1973. These artists created a video piece that year and titled it, "Television Delivers People."[1] It was both thought-provoking and disturbing.

The display consisted of canned music and electronically generated text scrolling over a blue background, conveying the same aesthetic as a public service announcement or a 3 a.m. infomercial. We've included a snippet of the text (Figure 3.1), and the whole video can be viewed on YouTube.

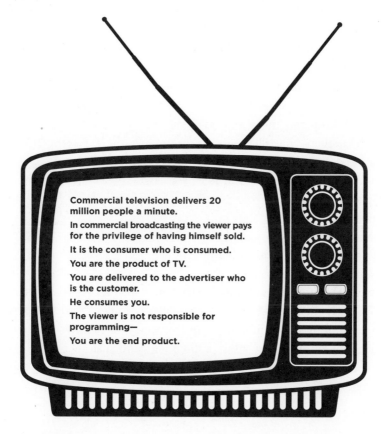

Figure 3.1 Example of the text from the video "Television Delivers People."
Source: YouTube[2]

Serra and Schoolman felt that the corporations behind television broadcasting were manipulative forces solely interested in gaining power and profiting from the customer. Corporations packaged advertising and marketing messages in easily consumed narratives and catchy brand slogans. By hiring experts on human psychology and curating their messages to tap into our hopes, dreams, and insecurities, companies were able to affect how we thought and felt about our place in the world, what products we wanted, and our innate desire to "Keep up with the Joneses." They began to shape our perceptions of the world, ourselves, and each other.

Television was the technology used to transmit these messages, and the process of influencing the consumer's psyche became an ingrained aspect of the television customer experience. While consumers received programming that was ostensibly "free," advertisers got to showcase their products to large, profitable audiences. This model was the precursor to our current world of digital customer experiences in which we now disrespect and talk at the customer with nonstop digital ads and "free" content that follows them around the web via their smartphones and computers.

More and more, we are hearing that people are tired of this. New technologies aimed at blocking ads and corporate content from consumers' screens are being developed every year, and the

> **Blind Spot**
>
> Historically, companies have treated customers as commodities, which results in them choosing price or product features over loyalty to a brand because of the experience.

younger generation is making it clear that they won't accept this aggressive, manipulative customer experience model any longer. And yet, despite a corresponding boom in books, conferences, and seminars explaining the need for companies to adopt authenticity and customer centricity as their central business model, the old trend continues without any sign of slowing down.

"Why Should I Care?" Contextually Irrelevant Content Is Not New

Looking for similar patterns in the evolution of the digital customer experience, we find more indicators that something is amiss.

Usenet was an early internet discussion platform conceived in 1979 and publicly established in 1980 at the University of North Carolina at Chapel Hill. Duke University followed a decade later with what we know today as the World Wide Web.

Over time, Usenet moderators became concerned about the customer experience on certain newsgroups, predominantly as it related to spam. The moderators were aghast that a platform meant to inspire vibrant, intense global conversation was being turned into a giant infomercial for get-rich-quick schemes and pornography. They couldn't completely fault those looking for a way to monetize Usenet, but they wondered if any of them were respecting the customer in the way they went about it.

In 1999, AllAdvantage launched a service that showed advertisements to customers at the top or bottom of the computer display while they browsed the Usenet newsgroups—and paid them for it. Viewers could receive 50 cents per hour compensation with a cap of $20 a month.[3] In December 1999 Steve Atkins, moderator of two drama and theater Usenet newsgroups, sent a message via the Usenet discussion groups that contained a similar sentiment to that of Serra and Schoolman's statement about television:

> *If you want to sell crap, AllAdvantage punters are not a bad demographic to advertise to. This isn't meant to imply anything about any individual AA punter, just about the demographics. The punters are not the customer, they're the product. Anyone who's an AA punter is being sold for a few pennies an hour.*[4]

So even back then, there were concerns about contextually irrelevant content and the type of customer experience being created by it. A reaction article on ZDNet noted, ". . . in forums of public discourse, the users of Usenet are learning that freedom of speech comes with a price . . ."[5]

MLMs, Spam, and Unintended Consequences Galore: Misusing Customer Data Is Not New

Following Steve Atkin's post, author Claire Wolfe wrote an article titled "Little Brother Is Watching You: The Menace of Corporate America" in which she discussed another indicator. It centered around the way digital marketing had become very business-centric and was being used to collect people's personal data through biometric systems, black box recorders in cars, and records of credit card purchases:

> *[...] you're not the customer anymore. You're simply a "resource" to be managed for profit. The customer is someone else now—and usually someone without your best interests at heart ... Who is the customer? Not you, whose life is reduced to someone else's salable, searchable, investigable data. The customer is everyone who wishes to own a piece of your life.[6]*

When the Customer Becomes the Product

In June 2001, a Usenet user named Tom Johnson posted in a newsgroup called "rec.arts.tv. interactive."[7]

> **Subject:** You're not the customer, you're the product.
>
> **To review:** Television viewers aren't the customers, they're the product, and younger demographics are more desirable to advertisers because they're dumb enough to pay attention to ads.

In September 2010, influential publisher Tim O'Reilly tweeted the remark below while crediting Andrew Lewis' article on MetaFilter's webpage about news aggregator Digg:

> Yes! RT @bryce love this quote "If you're not paying for it, you're not the customer; you're the product being sold."[8]

In their 2012 book, *Fake It! Your Guide to Digital Self-Defense,* authors Steffan Heuer and Pernille Tranberg made the following statement:

> *"If you are not paying for it, you're not the customer;*
> *you're the product being sold" so said an internet user*
> *with the screen name blue_beetle, whose supposed real*
> *name is Andrew Lewis, in a post in August 2010. It caught*
> *on as a meme and rallying cry for people who don't buy*
> *the "free" tricks anymore that web companies play on us.*[9]

Today, we annoy customers with chatbots that pop up on the screen before they've even indicated they need help. The result is often negative interference with the customer's experience. Companies end up blocking the thing customers want to accomplish as they angrily try to close the pop-up window—or just give up and go to a competitor whose user experience isn't so annoying.

Brand Advocates vs. Badvocates

Instead of creating customers who become fans or brand advocates and, hopefully, brand ambassadors, manipulative companies are creating negative PR outcomes and "badvocates." Customer trust has become so abysmally low that they tend to believe other customers (even those they have never met) more than a company's most recent, clever marketing message or value statement.

Badvocates are the opposite of brand ambassadors; they are customers who will loudly and openly talk or post about their negative experiences with a company, most often through social and digital media. Badvocates'

> **Blind Spot**
>
> Tired of bad experiences, customers become badvocates instead of brand advocates, leading to negative in-person and online word of mouth.

public dissatisfaction leaves a major dent in a company's reputation. Even carefully crafted messages from a brand's talented (and expensive) PR, advertising, and marketing teams can't compete with thousands of easily accessible posts from real and unhappy customers.

Review and recommendation sites have become incredibly popular for the simple reason that customers relate to hearing from people like themselves, and they trust their community's statements about doing business with a particular brand.

This global phenomenon is illustrated by the popularity of sites like Angie's List, Amazon Reviews, Thumbtack, HomeAdvisor, Houzz, Kaodim, Travaux, Werkspot, My Builder, 58.com, Yuedan, HomeStars, and more. You can gain a great deal of insight from these sites and the reviews posted on them. If you are operating in the Empathy Era, you will have taken these lessons to heart and turned your brand advocates—and your badvocates—into brand ambassadors. No extra money needs to be spent on PR crisis aversion or fancy marketing. These ambassadors spread the word simply by using their sphere of online and off-line influence in their normal, authentic way. People talk about their experiences. That's truer in today's highly networked world than ever before.

Another side to bad customer experiences is the demoralization of employees who have to deal with the fallout. Constantly handling upset customers leads to poor morale and lower productivity, even poorer customer experiences, and high employee attrition—all of which is extremely costly for the company as a whole. Embarrassed by the company's lack of integrity, employees become apathetic instead of being champions of the company or its brand.

Producing Disaster: Why Are Customers Still the Product?

Despite the success of Amazon, Zappos, and a respectable host of innovative business-to-consumer brands such as Carvana and Warby Parker, the same old Big Brother manipulation practices continue to be common across many industries, now based on internet technology. Poorly designed freemium campaigns and "manufactured consent" are far more common now than ever before. Unfortunately, too many customers are still the product—and now, they know it. In the digital age, you can depend on customers being hyperaware and even more informed than your own marketing departments when it comes to your brand's reputation.

We are at a turning point, and it calls for a reimagining of the corporate model from the ground up. It's not about getting new customers (Figure 3.2); it's about getting a new way to think about them. Through a determined commitment to empathy across the entire organization and a focus on experience at every customer touchpoint, a whole new culture can emerge. With it, companies have the opportunity to become more than just successful. They have the chance to become meaningful. And meaning, more than anything, drives profit in today's market.

> **Blind Spot**
>
> Most businesses design customer experiences with a business-first mindset vs. a customer-first mindset.

© 2021 Ted Goff

"Our customers have told us that everything we do is wrong. Therefore, we need new customers."

Figure 3.2 It's not about finding new customers; it's about shifting the way companies think about current and potential customers.

Noncustomer-centric cultures lead to lower customer lifetime value (churn). In marketing, sales, service, and all the way to back-of-the-back-office operations, noncustomer-centric companies waste enormous sums of money. Businesses acquire customers with empty promises, then turn them away by mistreating them.

To review:

- Since the First Industrial Revolution, companies have been organized around company/shareholder profit (vs. customer/employee value).
- This has driven companies' decision-making processes, leadership styles, organizational structure, employee hiring practices, training recognition, and rewards.
- Customer practices (how to treat and serve customers) are, unfortunately, designed with a company-first mindset.
- Most companies don't make customers feel special, heard, or acknowledged when they interact with them.
- Businesses often mishandle customer data via data breaches or misuse the 2.5 quintillion bytes of customer data generated daily for astronomical financial gain.
- Companies, operating solely on a price-and-product paradigm for so many years, don't realize they are selling experiences—as a result, they don't put enough emphasis on these experiences, even when research consistently shows that customers will happily pay more for better ones.

The Exponential Business Model's Urgency Factor

Applying the lessons of the past and integrating the potential of exponential technology and people-centric strategic revolutions is key to differentiating yourself from competitors. Situational awareness is a matter of survival in today's

> **Blind Spot**
>
> Most businesses don't realize their agile competitors are eclipsing them, leaving them far behind and standing in the dust wondering what happened.

hyper-speed culture, and you must be aware of how market dynamics have changed since the days of early industrial business titans. This means evolving your business strategy from:

- A B-centric to a C&E-centric, empathy-centric, people-based model
- One that uses linear technology to one that integrates exponential technology
- Using linear business growth models to exponential business growth models
- One focused on B-centric efficiency and effectiveness metrics to one that sees these through the lens of empathy (the customer/employee point of view)

Defining Linear vs. Exponential Business Growth on Your Terms

We can better understand the urgency to become an empathically based, customer/employee-focused company by comparing linear and exponential business growth models. Linear business growth is dependent on using linear technology, whereas exponential business growth comes from using exponential technologies that accelerate its business growth rate.

Good Things Come in Threes: Components of the Exponential Business Model

Because business growth rates are directly related to the type of technology used to achieve them, let's look at the three components of an exponential business model (Figure 3.3). The x-axis is time, and the y-axis is the increase in the capability of the technology—which eventually expands exponentially with respect to time.

Many experts have used the graph to depict how exponential technology's capabilities sneak up on industries, and they tie this to three distinct points in time:

- No sense of urgency (Disappointment Zone)
- The point of no return
- It's too late (Chaos Zone)

Blind Spot

Not understanding the three parts of the exponential business growth model means businesses are left blindsided by competitors who are using it to their advantage.

The first part of the graph, the Disappointment Zone, correlates to the linear growth business model. The line appears straight because the rate of change in technology's capabilities is too slow to make any noticeable difference. This perception often leads to a lack of urgency in corporate leadership circles. It's also why many companies either ignore exponential technologies or don't consider them a business priority. They don't realize something phenomenal is brewing.

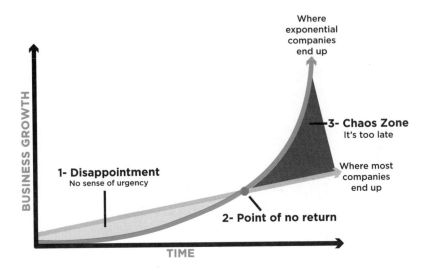

Figure 3.3 The three parts to the exponential business growth curve:
1. Disappointment; 2. Point of no return; 3. Chaos Zone.

The second part of the graph is where things get interesting. As we follow the curve, we first see the doubling of a given technology's capabilities (.02 -> .04 -> .06 -> .08 -> 1.0). When it breaks the whole number barrier (the point of no return), the capabilities then increase exponentially compared to the Disappointment Zone. With this increase in capabilities comes the opportunity for visibly disruptive, exponential business growth as the technology is applied in a business setting, regardless of its initial or intended purpose. The point of no return is where competitors get caught off guard and are often completely blindsided.

The third part of the graph, the "It's too late" area, is unfortunately where many businesses eventually find themselves—in the Chaos Zone. With the technological capabilities developed into practical business offerings, those using them experience exponential business growth compared to those using linear technologies and strategies. This business growth rate is so much faster than prior time periods that it's nearly impossible to catch up to it once it passes the point of no return. When we compare the linear business growth model to the exponential growth model, we see the difference between the two rates expressed as the "digital disruption" (Figure 3.4) referred to in Chapter 2 (Figure 2.2).

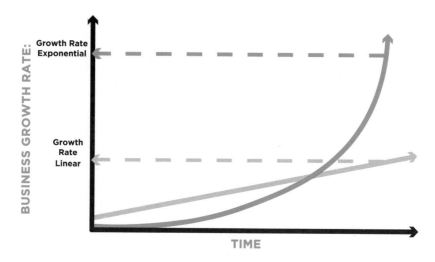

Figure 3.4 Comparison of companies with linear and exponential growth.

What If's and What Then's: Disrupting Kodak's Business Model

True disruption of an industry or business requires not only new technology, but also new business models to go with it. Let's see how this applies to our Kodak case study, which perfectly demonstrated the disruptive potential of exponential tech through the rise of Instagram and other smartphone-based applications.

To start with, Kodak kept using linear technologies: film to capture the image, chemical processing to develop the film, and special photographic paper for printing pictures. Their business model stubbornly clung to these technologies as their foundation, priming them for disruption. Kodak's revenue came from customers buying film as well as from companies buying the chemicals and special photographic paper that developed and printed pictures for those same customers.

With the advent of digital camera technology, customers no longer needed to buy film, and the companies developing and printing the pictures no longer needed to buy Kodak's chemicals or special photographic printing paper. Customers could even print pictures at home with their own printer.

At the same time, social media platform founders and digital camera makers asked, "Is there another way to be in touch, to preserve and share memories? Is there a way to share pictures digitally so people don't need to print or make copies to send them to friends and family?" Creating these new digital platforms and technologies greatly reduced the demand for processing chemicals and photography paper. Almost overnight, the main ways Kodak made money—selling film, photographic chemicals, and paper—all but vanished.

Late to the Game: Missing the Exponential Tech-to-Business Model Shift

How does this happen to a company? Well, it doesn't happen all at once. If Kodak had cultivated an exponential business mindset, they might have seen the signs that were popping up for years before the major market shifts occurred. After all, markets don't change by themselves. There are always forces driving their patterns—and the key is learning to spot those forces early on.

When the technology for smartphones was first being developed, it didn't look like much was happening (the Disappointment Zone). But some digital device companies were paying attention to Moore's Law. As these companies invested in the development of digital device technologies, the devices' capabilities—processing speed, memory capacity, sensors, and even the size and number of pixels in digital cameras—doubled quickly and advanced to the point that it could be made into a practical consumer device (the point of no return).

Unlike the companies making these investments, Kodak's executives didn't see around the corner. They couldn't bring themselves to look beyond the film, chemical, and paper business. They didn't investigate the use of exponential technologies, and they didn't stop to consider the advantage they would have if they used these technologies to create a digital camera—an invention they had a 30-year head start on and were perfectly positioned for bringing to the market. Those 30 years represent a lot of missed opportunities, all arising from the company's flawed lens of perception.

Digital cameras, smartphones, social platforms, and related software and applications such as Instagram not only used the exponential capabilities of digital technology, but also created new business models to integrate them. They were able to reinvent how memories are captured, stored, and shared. Kodak lost market position because they didn't shift their revenue model from selling film, chemicals, and photographic paper to selling digital cameras or developing a social platform to share memories.

In the end, exponential models always come out on top. Linear models end as soon as a new dimension is added to the market.

Lessons Learned from Exponential Business Growth

What does this have to do with the CX/EX industry? The same type of exponential shift is happening through the exponential technologies used to deliver and scale empathy in CX and EX—except companies don't have to do any of the development themselves this time. The initial, critical development period of exponential CX/EX technology (the Disappointment Zone) has matured into feasible, scalable business offerings, which means we are at the point of no return. It also indicates that the acceleration of CX/EX technology will only continue to pick up speed and breadth in the very near future.

The critical lesson from the exponential business growth curve is a simple one: companies need to begin implementing exponential technologies as part of a systematic, empathy-fueled orchestration of the customer/employee experience. You can't wait to take advantage of these advances later on, when competitors have already integrated them and shifted to an empathy-based business model. You must incorporate them into your business, well, yesterday. Yes, you are already behind. That's where the "urgency" in "urgency factor" comes into play. If you are still using linear CX/EX technologies, you must make the decision to change now or be disrupted; when this happens, the best-case scenario is that you'll lose market share; the worst case is that you'll simply go out of business.

As a leader, you need to consider these questions:

- How can I change the agility of my business?
- Is my culture prepared to shift as quickly as the technology and the leadership team wants?

Just as we've reached a turning point in the current market's conditions, we've also reached a turning point in this book. From here, we'll start to deepen your understanding of how to implement what we've learned over the course of the past few chapters.

Chapter 4 explores the business advantages of deploying exponential CX/EX technologies. Chapter 5 looks deeper into the linear technology traditionally used in CX/EX, and Chapter 6 explores how poor experiences lead to "bad" profits—i.e., profits that were made at the expense of the employee's and customer's best interest. For companies that don't begin to take these strategies to heart, this "point of no return" will be followed by chaotic times, with competitors coming seemingly out of nowhere and taking the marketplace by storm. Make no mistake: they didn't come from nowhere. They are start-ups working in their garages using these principles.

Or, alternatively, they are established companies quietly reorganizing themselves and their CX/EX strategies and technologies as we speak, thus preparing to take advantage of the latest disruptive business methods the second they appear.

Shouldn't that be you?

Don't Underestimate the Power of Exponentials

Let's not be too hard on Kodak, or on any other company that's missed the exponential business growth train. It's easy to underestimate the power of exponential growth. It's something relatively new in the world of business, and it's part of why we spent so much time in the first two chapters observing the rate of change in technological advances throughout history. It takes plenty of background knowledge to understand how and why the rate of change is now exponential compared to that of the past. In fact, our grandfather's grandfather's business growth models were more linear without it ever becoming an issue. If something happened on the other side of the planet, people knew nothing about it. The market itself was linear, and that was because life was linear; things didn't change for centuries until the next revolution.

> **Blind Spot**
>
> Changes to exponential technologies are happening so quickly it's nearly impossible to remain competitive if a business isn't already incorporating them.

Without a relative comparison, we might not know how fast exponential change actually is. Here's a metaphor for perspective. Taking 30 linear steps, you end up 30 meters away. In the same amount of time, if you take 30 exponential steps, you could go around the world 26 times.

Even today, many of the people running businesses started their careers at a time when business models and technology were still largely linear. The ideas behind exponential technology and business growth models are extremely new when viewed on that timescale, and many entrepreneurs and executives haven't had the opportunity to learn about them. Few business schools and MBA programs include these concepts in their curriculum, so even new graduates "don't know what they don't know" about applying exponential business growth models to today's businesses.

Seeking out this type of information often falls on the shoulders of a few prophetic employees or leaders, often against a cultural backdrop where they seem to be outliers talking about some futurist nonsense.

The thing is, they aren't talking nonsense. They're speaking as visionaries. More than anyone, they see the future for what it can be.

Experiential Alchemy: Business Strategies to Focus on the Customer

It's not enough to have an exponential business model or use exponential technology to deliver on it. Yielding exponential results also requires a laser focus on customers and employees. A great example of what happens when you neglect this core aspect of the growth model is Groupon. Theirs is a cautionary tale of how not being customer-centric can hurt your

> **Blind Spot**
>
> Most companies don't make business decisions by considering the impact of their decisions on their customers/employees.

business, even if you're taking advantage of the latest, most innovative technologies. You need more than an innovative product or service that draws the market's notice.

The founder and CEO of Groupon, Andrew Mason, was fired only 15 months after the second-largest IPO in US history. He was the scapegoat for the company's plummeting stock prices and poor business performance, which had reached disastrous proportions by that time. As Mason resigned, he imparted this wisdom: "Have the courage to start with the customer."

On the opposite end of things, Jeff Bezos, the founder of Amazon (another company using the latest digital technology), is famous for leaving an empty chair at the conference room table. Why does he insist on this unusual practice? He ensures that everyone in attendance knows the empty chair is occupied by the "the most important person in the room"—the customer! The empty chair acts as a powerful cue for employees and executives to move away from a mindset based on what we all already think we know or groupthink to one that is intently focused on the customer's point of view.

To shift over to this paradigm, every company decision should be made through the lens of: What would that do for the employee and customer experience? What if this question became part of how you start every meeting and navigate every decision?

For most companies, it would be a major departure from how decisions are currently made. But it would also force them to think beyond the status quo, put the customer and the employee first, and lead the business with empathy as its guide.

It is imperative to incorporate a customer/employee-focused mindset into all parts of your business using the concept of design-thinking—the first core principle of which is to empathize, then to define, iterate, prototype, and test. This kind of thinking is particularly necessary in areas such as engineering, software coding, and manufacturing, which tend to be very business-centric and solely focused on linear measures efficiency and effectiveness.

Because it's such a new concept, an empathy mindset has to be enacted first by the highest levels of leadership, and then taught by example to all other parts of the organization. At this time, this is simply not the way most companies are led.

Staying Sunny-Side Up: Laggards Scramble in a State of Chaos

Companies investing in exponential strategies end up so far ahead of their competitors that the laggards end up in a state of chaos, scrambling to figure out how to stay afloat. They may find themselves losing money so quickly that they resort to severe cost-cutting measures as a method of revenue balancing—but we all know the key to business is revenue growth. Cost cutting doesn't grow a business; it just reduces the cost to run a business. It's the precursor to a revenue decrease, which, in this context, almost always follows.

It's challenging to catch up to an exponentially changing marketplace and to face competitors who are constantly evolving their business models, growing their revenue exponentially, and preparing for digital disruptions. These competitors are not only open to change but are actively seeking it.

These examples are shared to create a sense of urgency and to fuel your drive to incorporate exponential technology as a flywheel or an exponential-forcing function, thereby transforming your business strategies. They should also remind you, your team, and your company about the importance of:

> **Blind Spot**
>
> Without adopting exponential business models and technology it is exponentially more difficult—if not impossible—to remain competitive.

- Encouraging collaboration and innovation in new ways
- Creating a new type of organization
- Having a sense of conviction, belief, and desire for your team to be on the forefront
- Learning to see around corners using an empathetic approach
- Taking advantage of everything you can
- Using these capabilities with empathy as your guide
- Becoming an exponential, digital organization hyper-focused on empathic customer and employee experiences—with exponential success as the result

TAKEAWAYS

- There have always been early warning signs indicating when businesses have lacked a customer-centric mode of operation.

- Businesses must evolve their business strategies/ models from business-centric to customer/employee-centric.

- Exponential business growth models and customer/ employee-centric technologies allow companies to make experiences a top differentiator in an increasingly competitive marketplace. Those that don't will be blindsided.

TONY'S
LEADERSHIP CORNER

Blind spot: Know when to push and when to let go
when driving market transitions and innovation

One of my greatest career successes was leading the team that built the Cisco CRS-1 router, which became a multi-billion-dollar business. It started in 1996 when I was a consulting engineer at Cisco and was brought into an executive meeting to represent the voice of the customer. It was a wild meeting with executives arguing over the next piece of engineering greatness. The problem was we had built all this amazing networking technology with the newest operating system, the newest silicon chip, and the best engineers in the industry—but nobody really knew how it needed to operate with the rapidly rising internet.

The typical engineer didn't connect to the customer. It's a classic gap; what a product does and how a customer or operator uses it. I was willing to call them out on this and, as a result, was named head of product management of the company's high-end core router (code named BFR), the Cisco 12000. From there, I went on to lead the next generation core router (code named HFR), the Cisco CRS-1. This was a five-year project that was like building the space shuttle. In the first year of the mission, it became clear that Cisco's proprietary internetworking operating system (IOS) would not scale to reach the needs of our new router.

I remember the meeting when I let then-Chief Development Officer Mario Mazzola—the man responsible for leading Cisco's overall R&D strategy and 11 technology groups, the former president and CEO of Crescendo, and the holder of a master's degree in electrical engineering and several networking patents—know that my team needed to divorce from Cisco's core IOS platform as the path forward. We were coming up against the blind spot of losing perspective and losing sight of where the market was going because we were too attached to the technology; coveting technology at the expense of solving real-world problems. Challenging the CDO in this way could have been a career-limiting move.

But, when it comes to innovation, a customer-first mentality is critical. It might require you to push the boundaries of status quo thinking and go up against the most powerful forces within the enterprise. On the flip side, there are times to let go.

Another time at Cisco, I worked with a team of incredibly talented engineers who invented a new MAC layer technology for self-healing rings, which we patented and became the de facto IEEE standard. I loved working on it and, at the time, considered it the greatest creative invention in my life. My boss empowered me and everyone believed in me. I was asked to lead the development of the hardware even though I had no prior hardware experience. However, as we became more successful, I recognized that I didn't have the right experience to see the project through to large-scale success—even with everyone rooting for me.

The lesson here is "know when to let go." Be bold and go for it, but understand what it takes. Check your ego at the door and build the right team. Further along in my career now, I see this blind spot with many company founders. The genius who created the brilliant invention may not be the leader who can create a profitable, global company with a strong culture that's built to last.

> **"** The status quo
> is tenacious. The
> human mind prefers
> continuity rather
> than change.
>
> —Roger Martin

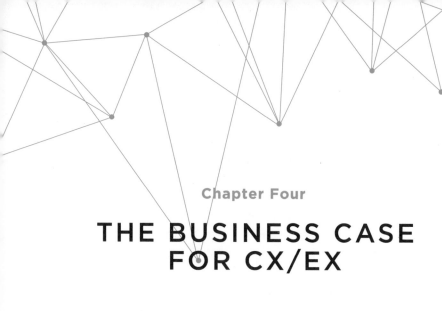

THE BUSINESS CASE FOR CX/EX

Blind spots are dangerous when we're changing lanes at 60 mph on the highway, and the blind spots limiting a company's customers and employee experiences are just as dangerous in context. You need to develop a strong set of rearview mirrors and other tools to prevent them from crashing your business model into the median.

Before we get started on the exact steps to achieve this, let's look at how rapid changes in the exponential technologies governing customer and employee experiences provide the opportunity to build better businesses, create competition differentiation, and drive the urgent need to transform your business—or be left in the dust.

What Happened to the Customer Experience Movement?

Mom-and-pop stores were plentiful in the eighteenth and nineteenth centuries—from general stores that carried just about everything to specialized stores like bakeries, jewelers, and butchers. These shops appealed to customers' desire for a personalized experience with human connections: store owners knew everyone's name and their preferences. As department stores entered the landscape, Americans flocked to Macy's, Bloomingdale's, and Sears, not just for products, but also for the in-person experiences they offered—lectures, entertainment, demonstrations. Relevant, personalized experiences were expected.

However, twenty years ago, the idea of a "one-to-one digital experience" was considered radical thinking in marketing. Organizations attempted to personalize customer experiences by segmenting, targeting, and retargeting customers with digital content and ads. In concept, it's a great idea. In practice, it's difficult to execute. Compared to what exponential technologies can deliver, linear technologies are severely limited in creating highly personalized customer or employee experiences.

Previous personalization attempts were driven by company-focused goals such as attaining higher customer acquisition rates (leads) and sales closures. From the customer's perspective, however, the interactions didn't always result in a better experience. Targeted ads or offers leveraging personal information can be invasive and turn customers away. Known colloquially as the "creepy factor," customers often feel that companies know way too much about them without their permission to access or use that information. In fact, in a recent study by the PEW Research Organization, half of Americans decided not to use a product or service due to privacy concerns.[1]

> **Blind Spot**
>
> The idea of providing one-to-one customer experiences is decades old, yet many organizations' attempts to personalize a customer's experiences fall short by using a business-centric vs. customer-centric POV.

Even with the 2.5 quintillion bytes of customer data gathered each day and the behavioral insight this data provides, most companies miss the mark when it comes to using it to create amazing customer experiences. It's partially due to their blind spots about what constitutes a great customer experience in the first place—at least from a customer's point of view. Research shows that most consumers are willing to exchange their data for more connected, empathetic experiences. Two out of three consumers worldwide believe that when companies collect data with consent and customer-centric intent, it improves the service experience.[2] But not very many companies have found a new way to do this. We will show you how (more on this in Chapter 9). If providing products, services, and experiences is how you make money, shouldn't the thoughts and feelings your customers have about those experiences be the most important indicator of your long-term financial success?

What Is an Empathic Customer Experience?

We've all been on the receiving end of bad customer service. In fact, research shows that the majority of consumers have been driven to tears by a bad service interaction. Clearly, companies need to reevaluate their strategies and respond to their customers in new ways. Whether an experience is delivered by a human employee or designed into technology-based experiences (like an AI chatbot or an SMS message), the design process should begin with one simple question: How can I put myself directly into my customer's shoes and understand what they are trying to do?

If you remember a great experience, it probably means you were heard, recognized, and even delighted by the engagement. In talking to customers, we find that great customer experience begins with an empathic approach. These customer-centric encounters grow customer's trust in a company and drive their loyalty toward a long-term commitment. This is the foundation of Empathy in Action.

> **Blind Spot**
>
> If providing products, services, and experiences is how you make money, what your customers think about their experiences is the most important indicator to your long-term financial success.

Empathy requires an understanding of what customers are looking to achieve and the context of the steps they have taken so far. A company needs to engage customers in real time, in preferred channels, and without losing context—even when a customer changes channels altogether.

This can be done through orchestrating personalized experiences (Figure 4.1). Until now, true personalization often required the extra effort of exceptional employees. While individuals acting in sympathetic or empathic ways can be critical to great customer experiences, businesses need more than one or two employees' empathetic mindsets. Otherwise, it's not realistically scalable or consistent. That's where exponential technology—if designed and implemented with an empathic, customer/employee-first point of view—comes into play.

Figure 4.1 Orchestrating personalized experiences drives empathy, trust, and loyalty.

Foundations and Walls: Why Do Customer Experiences Matter?

When we talk about delivering great experiences, we're also talking about the way these experiences deliver better business results for the company. Customers and employees form the foundation of your business as well as the walls, ceilings, and well, everything else. And since employees determine the way your company interacts with those customers, they are just as important.

How do you know for certain what customers think about their experiences with your company? Businesses often measure opinions through surveys or focus groups, but these often rely on what customers say they will do versus what they actually do. According to experts like Diana Lucaci, the neuromarketing strategist, founder, and CEO of True Impact, science has shown that emotion is a better indicator of behavior.[3] We act on how we feel, not what we say. When companies ask customers about what they would do, they are not getting the right data. Companies gain a more accurate picture of their performance as a business when measuring customers' actions with neuromarketing. By tapping into emotional data, we can create real-time, relevant, and authentic experiences while simultaneously improving employee experiences by using exponential technologies curated for that purpose. Simply put, we can deliver on the promises of Empathy in Action in ways never before possible.

The new empathic customer experience approach makes business sense for the simple reason that emotional and human connections lead directly to customer retention, lifetime value, and loyalty, which equates to repeat purchases over long periods. These emotional connections don't have to be super-deep, heart-filled interactions. They can be as simple as the feeling of, "That was fast!" or "That was easy!" or "I'm glad I didn't have to repeat myself; they got it!"

And yet, despite its simplicity, creating a customer experience that results in such positive reactions requires a lot of context.

> **Blind Spot**
>
> When businesses don't understand how important great experiences are, it leaves them vulnerable to customer attrition, lower lifetime customer values, and reduced new revenue.

The Business Impact of Empathy

Empathic businesses can boost their profits, keep costs under control, and improve employee morale—all by putting their focus where it belongs: on the people who make their success possible. Studies on customer experience by Forrester Research show that empathic companies' cumulative total returns beat the S&P 500 Index by an average of 27 percent, blowing away customer experience laggards by a whopping 128 percent.[4]

A survey by Gartner revealed that 89 percent of companies say they compete primarily based on customer experience.[5] But in a Bain & Company research report, 80 percent of their studied companies reported providing good customer experiences, yet only 8 percent of customers agreed.[6] Why does this matter? When customers don't think companies offer them great experiences, those companies are vulnerable to customer attrition, lower lifetime customer values, and less new revenue. Customer experiences can and often do determine whether a company stays in business. It's an investment you can't afford not to make.

But customer experience transformation is not a one-time event. It is an ever-evolving, strategic investment in your company's future business and financial success. The world is constantly changing. Companies must become current to survive, but they must be ahead of the change to truly thrive. This means becoming a lifelong learner and keeping pace with the exponentially changing business and technology world.

How Companies Make Their Money

To understand the financial impact of experiences, you need only to consider the ways a business earns and increases its profit. One way to make money is to reduce costs, but this often puts CX/EX at risk.

A second way to make money is to increase new revenue while simultaneously reducing costs where possible to increase profits and other margins. Our focus is on doing both, but in new ways that use exponential technologies to maximize cost savings while, at the same time, improving both business results and CX/EX.

Suppose your organization is focused on cost-reduction as a way to boost margins. To start your CX/EX journey, you could do a comparison of the cost of customer/employee attrition versus the cost of customer acquisition and the price of hiring top human capital.

> ### Blind Spot
>
> When businesses don't report customer value to investors, they are part of the problem. By collecting data on customer value as part of financial reporting, business leaders can transform how shareholder value is reported, driving shifts in all aspects of business.

If your organization is growth-oriented, as most exponential organizations are, improved experience delivery can serve to drive awareness and sales via a viral loop of customer brand advocacy (through word of mouth—both online and in person). This allows you to generate more new revenue and drive higher customer lifetime values while minimizing unnecessary costs and increasing margin and profit. It's this balance of factors that ultimately drives success.

Creating Value from Customer/Employee Experiences

The economic opportunities available through brand advocacy and its resulting value creation is unprecedented. And it all begins with crafting and sustaining unique, amazing experiences for the people your business is built on. According to the Young & Rubicam Brand Asset Valuator, companies focused on increasing their brands' differentiation have an approximately 50 percent higher operating margin on average than companies that allow their brands' differentiation to decrease.[7] A brand's ability to create new jobs, add to the economy, and excel financially—not only for themselves, but for employees and shareholders, as well—is a direct indication that they have shifted strategy and made customer-employee centricity and experiences their primary objective.

Though many have suggested that CX/EX is a major key to business success, authors Pine and Gilmore of *The Experience Economy* were some of the first to suggest businesses must orchestrate memorable experiences.[8] In the book, these strategy experts explain the power of experience memory itself. The positive interaction customers receive becomes the product and secures their loyalty. Pine and Gilmore's message is even more relevant today than it was when the book was first released. That message also places CX success where it belongs: at the center of a long-term picture and shows why businesses can't use customer experience as a one-trick pony or a one-time campaign. It must become how they always do business; it has to be ingrained in their DNA, at the core of their most foundational processes. It's no less than how employees collaborate with customers from the get-go, and it's how companies then deploy technology to scale those experiences beyond the level of one-off interactions.

Pine and Gilmore's work goes into great detail while examining how customer experience is a real offering—as real as any product or service. Unfortunately, some companies mistake customer service as customer experience. Realizing the full benefit of customer experience means businesses must deliberately design engaging experiences across the whole enterprise. It can't be limited to the contact center or service department.

The Experience Blind Spot

If experiences matter so much for every outcome a business cares about, why aren't companies truly focused on them? In 1999, Pine and Gilmore explained how undifferentiated, commoditized goods and services are not a sufficient basis for businesses to grow on. Their groundbreaking insights are the roots and sturdy trunk of our approach in the context of this new, exponentially fast-paced, and competitive marketplace. And we are passionate about this approach for the simple reason that many companies still rely on old economic standards, stubbornly clinging to a model that prioritizes the offering of products and services instead of empathetic experiences. They have not shifted their business models to be customer-centric, dynamic, or engaging. Pine and Gilmore wrote, "As goods and services become commoditized, the customer experiences companies create will matter most."[9]

In today's digital economy, the cost and time it takes for customers to switch between market options are minimal. This is a key driver behind why their experiences matter so much, but many brands' decisions, choices, mindsets, processes, and technologies are centered around benefiting the company first. Whether their decisions actually serve to help the customer in the long run is, at best, an afterthought. Such businesses haven't realized the full scope of how vital customer-employee centricity is to their improved financial outcomes.

Why Don't Companies Shift Mindset?

Up until now, it was possible to provide less-than-sufficient customer and employee experiences while remaining profitable. When we looked at why changing the customer experience hasn't been prioritized more significantly, we found seven key factors that hold back progress:

1. Noncustomer-centric accounting principles and too much emphasis on reporting to investors/Wall Street
2. Trapped loyalty (customers who are cornered into buying from one source)
3. Resistance toward the level of effort required to make real changes toward customer centricity in everything an organization does
4. A lack of technological advances capable of driving contextually relevant, real-time, personalized, and one-to-one experiences that aren't "creepy" or invasive
5. Static, linear business plans and strategies that aren't agile enough to change with the changing global market conditions, or with competitors who are already using exponential strategies and technology
6. Failure to use data and AI/ML as an exponential flywheel to continually listen to, understand and predict, act on, and learn from the current customer/employee experience
7. Unchanging management styles (from command-and-control to collaborative) and a lack of effort toward creating cultures that reward customer/employee-centric behavior

Lighting a Fire: Urgency Drives Positive Change

While transforming the customer experience has been discussed for years, changing the hearts, mindsets, attitudes, and business practices of an organization can be a major paradigm shift for many executives. When we ask our clients why they haven't transformed to a customer/employee-centric business model, many have responded: "Why do we need to change? Clearly, what we are doing seems to be working right now."

In part, this is the case because companies have been successful even if they haven't provided great experiences. This is often due to what's called trapped loyalty. For example, customers of a utility company are forced to buy gas or electricity from their local energy company because there is little to no other choice; loyalty is driven by availability.

Other scenarios involve issues of convenience, such as a customer who has set up an account at a bank or with an online retailer and perceives moving their account to be too much effort.

Finally, there's the issue of market variety. When no one offers customers a sustainably different experience, they choose by comparing price, product, or availability rather than brands themselves.

The paradigm shift that's exploding now is not just about transforming business, but also disrupting it by differentiating your customer experience to the point that customers choose your company, hands down, over your competitors. As mentioned previously, causing disruption means not only developing a new business model, but also applying new technologies. This type of disruption is what initially took the taxi industry by surprise. Rides-as-a-Service exploded onto the scene with ride-sharing services like Uber and Lyft providing a better customer experience via mobile apps that matched passengers with drivers for hire. The new rideshare business model did not require these "matchmakers" to own cars or hire drivers.

It balanced experiential strategy with a perfect model of cost-reduction and profit-generation, making these new players practically unbeatable by the traditional taxi services they were competing against.

> **Blind Spot**
>
> Not understanding that the urgency to transform your business into a customer/employee-centric strategy is powered by inescapable exponential change.

Urgency Driver: Exponential Technologies

When thought leaders like Tom Peters, Peppers and Rogers, Joe Pine, Fred Reichheld, and others started conceptualizing the importance of the CX/EX, the world was in a different place. Change happened much more slowly. In theory, changing things seemed like a great idea. Though many had formal transformation initiatives, businesses rarely changed from a business-centric to a customer/employee-centric business strategy in any fundamental way.

The slow pace of the world prior to the advent of digital devices, social media, and exponential technology allowed companies of the past to have more financial padding through the function of time. This simply means that, if a company was eclipsed by a competitor in a particular situation, they had time to react and replenish the financial resources needed to weather the hit while staying in business. Before the democratization of technology, a company might also have more competitive power thanks to a lesser populated and more static playing field. But that's no longer the case. There are start-ups and companies disrupting industries every single day.

As a result of all these factors, the competitive landscape is far more challenging than ever before. The CX/EX empathy-based business mindset, the prowess to successfully lead experiential change, and exponential technologies are allowing competitors to eclipse one another more and more quickly.

Progress Hurdles: Organizational Inertia and Resistance

Organizational change, which is often fraught with internal inertia and stubborn resistance—especially when things appear to be "working fine"—meant changing CX/EX was a lot of work. Change is an interdepartmental, cross-functional and, above all, collaborative effort involving IT, customer service, marketing, sales,

> **Blind Spot**
>
> Not understanding the level of effort required to transform your business to become customer/employee-centric is often why companies have low success rates with transformation projects.

e-commerce, and back-office operations. The level of effort required to change the strategy, mindset, process, and technology of all these departments can be enormous. Often, the lack of organizational readiness for and magnitude of the change (i.e., the number of systems and processes changing, the number of people affected and shifts in how they work) translated into giving CX/EX more lip service than leadership. As a result, experiences fundamentally remained the same—business-centric.

Some organizations really did try to change, but only ended up with cosmetic changes. Actual change is hard work and it's often messy. It takes serious alignment and internal fortitude. Unless more experienced change leaders take firm charge of the operation, change initiatives can pit people against each other, leaving employees disenchanted and more determined than ever to keep their heads down. Nothing new gets accomplished in such an environment.

Urgency Driver: Accounting for Customer Value

What else has limited companies from becoming part of the empathy economy? Outdated accounting methods, for one thing.

Traditional financial-valuation methods usually require quarterly financial projections, most notably of revenue. But under these models, the vast majority of a company's revenue projections are not based on customer value or an assessment of its underlying value.

Markey's customer-based corporate valuation method (CBCV) indicates a change in the old methods by giving sharp focus to how customer behaviors and success metrics drive the top line.[10] Using the four capabilities from Markey as mentioned in Chapter 1, we developed a similar list to guide businesses to grow and disrupt industries via a customer/employee-centric approach, which is achieved by using the first part of the Empathy in Action Flywheel, EBBV (empathy-based business value) (Figure 1.4):

- Energize customer/employee-centric leadership
- Engage customer/employee-centric cultures
- Evolve to design-thinking and exponential, loyalty-earning technologies
- Earn customer-employee financial value

Without these capabilities, a company's ability to report on customer value-related business outcomes and, as a result, to achieve consistent and sustained growth in that value, is inhibited. Let's examine all four capabilities in detail.

Earn Customer-Employee Financial Value

Companies need management processes, tools, and capabilities to understand their customer base's current total lifetime value (CLV). They need to correlate how the changes in customer experience result in changed customer behavior, increased loyalty, and the financial results connected to them. It requires dedicated measurement of the following metrics both before and after the customer experience is changed:

- Cost to acquire new customers in each customer cohort
- Percentage of active customers in each customer cohort
- Frequency of each customer cohort's purchases
- Cost to serve each customer cohort
- Amount of revenue per customer

The Experience Index

Customer loyalty is created through a company anticipating, meeting, and exceeding customer needs (sometimes unexpressed). Companies can do all of this by moving away from being reactive and toward a proactive, predictive, and prescriptive customer-centric approach. To change the customer experience on this scale, you need a framework to design optimal experiences—we call ours the Experience Index.

Customer behavior has often been measured by the Net Promoter Score, which is related to what they said they would do. But if you'll recall, current neuromarketing research shows that customer behavior correlates to how they feel about a company, not what they say about it in surveys or focus groups, and how a customer feels about a company correlates directly to their experience and thus their behavior.

The Experience Index is a standardized, universal methodology to measure the empathy, efficiency, and effectiveness of an experience from the end user's point of view. The Index identifies the key aspects of an experience and measures the degree to which customers (the end user) feel their experience delivered on these key aspects. The Index then analyzes how the experiences companies deliver impact customers' overall brand perceptions and relate them to key performance indicators. From those scores, a brand's index is calculated and can be compared to the ideal from the end user's point of view.

By surveying and benchmarking many vertical industry customer experiences, we have compiled a library of ideal experiences from various perspectives. Based on the business outcomes a company is looking to optimize, we can provide guidance on where they stand compared to their peers. Peer benchmarking reveals opportunities to optimize the customer experience with those specific desired outcomes and unique customer bases in mind.

This information represents the customer value metrics that feed into your accounting and investor/board/market evaluations to calculate the CLV and EBBV. This approach is extremely useful but requires your team to work in perfect harmony with your CFO and the financials to report on customer value creation.

Applying the Experience Index

How would this process play out in the real world? Let's say you are a bank, and you want to increase the number of customers using your mobile application, because such customers are more profitable. Your current customers, who fall into the innovators and early adopters cohorts (generally, 15 percent of your customers), are already using the mobile app. Let's say you'd like to increase usage among skeptics who are often the most extensive customer base but also the most reluctant to trust a mobile app (often 60 to 65 percent of a customer base).

Using the Experience Index, you would be able to compare the experiences your company currently delivers to these skeptics with industry-optimized, customer-centric metrics, and once analyzed, you would be poised to understand this customer cohort's mobile app pain points on a deeper level. You could then craft an informed strategy that would transform the experience, removing the issues that stopped your skeptics from using the mobile app in the first place.

By changing the experience, you gain the skeptics' trust and foster behavior changes like using facial ID recognition to sign into a mobile app or adoption of mobile features to deposit checks, transfer money between accounts, set up auto-pay, or make minimum payments so they are never late.

You'd then have the data to show how these changes to the customer experience increased the use of your bank's mobile app (customer behavior) and improved the business value of this customer cohort (financial outcome).

Evolve to Design-Thinking and Exponential, Loyalty-Earning Technologies

A customer/employee-centric company requires a systematic way to listen, understand, predict, act on, and learn from people's perspectives to deliver highly personalized experiences, products, and services—all of which culminate in lifelong loyalty. With the advances in exponential CX/ EX technologies (AI and ML-enhanced data in the cloud), we can enable these highly personalized, contextually relevant experiences at scale.

When a company uses exponential, loyalty-based technology systems orchestrated by AI-enriched data to produce galvanizing experiences, they already know where the customer has been on their journey. This might include their latest web, mobile, and voice interactions; social media posts; and purchase history. This kind of technology garners a robust customer profile from many different data sources.

As the customer reaches out to the company, the system analyzes their information, calculates their intent, and assigns a routing choice based on the probability of the best outcome. It may be an AI chatbot or voicebot. In the case of an employee, the system provides an intelligent matching of which employee's experience and capabilities can most easily and best handle the question at hand. In short, both customer and employee are provided with the best possible experience.

As employees talk to customers, AI-enabled capabilities analyze the customer's voice tone, rate of speech, next-best actions, and knowledge content—providing the employee with real-time guidance. Over time, the technology gains more and more perspective, context, and data, further enhancing its ability to provide optimal outcomes for everyone involved.

While digital or self-service channels are often used as a financial cost-cutting method, speaking to the right person (though antithetical to current best practices) could be considered the best option to reduce experience costs. Companies need to discern which interactions are best handled in digital channels without employees versus those in which reaching the right person is a better option for both the company and the customer. Moving from a cost-cutting strategy to a loyalty-based approach helps companies decipher how each unique interaction should be handled.

The use of loyalty-based, AI-data enriched orchestration technology platforms and systems is a new concept for most companies. Teams often face legacy technology systems and data challenges, which can be very intimidating and complicated to face. We'll talk about overcoming these hurdles in the following chapters so they don't become the reason you fail to personalize your employees' and customers' experiences.

Engage CX/EX-Centric Cultures

Typically, businesses are organized around functional departments. That type of organizational structure provides localized accountability and expertise based on B-centric efficiency and effectiveness models. But using a conventional functional organization model means you can't meet the ever-rising customer expectations, which often require cross-department collaboration. Unfortunately, many managers lock the business into silos, each of which is incentivized to optimize their performance instead of focusing on what's best for the customer and the employee experience—and therefore best for the company. These siloed operations often lead to conflicts, biases, and office politics, redirecting focus from what is essential and isolating silos' priorities more and more from those of the company as a whole.

Let's take the example of a new product launch, with three sizes of product to see why siloed functional departments mean a substandard customer experience. The goal of this launch is larger orders of the largest product size, because there's more margin to work with when these are met. But as the campaign results come in, the larger product box orders are physically crushing the smaller product orders, often damaging both. If the company was customer-centric, they'd reduce all the crushed orders, especially those in smaller boxes.

However, each individual department is solidly focused on metrics that make them look better. Sales, bent on exceeding targets, refuses to charge more to stabilize the packaging so they don't fall and crush the smaller boxes. To keep calls to a minimum, customer service makes it challenging to find the company's contact information on the website and limits claim filing to speaking directly to an employee. Finance risk managers are instructed to reject many of the claims. When viewed by individual departments' metrics, they did well; shipping and customer service costs were kept in line and revenue grew in the short-term.

However, when the experience is viewed from the customer's point of view, it's not so nice. What isn't apparent in a business-centric operating model is that, while short-term metrics may look like a win in the moment, the company also loses in the long run.

Customers, who are now deeply frustrated by their experience with the business, search for competitors. They find companies whose price is similar but who offer a better experience—large and small packages are delivered safely. There are lower shipping damage costs for the company, higher order volume, larger margins, and continuous orders, both new and ongoing. This means their CLV and EBBV are continuously increasing because customers are loyal—they return and buy more over longer periods of time.

What can we learn from this example? First, you can have all the customer value-related data but still fail to have your objectives aligned around what's best for the customer. The "gold" remains locked in the departmental silos, driving internal politics and departmental bias regarding what's most important to the company as a whole. On the other hand, a cross-functional collaboration, with decision-making and responsibility focused on improving customer outcomes above all else, can result in wins for the customer and the company.

Objectives based on customer needs must sit alongside product and operational goals; leaders must measure success across critical outcomes such as customer satisfaction, loyalty, and product sales before they consider secondary metrics, such as those relating to specific departments.

Energize Customer/Employee-Centric Leadership

Although a customer-centric focus requires that employees at all levels embody this vision, that doesn't mean that leaders are off the hook. In our experience, which includes working on building a more customer/employee-centric culture in a business that was 30 years old, all of the largest shifts start with good leadership.

Loyalty leadership demands persistent attention. It requires the executives to constantly signal their commitment to new customer-centric strategies through their own actions and principles. When that message is transmitted effectively, it gives employees confidence that customer loyalty is not merely a management initiative of the moment. They come to feel that it is how their organization will do business today, tomorrow, and forever.

When employees realize that this strategy is not going away, it helps them to align their actions across the whole organization—changing decision criteria, supporting policy changes, and celebrating customer loyalty wins regardless of which department achieves them.

When employees know for a fact that customer centricity affects every single decision at the top levels of their company and that the investors and the board are banking on it, it solidifies and invigorates their commitment and provides them with the resilience required to make it through the transformation zone. By creating an inspiring vision, laying out a path, and engaging all employees, corporate leaders can begin to get the change agents on board and excited about their shared destination.

Taking a page out of the book of the world's best entrepreneurs, we found that their transformation zone began with a vision of what they were doing and what it would look like when they got there. They then demonstrated relentless motivation and a passion for taking risks, and they showed determined persistence in the face of challenges and unforeseen circumstances like COVID-19. No matter what happened or what people said, they stayed on point while empathizing, pivoting, and iterating daily. This is the story of our own journey, and it's the story of many of the companies we've worked with and seen transform over the years.

This kind of initiative also calls for top leaders to maintain the support of their board members and investors by educating them about loyalty-based strategies and methods for evaluating progress in that arena. This is key to customer value transformation, because the decisions that management makes (like investing in technology) can temporarily reduce short-term earnings. As leaders demonstrate to investors and boards that those decisions pay off through increased customer acquisition/retention, increased revenues, and lower service costs, it becomes evident that choosing customer-centric goals versus individual department goals is a better choice overall.

Transparency and reliable disclosure are key throughout this process, as they give investors and management teams the confidence to strike at the heart of short-termism and run the business for sustainable value.

We'll cover more on leadership in Chapters 10 and 11.

Case Study: Earn Customer-Employee Financial Value

Telstra's former CEO, David Thodey, led his company's growth by committing himself to customer experiences. He began each business unit review with a discussion on the progress of customer advocacy. He spoke to customers. He insisted his leadership team devote time in meetings to knock down barriers to great CX, supported policy changes and pricing to improve CX, and often did so at the expense of short-term business performance. He achieved this with support from investors because he took the time to educate them on the company's efforts to solidify customer relationships for the sake of long-term value.

During his six years at Telstra, Thodey improved customer loyalty in every major product area, customer segment, service process, and interaction base. The company gained 10 points of market share in the lucrative mobile business, and the stock increased by more than 70 percent. Unfortunately, after Thodey's retirement, the company went back to its old ways and slipped to the middle range of loyalty rankings.[11]

Looking from an outside perspective, Telstra's example is a perfect and neatly packaged comparison of how experience centricity impacts outcomes versus how linear thinking holds them back.

Agile Business Strategies and Plans

Most business strategies involve a carefully planned document that predefines competitive threats (a SWOT analysis of an organization's business and market strategies). By the time companies finish writing these plans, however, they are often out of date. In this fast-paced, exponentially changing world, strategies must be both agile and proactive. And yet, most business strategies are not nimble. Static strategy plans are both a liability

> **Blind Spot**
>
> Businesses must be able to change their business strategy and plans on a dime (be agile) with rapidly changing market conditions.

and a blind spot. They can easily be exploited by a quicker, more agile competitor. Once you identify the opportunities and the threats laid out in front of you, you need to figure out how to take advantage of the opportunities and overcome the risks with an agile plan of action, and a process that allows you to iterate and pivot at a moment's notice.

We'll cover this concept more in Chapter 12. For now, just remember what our case studies and examples have shown time and time again: slow, traditional, and above all, bureaucratic businesses don't survive in today's market. Only the agile can truly run the gauntlet and come out on top.

Recently, we found ourselves having to reevaluate our business strategy due to the onset of the COVID-19 pandemic. With businesses scrambling for answers on how to provide effective customer service—traditionally delivered by contact centers with 10 to 1,000 or more people in a room—we decided to be agile in our thinking and offer cloud contact centers that could be set up in 48 hours for free for the first two months. Employees could either work from home or, where the country's infrastructure didn't support working from home, businesses had their employees work from hotels.

This allowed companies to keep their employees safe by adhering to social distancing requirements while still providing the help customers needed. Employees felt cared for, cherished, and motivated, and customers felt prioritized. We did what was right by the customer and their employees. What's interesting is it shows that by doing that, it's also good for the company; we experienced an astonishing 83 percent conversion rate.

Reshaping Business Models

Looking through the lens of hindsight can help you see how important it is to reshape your business model. As products and services become commodities, margins grow slimmer, and revenues and profits decrease, it's far more difficult to turn a large, stubborn ship than a well-designed and proactive one. In the grand scheme of things, it's much easier to have an open mind toward the adoption of exponential technologies and organizational design than it is to resist them until it's too late.

> **Blind Spot**
>
> Businesses must transform their culture, leadership style, and organizational structures to become customer/employee-centric to accommodate rapidly changing marketplace shifts.

Without understanding these challenges and, in response, changing how the business is run, companies can find themselves financially ruined. Where should you start in order to learn about the changes necessary to disrupt your business model and increase your market share? Simple: you begin with customer and employee feedback.

TAKEAWAYS

- Even though customer expectations have evolved from merely desiring products and services to demanding great experiences, there are several common reasons companies give for not adopting customer/employee-centric strategies.

- The urgency to transform business from company to customer/employee centricity has never been greater; financial models that account for customer value are a critical component to deriving a company's value.

- Businesses that do adopt customer-centric strategies, new investor reporting processes, and exponential technologies are able to drive more value to the customer, the employee, and the company.

TONY'S LEADERSHIP CORNER

Blind spot: Believing leaders have all the answers

I was privileged to learn the essentials of leadership at Cisco. Those 14 years, when I was in my 20s and 30s, were the formative years of my career.

Then-CEO John Chambers is famous for being the top salesman for Cisco. From an insider's perspective, he was also a master at mobilizing the leaders of the company. Every year he hosted the "Strategic Leadership Offsite" for the top 1,000 leaders of the company, where he and the executive team shared the strategy for the year. The event always featured an exceptional guest speaker along the lines of former US President Bill Clinton, Duke University basketball coach Mike Krzyzewski, and Carly Fiorina, the former CEO of Hewlett-Packard, which, at that time, was the world's largest seller of personal computers.

The speaker who made a lasting impression on me was Lee Scott, former CEO of Walmart.

Scott led Walmart for nine years, from 2000 to 2009. Walmart was ranked number one on the Fortune 500 list during his tenure and, by the time he left, Walmart had net sales of $400 billion. He was one of the most successful business leaders of the time, yet he was incredibly humble. He came to the stage with a single slide with text and no fancy graphics outlining his "10 Top Lessons in Leadership."

This is the best leadership list I've ever seen, and I think about it often as I'm building and leading organizations:

- Hiring people better than yourself will make it easier to achieve success.
- Reign in ego because it is an impediment to leadership.
- Tell people what you want, and you will often receive it.

- Give others honest, constructive feedback.
- Remember, few people feel as though they have a handle on things.
- What is heard and how it is heard is more important than what you say.
- You can be wrong about things you feel strongly about.
- Harsh critics may be saying the very things you need to hear.
- Don't look to share praise; give it all away to others.
- Integrity is the most important thing.

The one I'd call out as a personal blind spot is remembering that few people feel as though they have a handle on things. Earlier in my career, I had a bit of a chip on my shoulder because I dropped out of college after one year. It seemed that along with a degree came the confidence of knowing the answers. I've learned there's nothing like on-the-job training. There is no playbook in business. We're all creating and making it up as we go, especially in high tech. Things are moving so fast that there's no way anyone can know it all. Once you realize that even Lee Scott didn't feel like he had a handle on things in every situation, you're really free to lead.

" Real change,
enduring change,
happens one step
at a time.

—Ruth Bader Ginsburg

THE TECH WE USE MATTERS: FROM LINEAR TO EXPONENTIAL TECHNOLOGIES

Customer service complaints are as old as time. Or at least as old as 1750 BC, when the first recorded customer complaint was filed against Ea-Nasir, a big-time copper and finished metal products trader. Known as the worst businessman of the century due to constant complaints, Nasir evidently received a stone tablet—covered front to back in angry cuneiform writing—from his customer, Nanni, who demanded a refund for the delivery of the wrong copper grade (Figure 5.1).[1]

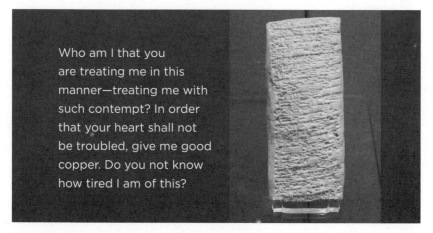

Who am I that you are treating me in this manner—treating me with such contempt? In order that your heart shall not be troubled, give me good copper. Do you not know how tired I am of this?

Figure 5.1 Customer service complaint from 1750 BC.
Source: Creative Commons[2]

It's uncanny how familiar the complaint sounds. While this particular example of poor customer service is ancient, the human desire for trust and fair treatment with brands is not. Just like Nanni, customers today need to be heard and understood by the companies they interact with, and the technology we use plays a key role in facilitating those exchanges—whether the technology is using a sharp object to chisel a complaint in stone or sending an SMS.

History has proved that advances in technology can be empowering and enriching across civilizations and societies. But as society advances, values change. What's wanted and needed naturally evolves, driving innovation to meet current and future demands. For example, we saw how George Eastman invented the technology for photography and the ability to preserve memories. Fast-forward to today, and digital cameras and social networks have taken preserving memories to a whole new level. As hindsight often provides insight, let's look at some key points in the evolution of customer/employee experience technology, bringing to light past limitations as we put into perspective what's needed now.

The origins of customer/employee experience technology began with a B-centric efficiency and effective mindset as being the predominant paradigm in management thinking. Though state of the art at the time, B-centric, linear technologies cannot deliver on the expectations customers or employees have today. Driving the most recent customer/ employee experience change is the consumerization of technology—a metamorphosis of product, service, and experience designs focusing on the end user as a person, in contrast to focusing on the company. The consumerization of technology has driven the necessity for companies to use design-thinking to reconfigure the technology employees use when interacting with customers. Keeping in mind the customer/employee experience industry's technological past, we'll see that what companies are doing with exponential technologies now in the Fifth Industrial Revolution far surpasses everything we've had to date.

The Evolution of CX Technology (and How Companies Used It)

Long-distance communication was revolutionized in the 1830s and 1840s when Samuel Morse and others developed the telegraph, and by 1866, a telegraph line stretched from the United States to Europe. People and organizations exchanged messages almost instantly, transforming how companies conducted business.

Technology evolution is personal. Alexander Graham Bell had a deeply rooted interest in sound technology. Both his wife and mother were deaf, a fact that greatly influenced his work as a scientist and engineer. His research and experimentation improved the telegraph and led to the creation of the telephone. Once connections between a phone and a wide-scale telephone system became possible with the first private manual branch exchange, or switchboard, horizons for customer experience expanded. Boston inventor and entrepreneur Edwin Holmes developed the first commercially viable telephone network and adapted it to work with a telephone switchboard. And after founding the Boston Telephone Dispatch Company, Holmes collaborated with Bell to create the Bell Telephone Company.

But as new technology emerged, so did issues relating to the customer experience. Holmes hired teenage boys to operate the switchboard and identify the caller, their intent, and plug the phone cord into the correct jack. This arrangement worked well behind a silent telegraph line, but things changed once the boys spoke to people. Customers found their attitude, lack of patience, and cursing unacceptable for live phone contact—and it hurt the business' reputation. Bell intervened. Bell hired Emma Nutt (and her sister, hours later) as the first female telephone operator. Long before Siri, Nutt's soothing tone was the first patient, polite, and kind female voice in what has become the field of telecommunications. Putting herself in the customers' shoes, Nutt became a trusted, familiar voice by listening and understanding her customers' needs. Her approach was customer-centric, which elicited positive responses from customers. Unfortunately, this may be one of the most recent examples of a company genuinely thinking about empathy and their customers' experiences (Figure 5.2). (Interestingly, Tony's grandmother was a switchboard operator for the London Underground.)

Figure 5.2 Female switchboard operators in London around the 1880s.
Source: Alamy

With such innovation in communications, it didn't take companies long to realize the telephone's sales and marketing potential. The Multi-Mailing Co. of New York is an early example of a company leveraging this technology. Compiling and selling lists from local phone directories, they profiled, segmented, and targeted customers who owned telephones, viewing them as part of an influential class.

The 1920s brought rotary dial phones, negating the need for operators. The 1950s brought outbound call center agents, many of whom were housewives augmenting their family income by selling baked goods. In 1957, DialAmerica was the first-ever telemarketing firm with a call center.

With the arrival of automated call distributor systems, companies created large groups of generalists to answer customer inquiries. The pooling principle led to efficiency gains, although many were at the expense of customer experience. A customer could get a different answer from each employee they were connected to, and often, customers sat on hold for long periods while an employee researched a response or transferred the call. With each transfer, the system forced customers through the validation process again, and they had to reexplain their reason for calling.

The private automated branch exchange replaced the manual switchboard to automate connecting calls, and in the 1970s, the interactive voice response (IVR)—the "press one for . . . press two for . . ." technology—helped direct calls. Later, the development of Wide Area Telephone Service allowed companies to deliver outbound calls across the country, growing the telemarketing industry.

But what started as a good idea for the efficiency of companies soon became a source of frustration for customers. When companies assured callers waiting on hold that "your call is important to us" but then left them listening to a 40-minute violin solo, customers were understandably perturbed. While this scenario is the target of parody, it's also a symbol of the ultimate lack of empathy for the customer.

The Bell System telecom monopoly next offered toll-free numbers with dedicated area codes, allowing call centers to manage more inbound calls from customers responding to advertisements and marketing, which created the role of the inbound call center agent. Ray Tomlinson created the first email program in 1971, and in the 1990s, email and telephone served as the primary customer experience channels. Computer sales rapidly increased in the 1980s, and relational database systems became a commercial success. Database software evolved into the customer relationship management (CRM) software that marketing, sales, and service departments used to record and store customer information.

The emergence of the World Wide Web was the biggest game changer for the customer experience since the telephone. For the first time, customers could shop online from the comfort of their homes. With the 1990s dot-com boom, online shopping disrupted many companies' business models, which had been in place for centuries. With companies operating online, customers no longer had to go into stores for support—they turned to contact centers instead. With the mobile phone, internet, and e-commerce, businesses began digitizing services to stay competitive, leading to the proliferation of customer support software and the online help desks.

This increasing customer demand meant expanding the number of contact centers and agents to accommodate customers' needs, making it increasingly expensive to serve the customer. As a result, these centers became known as "cost centers," which led to outsourcing to other countries, which led to American customers becoming frustrated by poor service and language barriers. And a company might have dozens of contact centers scattered across the globe, and the databases that stored customer information—orders, billing, and shipping—were not always connected. Depending on which contact center a customer's call was routed to, the information an employee had access to varied significantly, degrading the customer experience.

By the 2010s, social media platforms abounded. With social media's public nature, customers recognized these channels as a way to get a company's attention, especially when using other avenues led to unsatisfactory responses. It became commonplace for customers to broadcast complaints on social media, forcing companies to respond. Companies quickly realized that if not handled carefully, these channels could generate enormous brand damage. Eventually, the technology used to route calls and emails began routing social posts to employees, allowing them to respond directly. Digital interactions like SMS and chat features also became pervasive, allowing for business-focused messaging programs like reminders, offers, and other notifications via mobile devices. By using self-service channels, customers could serve themselves, and in theory, companies could cut the cost of interacting with consumers.

Most contact center software solutions were developed as point solutions, meaning a single interaction channel. As vendors began using a solutions-first approach, they brought many channels into one solution. This was then packaged and sold as a specific service offering. Despite the inconvenience for both customers and employees, many contact centers today still use between 10 and 30 vendors—and sometimes more—to provide customer/employee experiences.

All these developments in technology affected the customer and employee experience; it isn't difficult to see how these changes produced benefits primarily for the companies using them. They focused on the B-centric version of the two E's—efficiency and effectiveness—but not on personalized experiences for the customer.

The Four Eras of Customer/Employee Experience

While customers no longer etch complaints in stone, businesses still have a long way to go to provide more personalized, empathic experiences. To illustrate, let's look at experiences from a customer's and employee's point of view. Like the four industrial revolutions, when looking at the evolution of customer service, we noticed four experience eras emerge—from the old business-centric paradigms to the newest era—the Empathy Era.

- Transaction Era
- Interaction Era
- Engagement Era
- Empathy Era

To evaluate the customer/employee process of delivering experiences, we created four Empathy Pillars™:

- Listen
- Understand + Predict
- Act
- Learn

Think about the conversations you have with family and friends. As you interact, first, you listen. You take in all the necessary information. Then, using your brain and experience, you translate that information into understanding and predict how to respond to add to the conversation. Next you take action by providing a response. Throughout your interactions, you learn from their responses, continually improving the relationship over time. With some care, doing this leads to the other person feeling known, heard, and understood. You personalized the experience by seeing the world through their eyes, which results in gaining or maintaining their trust and thus their loyalty (Figure 5.3).

Figure 5.3 Orchestrating personalized experiences drives empathy, trust, and loyalty.

Using these Empathy Pillars, we can analyze how customer-employee centricity varies in each era, based on the predominant technologies (Figure 5.4).

The empathy continuum (the *y*-axis) represents the level of personalization. In the early eras, experiences were very B-centric, very generic, with little personalization. As companies shift to a C&E-centric approach, experiences become more personalized, increasing the area under the curve.

The Transaction Era

As with the other eras preceding the Empathy Era, the Transaction Era was based on B-centric efficiency. Companies tried to balance the cost of their workforce to service customers on the available channels against business outcomes centered on the labor costs to deliver service. Companies had to work hard to find a balance between forecasting the numbers of interactions with the available resources. If there were too many customer interactions, the business became overwhelmed.

Between the company focusing on reducing costs and the lack of C&E-centric technologies available, the level of personalization or empathy toward the customer and employee was low. Companies didn't have the data to listen. Routing was largely through a toll-free number, indicating, at most, whether it was a sales or service call. With interactions lacking context and intent, calls were long—customers had to get the employees up to speed before any action could occur. And methods of evaluating the transactions were based on manually evaluating historical, static business intelligence reports at month-end to learn what to improve.

COMPARISON OF THE OLD AND NEW PARADIGM IN THE LEVEL OF PERSONALIZATION

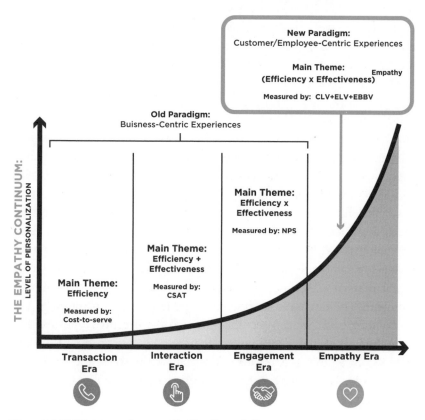

Figure 5.4 Various eras of personalization through time.

The Interaction Era

Businesses were still B-centric in their approach to customer experience in the Interaction Era, but they sought to optimize company-oriented effectiveness to improve business performance by finding a better balance between efficiency and effectiveness. Thanks to new self-service channels like FAQs and bots, the ability to provide slightly more personalized experiences began to emerge. However, primitive bots often delivered canned responses, leaving customers without answers to specific questions. While the customer's experience improved in the Interaction Era, companies still fell short as they measured customer satisfaction (CSAT). Companies could process data (listen) in a few channels but still lacked a broader understanding of the customer's intent and context. Actions were siloed, and learning about what would make the interactions better was still done manually with static business intelligence reports.

The Engagement Era

Shifting to use new technologies to understand and map the customer journey, companies sought to increase customer loyalty by implementing modern customer experiences using social media, synchronous chat, and SMS in the Engagement Era. Though this era moved closer toward customer/employee centricity, it was still largely driven by business-focused efficiency and effectiveness, cost reduction, and the same linear technologies. While companies could listen to incoming data from more channels in a broader way, employees still needed to clarify context and intent manually. Actions targeted to business rules were reactionary. Companies graduated to scoring customer interactions using NPS.

Looking back, we can see that although the B-centric optimizations were the best available options at the time, they compromised the very individuals who make business possible—employees and customers (Figure 5.5). Sadly, many companies still operate in the first three eras.

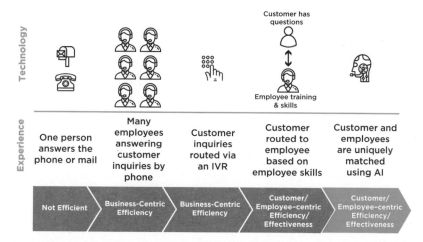

Figure 5.5 Evolution of the customer experience through time and advancing CX/EX capabilities.

The Empathy Era

It's not until we rethink how we design customer/employee experiences by using exponential technologies that we see significant changes in the ability to personalize experiences for each customer. Companies systematically and holistically listen in the Empathy Era by connecting data across all customer channels as the customer moves through awareness, consideration, purchase, onboarding, fulfillment, and support. Using smart automation like AI, companies clarify, understand, and predict what customers want, allowing employees to take proactive, predictive, and prescriptive actions.

The company's ability to understand and foresee unique customer needs is enhanced by using predictive models to identify customers and clarify intent, enabling employees to surface the right content and resources at the right time. With all this information, the brand can engage each customer with the proper support and relevant content, minimizing effort and friction and accomplishing what needs to be done from the customer's point of

Blind Spot

Organizations need to understand the business advantages exponential technologies provide to successfully deliver better experiences and business capabilities.

view. Empathy Era companies are also leveraging AI and ML to aggregate hundreds of thousands of interactions to evaluate performance and quality so they can constantly learn and improve.

What did we miss in the first three eras that's critical to achieving positive customer/employee interactions? What aspects of the deployed technologies limited personalization and the ability to provide great customer and employee experiences? Let's take a look.

Self-Service? Not All That Great

The self-service movement originated to reduce the increasing costs to service customers. Besides technology, employee salaries form the most expensive part of running a contact center. Self-service—whether it was confusing IVR trees, dumb bots, or unhelpful websites—was touted to significantly reduce the number of contact center employees required; customers could serve themselves. The initial attempts at self-service were great in theory, but in retrospect, we see that customers who couldn't get what they needed were stymied (Figure 5.6). They figured out how to escape the IVR or gave up on the bot, dialing to speak to a human instead. This defeated the "self-service" savings, often costing the company more money because of the increased number of contacts required for customers to get their issues solved.

© 2011 Ted Goff www.tedgoff.com

"For a real person, press 1. For a real person who knows anything, press 2. For a real person who knows anything who has time to talk to you, press 3."

Figure 5.6 Business-centric self-service often prompted customers' frustration.

IVR Trees

Companies embraced the promise of the IVR to make serving customers more efficient. But if the customer could find the phone number on the website, dealing with an IVR was often frustrating. Confusing options made it difficult to determine which menu button to press. Waiting on hold for long periods with elevator music playing led to customer anxiety (Figure 5.7). And many consumers, distrustful of self-service, didn't want to figure out which buttons to push to get what they needed. The experience was so poor that websites like PleasePress1.com and GetHuman.com began appearing, where people mapped out how to get directly to an agent. This circumvented the company's supposed cost-reduction self-service options.

© 2021 Ted Goff

"Oh. You're obviously still angry. Please hold while I play another five minutes of soothing music to calm you down."

Figure 5.7 Companies tried to calm customers using Muzak instead of truly changing how they delivered experiences.[3]

Why was the experience so poor? IVR technologies were linear technologies, and from the customer's point of view, they were not efficient or effective. By the time they talked to an employee, customers felt thwarted. With the conversation starting on a sour note, employees had to interact with angry customers, driving employee attrition.

Tricky Websites

When companies began using their websites as a customer experience tool (versus an online brochure), there was little to no personalized engagement—the customer was essentially on their own. Customers found themselves going from one page to another to find answers, and the site often forced them to navigate through layers and layers of FAQs.

Many companies removed their phone number from their websites (or "buried" them) to reduce call volume, asking the customer to reach out via email instead. Customers shared their intent (the specific need or question) with companies only to feel like their efforts fell upon deaf ears. In part, that's because most customers on a website want to make a real-time connection, a desire email can't fulfill. If a customer has a question about something in a shopping cart, they need an immediate answer. Without the ability to reach out intelligently, companies ended up with a high number of calls or abandoned shopping carts, resulting in lost revenue.

Dumb Bots

A dumb bot provides a concrete example of the old paradigm, the business-centric, cost-cutting customer experience. Before the advent of AI, bot technology was pretty limited. Companies saw bots as another less expensive self-service channel to help serve customers. But these bots didn't have the interaction channel history, customer data, or AI to deliver contextually relevant, real-time experiences. As a result, dumb bots delivered generic FAQ responses that often did not provide the information needed in context with the interaction. While this was the best technology at that point, customers repeatedly tried other channels or switched to competitors.

In reality, using a dumb bot wasn't efficient for the company, and it wasn't effective. The technology didn't deliver on the promise (greatly reduced call volume), and first contact resolution (FCR) was not nearly "one and done." The customer had to try other channels, which cost the company more. And the customer never knew if the next channel would provide the information or the value they wanted.

Employee-Assisted Service

We looked at the effect of requiring employees to serve customers without all the necessary information and tools. It creates employee frustration, dissatisfaction, poor customer experiences, and eventually, agent attrition. Because agent attrition is such a costly aspect of running a contact center, it doesn't make sense to use systems and technology that frustrate employees.

Often, the employee didn't have access to the customer's actions on the company website; they had to ask for the customer's account number, manually search the database for the customer's record, and then ask what they wanted. If the call wasn't routed well, this employee had to transfer the call to the next employee. Because the context of the interaction wasn't kept intact, the customer had to reexplain the situation to the next person.

As the customer was shuffled from employee to employee, getting more frustrated by the minute, they'd begin to doubt that this next employee would be able to solve their issue. If the interaction escalated and the customer asked to speak to a manager or supervisor, they had to again start from scratch, explaining their issue and wasting more time. With this amount of customer effort, trust and loyalty were lost.

Most companies operating contact centers shared the efficiency mindset to make interactions with customers as short as possible. In many industries, this often meant a four-minute call. Employees were expected to understand the customer's issue and resolve it in under four minutes or suffer the consequences, ranging from not receiving a bonus to being fired. It became obvious employees were hanging up at the 3:50 minute mark whether the issue was resolved or not to avoid getting penalized.

Contact Deflection

When contact centers went from calls and emails to many interaction channels, analysts predicted that opening new channels would reduce the volume of the traditional channels. The thinking went like this: I have 1,000 calls coming in per day/hour. If I open a chat channel, some portion of those calls will be deflected, and I'll end up with fewer calls. But experience has shown that opening a new channel doesn't necessarily mean it will deflect or lower the total number of calls or interactions.

Some companies have seen their interaction volume increase because some self-service channels did help, and calls focused on those needing help with more complicated questions. But when a company's goal in adding new channels is merely reducing call volume and costs, it's not focusing on personalizing the experience. It's focusing on costs. Even though vendors tout these linear technologies as being more effective and efficient from the company's point of view, if the technology leaves the customer or employee unsatisfied and less loyal, ultimately, it has failed, and the brand takes the hit.

> ### Blind Spot
>
> Often, businesses implement linear technologies, hoping they will provide cost savings. However, they are limiting their ability to drive empathy, trust, and loyalty, and provide contact deflection or cost savings.

© 2021 Ted Goff

"We've misshipped your order, but I'll be glad to give you the address where you can find it."

Figure 5.8 Employees are often frustrated because something in the experience goes wrong and it's beyond their control to fix it properly.

Isn't There a Better Way?

With linear technologies that focus on the company rather than the customer, B-centric contact centers gain a negative reputation, hated by employees and customers alike. Employees have to manage multiple screens (20 or 30 is considered normal) to access all the information and databases to serve a customer, frequently needing to apologize because the system is slow due to complicated connections to disparate databases or a process that is not customer-centrically aligned (Figure 5.8). As a result, contacting a company becomes a chore. Many customers don't want to face the automated phone trees in the IVR. They don't want to wait on hold or interact with employees disgruntled by the poor technology they are forced to use.

It's time to take off the rose-colored, business-centric glasses. How do customers and employees view your brand? What are their experiences? Is there a better way? Delivering on the promise of great experiences depends on our mindset and our technology; both need to evolve beyond the linear technologies and concepts of the past.

Do you know what your customers' preferences are: voice, chat, or messaging? Can you remember their personal preferences and use systems that allow you to personalize all customer interactions? That would be Empathy in Action. Gaining customer and employee loyalty is the result of customers realizing you have their back, that they can count on interactions where they feel heard and seen, and that they can trust you.

TAKEAWAYS

- The evolution of customer and employee experience has historically been a cost-cutting measure used to minimize interactions with customer technology and can be categorized into four general eras.

- Linear customer/employee experience technology has focused on the needs and priorities of the company, mainly using a business-centric version of the two E's—efficiency and effectiveness.

- Today's experiences can become more human by using methodologies focused on transforming typical business-centric metrics into customer/employee-centric versions of efficiency, effectiveness, using empathy.

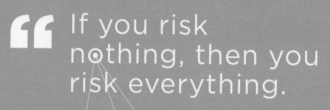

" If you risk
nothing, then you
risk everything.

—Geena Davis

EXPERIENCES DRIVE GOOD AND BAD PROFITS

In his book *The Ultimate Question,* business strategist and loyalty marketing researcher Fred Reichheld makes the distinction between good and bad profits. What are "bad profits"? To Reichheld, bad profits are when companies achieve profitability at the expense of the relationship with their customers and employees. He found that bad profits are created by delivering wearisome and somewhat deceptive customer/employee experiences and business practices.[1] From our point of view, bad profits could spawn from experiences like:

- Confusing pricing strategies
- Extracting value from customers rather than creating value (i.e., selling their data or constantly pushing sales offers)
- Misusing or not protecting customer data
- Providing unexceptional presale, at sale, and post-sale experiences
- Pushing company-focused efficiency metrics (like instructing employees to get the customer off the phone as fast as possible)
- Skimping purposefully on providing an amazing customer and employee experience to save on costs

These are all blind spots—ways companies operate that degrade customer trust and thus loyalty and the resulting empathy-based business value (EBBV), customer lifetime value (CLV) and employee lifetime value (ELV) we covered in Chapter 4.

No one disputes that companies are in business to make money. If more money is going out than what's coming in, companies can't cover costs, achieve operating margins, provide the budget for customer experience programs, deliver employee onboarding, training, and development programs, reward employees for hard work, implement innovative technology, fund R&D and acquisitions, or pay their stockholders, stakeholders, and investors. Ultimately, they can't grow their business.

The cost of bad experiences is not just customer and employee loyalty—it has a trickle-down effect on every aspect of your business. Remember? No customers, no business. Bad experiences are antithetical to the good business practices required to deliver and sustain the flywheel to amplify revenue, profits, and margins.

Bad Profits 101

> **Blind Spot**
>
> When companies degrade the customer experience by using techniques that only serve the company, they reduce customer trust, loyalty, and in the long run, customer lifetime value.

Reichheld provides a simple example of a poor customer experience and the resulting bad profits. Reichheld needed to reorder checks from his bank and found the charge was $120. His son suggested ordering checks from Costco because it was only $12. Reichheld wondered, "How could it cost my bank over $100 to print checks if Costco could do it for $12?"[2] And why didn't the bank realize they were abusing his trust by overcharging him? From Reichheld's viewpoint, this was a bad experience and bad profit.

Customers were once trapped because the only place to purchase checks was their bank. But as the marketplace evolved, customers could shop for alternative products and experiences—a new level of differentiation raised the spectrum of choice.

We define bad profits and bad experiences as a form of hoodwinking people, resulting in customer remorse. For instance, moviegoers pay much more for popcorn for the convenience of being served a buttery snack at the theater, but they may feel trapped in that purchasing decision because everyone knows you aren't supposed to bring food into the theater.

Sometimes, we choose to pay extra for convenience. We want the package expedited or we're willing to pay extra for milk at the local bodega rather than go to the supermarket. Unless the upcharge is excessive and the customer regrets the transaction, these are not bad profits—we have a choice in the matter. Having autonomy is key.

> **Blind Spot**
>
> Customers tune out the thousands of mass-produced, impersonalized customer experiences, numbing them to the unique value a company provides.

Personalizing every experience economically at scale is now possible, so why are companies still providing mass-produced customer/employee experiences? Because they aren't deploying Empathy in Action . . . yet. Emotions drive 90 percent of all customer decisions.[3] This means the perceived quality of a service or product has more to do with the feelings generated through company-customer interactions than with the objective quality of a company's offerings. The human aspect of marketing, sales, and service is just as important as objective quality. Customer experience can no longer be based solely on objective metrics like conversion rates or average handle times unless it also accomplishes what the customer needs and wants.

True success lies in delivering experiences that lead to loyalty and generate higher EBBV, CLV, and ELV. In the long run, higher EBBV, CLV, and ELV are not only better for the company but for the customer as well. It means the customer has gotten a better experience, and in turn, they are loyal. The result? The company derives more profit from its customers—and both parties get what they want. But having that long-term mindset is a paradigm shift from being hyper-focused on short-term business, Wall Street,

> **Blind Spot**
>
> Higher customer lifetime value means the company is doing things better for the customer while also benefiting itself and its stakeholders. It's a long-term mindset often missed in business today.

investor, and stockholder objectives. It requires refocusing on empathy-based customer/employee experiences that pay off for all stakeholders—employees, customers, companies, and in the end, Wall Street and investors.

Let's look at some specific examples of how companies use outdated customer/employee experience strategies, processes, and technologies to pave the way for bad experiences (resulting in bad or lower profits) and lead to business blind spots.

Mass-Produced Customer Experiences

An average customer receives over 10,000 business-generated messages a day. Companies target customers with personal data from their CRM (customer relationship management), MarTech stack, and analytics systems to break through all the noise. But businesses vying for customers' attention is not what overwhelms consumers—it's how companies go about attaining the customers' attention that leaves them numb.

Using a MarTech-type strategy to appeal to large target-market segments, old paradigm companies try to deliver the customer experience by using customer data to create five or six typical customer personas or target segments. By casting a wide net to get customers' attention, they use this impersonalized strategy to market, sell, and service customers.

This type of customer engagement looks great from the company's view of efficiency and effectiveness. What's wrong with it? Matching products or services with "average customers" can easily fail, as average customers simply do not exist. They never did. Until now, it was the most efficient way for companies to deliver some sort of personalization. But we can see how the first three eras (from Chapter 5) delivered relatively low levels of personalization (Figure 6.1).

> **Blind Spot**
>
> Executing interaction strategies that still try to match products or services with "average" customers can easily fail because average customers simply do not exist.

From the customer's point of view, averaged customer personas used to target and serve averaged customer market segments deliver unempathetic, marginalized customer experiences. When companies recognize every customer as an individual with unique needs, they realize the need for a way to tailor how they market and sell to customers, providing contextually relevant, real-time offers meaningful to each customer.

OLD PARADIGM EXPERIENCES WERE LIMITED BY THE AVAILABLE TECHNOLOGY

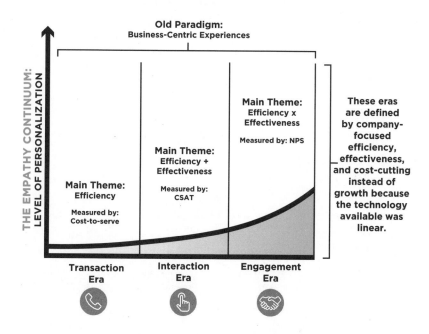

Figure 6.1 Cost-cutting eras were limited by the available business-centric, linear technologies.

Without thinking about how experiences affect long-term customer loyalty, companies create situations that businesses must recover from. These business-centric experiences are contrary to our point. Empathy means not only viewing but also delivering experiences from the customer's or employee's point of view—not the company's.

Customer-Journey Mapping

Companies often assume they know why perceived customers want to interact with their business, citing reasons like ad campaigns, marketing slogans,

> ### Blind Spot
>
> Company-centric customer-journey mapping designed using self-serving goals are often shortsighted, missing what the experience would be if customers designed it.

and service delivery options. But these tactics tend to be linear and don't reflect how people research, shop, buy, and engage service as individuals. Yet, it's how companies have grouped customers to serve them in the old customer experience paradigm efficiently. Exponential technology allows us to tailor customer-journey mapping and create accurate storylines about each customer's brand experiences, allowing for real-time, customized interactions in moments of need.

Multichannel vs. Omnichannel Experiences

There is a distinction between how a company interacts with customers when using multichannel and omnichannel capabilities. Though many use the terms interchangeably, they are very different in how the technology delivers interactions and the experiences they provide. Multichannel systems enable customers to contact and interact with a company using different channels, such as phone, email, SMS, chat, and social media. Omnichannel strategies and technologies allow for interactions on multiple channels while also tracking and preserving the context and intent of each interaction across all channels. It's an important distinction for companies to understand since customers often expect omnichannel experiences but continue to receive multichannel experiences.

The ability to move between channels without losing the context

> **Blind Spot**
>
> Multichannel customer experiences can't maintain the context of the interaction as the customer changes channels; a bot or an agent and the customer must repeat themselves, increasing customer effort and reducing loyalty and advocacy.

and intent means the customer doesn't have to repeat themselves, whether interacting with a bot or human, reducing the customer's effort and dramatically increasing customer loyalty and advocacy. Additionally, when the bot or employee has the customer context and intent, there's less effort to get the experience right—the solution matches the customer's intent. Shared context and intent are everything.

Losing Channel Context

An experience can be started, completed, and then effectively restarted by the customer using asynchronous technology, which allows the company to retain the context of previous interactions. Think of asynchronous interactions like your text exchanges with friends and family. Once that first text is sent, you don't have to start from scratch to send another message. You pick up where you left off; only now can that be done with companies, too.

But often, companies use limiting technology. For instance, a salon sends a text asking you to confirm an appointment, providing the ability to respond with a "Y" for yes, or an "N" for no. But there's no ability to carry on a conversation or pick up a previous discussion with all the content and intent of earlier interactions.

The best interactions are both omnichannel and asynchronous. Customers usually use multiple channels over time (even simultaneously) for one contextual conversation or during one transaction. Companies without the right technological underpinnings can't follow the customer experience across channels or pass on the context of the customer's previous interactions. The actions or needs get lost and must be repeated in the next phases of the customer's journey.

Disconnected Channels

Typically, a contact center has 10 to 50 vendors providing different capabilities for customer experience; it's simply how technology evolved. This often means the voice channel (inbound or outbound) comes from one vendor, while email, SMS, social, website, and messaging apps are from other, separate vendors. The back office also has a channel because the information needed to support

> **Blind Spot**
>
> As customer engagement channels increase, most companies don't have an orchestration experience engine to synergistically combine AI and customer data to drive contextually relevant experiences.

a customer—order management, shipping, and billing—is key to the customer experience. Separately, all these disparate systems are inefficient to manage and maintain. But an orchestration engine platform allows you to take all those otherwise disparate systems and connect them to deliver great customer experiences. It's the ability to deliver experiences as a service.

Experiences-as-a-Service capabilities require an engine that is always on, integrating all customer interactions in real time to avoid pitfalls, detect gaps, and shape experiences toward the customer's desired outcome. Avoiding experience pitfalls with preventive measures is better and cheaper than trying to restore a bad customer experience after the fact. If companies view customer experience as fragile, as something easily damaged, perhaps their mindset and approach toward it will change. As American business magnate, investor, and philanthropist Warren Buffett, said:

> *It takes twenty years to build a reputation*
> *and five minutes to ruin it. If you think about that,*
> *you'll do things differently.*[4]

Mass-Produced Employee Groups

In addition to grouping customers, companies have also organized employees into tiers or groups based on skill sets and knowledge. In this old paradigm, when customers reach out, the company tries to efficiently match and route them to a predetermined cluster of employees who are part of an averaged-skilled group. But the company is connecting the customer to the employee using the customer persona's perceived need. In the new paradigm, customers' actual needs and intent (not the perceived needs of the persona) are matched to the right employee for a highly personalized experience. And the employee gets more of the work they excel at, and the customer gets the resource that can best help them.

Poor Employee Context

Companies often leave employees or bots without enough context from the customer's real-time interactions. When bots or employees have to ask a customer who they are and what they've encountered, customers are forced to repeat themselves, especially if they switched channels (if the company isn't using omnichannel technology), creating a tremendous amount of customer and employee effort.

Striving for consistent experiences, companies have even created employee scripts to provide personalization (i.e., employees must say the customer's name three times during the conversation). However, this type of personalization makes employees sound like automatons. Without customer context or intent, employees can't be their best selves or use their problem-solving ingenuity.

With the technology available today, this isn't the type of personalization that should be delivered. While we don't blame companies for what they've deployed in the past, we do want to point out the limitations of past technology. Our hope is that the comparison illuminates a new path forward—one that's so enticing you won't wait or get caught off guard, surpassed, outperformed, and eclipsed by your competitors.

> **Blind Spot**
>
> When a company switches from company-centric cost reduction metrics to customer-focused loyalty-creating metrics, it not only saves costs, but also improves financial results.

Business-Centric-Only Metrics

With so many companies mass-producing experiences, customers expect mediocrity when they interact with a company. Governed by old paradigm key performance metrics (KPIs) focused on outdated definitions of efficiency and effectiveness, these averaged experiences are measured against the cost-cutting, business-focused interpretations of the average handle time (AHT), first contact resolution (FCR), and so on.

But seeing those metrics through the consumer's eyes has a different purpose—to improve the customer's experience. Looking at a metric like AHT, you can easily imagine how this KPI can conflict with the customer experience if the employee is forced to reduce contact time. The customer's issue may not be resolved, requiring additional contacts, thus additional costs and effort for the company. Or the customer switches to a competitor who has designed better experiences.

Imagine if we looked at efficiency or effectiveness measurements from the customer's point of view—our definition of empathy. What if all experience metrics were designed to deliver customer loyalty? Think about FCR. Customers, like companies, want shorter AHT and more FCR, but for different reasons. Higher FCR can improve the customer experience while not necessarily increasing the AHT. Customers want personalized interactions so their needs are met correctly. They don't want to waste time or expend considerable effort—not because it reduces costs for the company—but because it's a better experience.

Let's say a customer needs to talk to an employee. If the employee must ask a list of questions to identify the customer, understand their intent and context, and listen to the customer's story, the AHT is long. But suppose the employee is provided context and intent and has a set of next best actions and the right knowledge content. In that case, the AHT would be shorter than an experience that wasn't personalized. The benefit is lower AHT for the company (reduced cost) and a better experience for employees and customers, leading to both parties' loyalty.

We must decide what we are measuring and why. At the same time, we need to understand how to deliver experiences in new ways that don't shortchange the customer. In the context of the empathy economy, compromising the customer's experience doesn't make sense. Research shows only 12 percent of customers believe company messaging that says "we put customers first."[5] It's no wonder customer experiences don't meet or exceed customer expectations.

Misunderstanding Digital Proficiency

Customer experience no longer depends on digital proficiency. In years past, younger generations more familiar with digital technologies were more likely to interact on digital channels. But from online shopping to social platforms, the evolution of digital technology has made user interfaces and digital experiences far more intuitive, resulting in prolific use across all demographics. Customers no longer fit into prepackaged customer interaction preference-type groups that would have previously been associated only with a particular customer segment, like millennials, Gen Zers, or baby boomers.

However, if companies see customers as an averaged persona, segment, or profile, they make assumptions; for instance—only millennials want to primarily interact on digital channels via mobile devices or baby boomers via phone calls (Figure 6.2). For companies, this type of strategy is a way to organize and scale a company's multichannel strategy—by efficiently prepackaging experiences.

Gen Z	Gen Y	Gen X	Baby Boomers

Figure 6.2 Preferred interaction channels are assumed when a company uses averaged customer personas.

But customers often select channels based on ease of use or how applicable they are in different situations. For instance, customers may prefer to chat if at work or a noisy bar, but opt for voice calls when at home. Channel selection can also depend on the reason the customer is interacting with the company. In some instances, people don't want to bother talking to an employee and prefer using a self-service AI bot that understands intent and context. Those could be situations like changing an order or a delivery address. But when asking questions about an upcoming surgery, a customer may prefer to talk to an employee.

> **Blind Spot**
>
> Companies often implement chat that doesn't allow a conversation to be picked up later and requires a whole new interaction and explanation, wasting the customer's time and effort.

Savvy companies realize customers can't be pigeonholed into segments. A customer may indicate an interaction preference traditionally associated with millennials one minute and then with baby boomers the next (Figure 6.3). Today, it's about real-time, contextually relevant experiences versus demographic targeting.

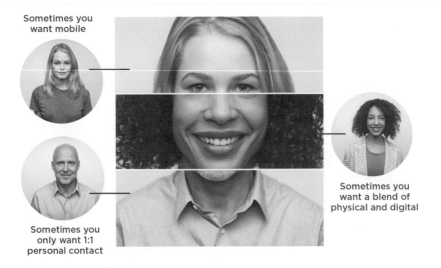

Sometimes you want mobile

Sometimes you want a blend of physical and digital

Sometimes you only want 1:1 personal contact

Figure 6.3 Customers are an aggregate of previous customer target personas.

Misusing CRM

CRM systems are a crucial part of the business ecosystem, but companies often forget that they are built to administrate company-focused customer relations and not real-time, customer-focused interactions. Traditionally used by salespeople to keep track of customer records (such as name, address, and account status), they cannot route real-time omnichannel interactions. Customer experience requires omnichannel routing that reflects how a customer moves from channel to channel, preserving the real-time context. Pre-built CRM workflows can't cut it.

> ### Blind Spot
> While CRM systems are an important part of the business ecosystem, they do not route omnichannel interactions in real time, limiting the customer experience.

Data Breaches

Imagine your company is hanging on the edge of a customer trust cliff by its fingernails. In the Edelman Trust Barometer Special Report *In Brands We Trust?*, company trust ranks as a top buying consideration—81 percent of consumers feel trust is a deal-breaker or deciding factor in purchasing decisions. And 67 percent of the respondents reported, "A good reputation may get me to try a product, but unless I come to trust the company behind the product, I will soon stop buying it." Fifty-five percent of consumers had concerns about companies using their data for tracking and targeting them.[6]

For many companies, there's a steep drop-off in customers' willingness to share data beyond the basics unless it's being protected. Studies like the *Consumer Intelligence Series: Protect.me* show that consumers are aware of cybersecurity threats like ransomware and remain skeptical of companies' ability to ward off attacks or prevent repeat occurrences post-attack. In fact, 87 percent of customers said they would take business elsewhere if companies failed to handle customer data responsibly.[7] Data breaches can result in downward spiraling consequences.

Not only do leaders need to treat customers with empathy to earn their trust, but they must also vigorously protect customers'

> ### Blind Spot
>
> Customers are increasingly aware of how their data is being used and do not want to patronize companies that do not protect their data.

data while respecting privacy. Between data trust issues and employee-customer apathy, it's time to rebuild the company trust quotient. Once a company has gone down the path of bad profits, it's tough to regain customer trust. The customer doesn't have time to see if you'll clean up your act. You've already cost them time and effort, and they aren't going to waste another precious moment on you. They've moved on.

Companies have an opportunity to transition from using customer data for company good to using it for customer good. Instead of focusing on effectiveness or the short-term opportunity to convert an offer or a sale, companies must harness customer data to deliver extraordinary experiences. And the data used for one-to-one personalization could even be based on customer consent that follows a "value-for-value" principle.

Great Customer Experiences = Your Brand's Igniting Force

Now that we've looked at how many companies orchestrate customer experiences, let's connect it to good and bad profits. A company derives good profits when it delights customers in ways that garner their loyalty to become repeat customers. These loyal customers want to tell others how great it is to do business with you; they become brand advocates.

When you consider the amount of money spent on PR, marketing, and advertising, the costs of acquiring a new customer can make it difficult to grow profitably. What if you compare costs for PR, marketing, and advertising against the cost of customer attrition due to poor experiences? You are essentially spending money to acquire customers you end up driving away with poor experiences. In contrast, consider a solid plan for customer-centric profitable growth, part of which includes the ability to ignite loyal customers to advocate for you, effectually becoming part of your extended PR and marketing team. This is only possible if you are operating under the principles of creating good profits by delivering empathetic experiences.

Today, the consequences of bad profits are more severe than when Reichheld first wrote about the loyalty effect in 1996.[8] Customers blog, tweet, rate, post, and text about their unhappy customer experiences in real time, often for millions of people to see. One bad experience doesn't only affect one person—it's witnessed by many.[9] In fact, the reach of social and digital media, smartphones, and browsers can expose your lack of attention to thousands—or millions!—of customers and publicly accentuate poor experiences by bad word of mouth.

> **Blind Spot**
>
> Customers use digital and social channels to publicly post their frustration and disappointment, exposing a company to bad PR.

Research shows that 95 percent of people surveyed would share their bad experience almost immediately with at least one person, and 54 percent said they would share it with more than five people.[10] Most companies realize customers talk to each other and that online interactions have tremendous power in increasing or reducing customer loyalty, yet they keep delivering poor experiences. A post on a social platform or review site (especially sites the company doesn't control) is like a cave painting. It could be there for everyone to see for years to come.

Even if you could take down a negative post, the backlash from removing it can be worse than the original post. Best practices are to respond to a negative post by understanding what happened from the customer's point of view, showing that the company cares about making it right. Responding with an honest explanation goes a long way to demonstrate good faith and commitment to quality.

> **Blind Spot**
>
> A company's financial and brand reputation is enhanced by creating great experiences that lead to brand advocates who influence other customers' purchase behavior.

No one wants to feel like a company is ignoring them. Companies are better off apologizing and offering to make a situation right.

At the same time, brands should use online comments as feedback to improve operations so they aren't constantly delivering poor experiences that require an apology. Social channels allow you to evaluate customer sentiment, providing input for everything from experiences to products, pricing, and quality.

When you realize customers are loyal to experiences rather than companies, experiences become the igniting force behind your brand. Research shows loyal customers love recommending a company to their friends, family, and coworkers if they have an extraordinary experience. That loyalty can result in repeat purchases from the original customer and future customers who hear about your company from brand advocates.

Most customers won't recommend a company unless the experience made them feel heard, acknowledged, and appreciated. After all, recommending a company reflects on their reputation within their circle of influence. When the experience is continually amazing, brand advocates turn into brand ambassadors. Because they are confident others will have great experiences, brand ambassadors spread the word about your company, increasing their own time spent with your brand and influencing others to follow suit—which generates long-term profits. Brand advocacy then becomes a business metric that drives CLV, ELV, and EBBV.

But We've Always Done It This Way . . .

What have we observed? Companies are under-delivering on the customer experience by over-targeting and over-segmenting their customers and employees. The facts are that 97 percent of customers globally are omnichannel users, using 5.6 channels on average. And 51 percent of consumers have switched companies in the past year due to poor customer experiences. Even though studies show 81 percent of consumers are willing to pay for a better experience, companies seem to be missing the business value of delivering empathic customer experiences.[11]

Why do we continue to over-segment and target customers? In part, it's because we've done it that way for decades. We were ticking the business-centric CRM and MarTech stack procedural boxes built to serve a now-outworn efficiency strategy, processing customers as if they were objects on an assembly line. We've ended up with averaged customer personas being served by averaged skill set employee groups leading to averaged experiences. We have to ask ourselves: What's in it for the customer and the employee?

Experiences lacking empathy lead to a reduced perception of the company's integrity, which then damages trust. The lack of trust leads to bad profits and lower CLV, ELV, and EBBV. While some companies work against themselves by sticking with business-centric paradigms, top companies realize they don't work anymore.

In this Empathy Era—especially in our subscription-based economy—customer loyalty is not a given. Your products and services are easily replaceable so maintaining trust over the entire customer life cycle is paramount. Focusing on short-term goals like converting a lead will not keep a steady revenue flow. Existing customers need to be continuously treated as prospects so they remain loyal and advocate. That's where your long-term revenue flow and good profits come from—repeat customers who buy more over longer periods.

The New North Star:
Empathy, Trust, and Loyalty

Why are companies missing the mark on customer and employee experiences? Many companies see the interaction as a transaction instead of a relationship with a human being. Poor customer experiences damage that relationship and break the customer's trust. In the end, this distrust leads us to bad profits—lower customer lifetime values, revenues, profits, and margins.

But personalized customer experiences lead to good profits and enhanced company reputation, customer trust, and long-term customer lifetime values, revenues, profits, and margins, all of which keep a company in business. Sooner rather than later, this bad profit paradigm must be broken. In the empathy economy, we can't look away anymore.

> **Blind Spot**
>
> Poor customer experiences affect customers' perception and trust of a company, leading to customer attrition.

We aren't suggesting patina or window dressing when we talk about personalized experiences. Experience-as-a-Service is a way to scale and make personalization real. And this means changing how you approach the people and process of experiences by using exponential technologies to deliver personalization, such as identifying the customer and providing valuable information so they feel heard and understood.

Companies keeping things as status quo are left in the middle of the bad profit paradigm, which must be shifted and shifted now. Part of that shift is the new paradigm of an intertwined triad of values: empathy, trust, and loyalty. This unique North Star triad provides a framework to shift the bad profit paradigm. Instead, companies deliver highly personalized, real-time customer experiences, returning the humanness to interactions once felt in marketplaces and bazaars in small towns and villages. With all of this in mind, we can develop what trust looks like and design customer experiences that garner loyalty in the company and its people and result in good profits.

We can develop company cultures and workforces that increase employee loyalty with these guiding lights, ultimately showing how the customer experience is delivered. When employees build and maintain trusted relationships with customers, it strengthens loyalty and saves time, money, and effort—for both the company and its customers.

Customers value their experience as much or more than the product or service, which is why customers are no longer loyal to brands, but rather to experiences. Reliably amazing experiences are what truly differentiate companies. While processes and technology facilitate customer experience, companies focused on harnessing them with empathy can distinguish themselves in a crowded field.

Chapter Six

TAKEAWAYS

- Bad experiences lead to bad profits.
- Bad experiences come from mass-produced customer and employee experiences, mistaking multichannel or CRM for omnichannel technology, business-centric metrics, misunderstanding digital proficiency, and providing poor context of the customer's intent and sentiment.
- Incorporating empathy into the customer/employee experience is paramount to creating great experiences and brand ambassadors, resulting in higher CLV, ELV, and EBBV, and profits.

" You never really understand a person until you consider things from their point of view . . . until you climb into their skin and walk around in it.

—Atticus in *To Kill a Mockingbird* by Harper Lee

IMPROVING EMPLOYEE EXPERIENCES

There's a saying that happy employees drive happy customers. When considering how to improve customer experience, an underappreciated aspect is often the employee experience. But to achieve the empathy-based disruption we outlined in the Empathy in Action Flywheel (Figure 1.4), one of the essential inputs is creating an empathy-based work culture. Parallel to customer experience, companies need to recognize how an employee's company experience directly affects the customer—and transform it, because devoted employees derive repeat customers.

History again gives us perspective. Until now, employee experiences have been delivered much like a manufacturing assembly plant is run—based on company-focused efficiency and effectiveness. This started with Frederick Taylor, widely known for his management methods to improve efficiency with his scientific management theory.[1] As one of the first attempts to systematically analyze and synthesize employee workflows, his theory optimized the workplace based on the business-centric efficiency and effectiveness paradigm.

> ### Blind Spot
>
> Company-only focused management theories drain purpose, passion, and engagement from employees.

Unfortunately, many employee management theories haven't evolved beyond that century-old foundation and therefore drain purpose, passion, and engagement from human capital. To thrive in the future of work, companies need to put themselves in the shoes of their employees and be able to amalgamate Empathy in Action into the employee engagement equation.

Frederick Taylor's Style of Work

As we look at Taylor and other management doyens' theories, we can see why they no longer work. In 1877, Taylor quickly advanced to a foreman at an armor plate plant. He felt the teams were producing one-third less than what he deemed a good day's work should produce. In 1915, Taylor published *The Principles of Scientific Management*, proposing that productivity would increase by adjusting and simplifying jobs (from the company's perspective). It was one of the earliest attempts to apply science to the engineering of work processes.

Determined to drive task-oriented work optimization in pursuit of company-focused economic efficiency, Taylor began using empirical methods to develop new procedures. Because workers' approach wasn't uniform, he thought the company was losing. He combined time-and-motion studies with rational analysis and synthesis to uncover "one best method" for performing any task, efficiently and effectively, from the company's point of view.

> ### Blind Spot
>
> When employees are managed only from a business-centric point of view, companies sacrifice employees' point of view, missing the critical components for buy-in, attitude and desire to go the extra mile.

After time-and-motion studies were complete, management rarely allowed workers to experiment or make suggestions for improvements. Taylor sought to provide better economic efficiency for the company because this was the paradigm. Unfortunately, one of many unintended consequences was that work would become monotonous and unfulfilling. Taylorism was later criticized for turning workers into automatons.

Taylorism forced workers to comply with rigid, narrowly scoped processes to complete a task, discouraging employees from using ingenuity to discover the best ways to accomplish their work with the available tools. Scientific management thinking appealed to managers because economic planning, budgeting, and compensating workers became

> ### Blind Spot
>
> Focusing only on old paradigm efficiency and effectiveness makes customer experience jobs monotonous and unfulfilling, reducing the ability of a company to provide great customer and work experiences.

more structured, and they thought the only goal was maximizing business-focused efficiency and effectiveness. But relying on the incentives of coercion and positional power left employees empty. Employee loyalty? If someone could find a better job, they left.

Company-Focused Management Theory

Management theories, based on B-centric efficiency and effectiveness, continued to be the mainstay. With the advancement of statistical methods, quality assurance and quality control began in the 1920s and 1930s. During the 1940s and 1950s, the body of knowledge for doing scientific management evolved into operations management.

Toyota established lean management in the late 1940s. Based on the success of their production line system, Toyota put into practice five principles to decrease the number of processes not producing value. It became known as the Toyota Way. Lean management systematically looked to achieve small, incremental changes in processes to improve efficiency and quality. Toyota and lean management practitioners sought to eliminate any waste of time, effort, or money by identifying each step in a business process and then revising or cutting out steps not creating value. They found significant improvements in company-focused productivity, cost efficiency, and cycle time.

> ### Blind Spot
>
> Management practices like Frederick Taylor's 1900s scientific management haven't evolved beyond that century-old foundation that drains purpose, leading to today's Great Attrition of the workforce.

While lean management did enhance some aspects of business, it wasted one of the company's most valuable assets: human potential. It overlooked employee talent and skills that, while not needed in the narrow definition of lean management, could have taken the company to the next level by using human ingenuity, passion, and innovation.[2] But the world hadn't discovered that new paradigm yet.

Similarly, in 1986 Bill Smith and Bob Galvin of Motorola developed the Six Sigma quality improvement process. Six Sigma's goal was to improve quality so that the number of defects becomes so few they are statistically insignificant. And in the 1990s, the reengineering movement became a widely popular management theory viewing people as a pair of hands without an opinion on their job. Unfortunately, it became known as the management fad that forgot the people.[3] Suppose they had used an organizational learning approach to reengineering. They could have discovered how to improve the process while also including the motivations of the people directly responsible.

> **Blind Spot**
>
> Management theories, focused on business-centric values of efficiency and effectiveness without considering individual's motivation, are missing the contribution of human ingenuity.

The Military Effect

Some of the structured approaches to managing people in corporations resulted from a world ravaged by war. Military leaders who had gone through WWI, WWII, the Vietnam War, or subsequent wars transitioned from their ranks into corporate leadership roles and managers. They brought with them a hierarchical, command-and-control, authority-oriented leadership style. Having the power to give orders, make decisions, and enforce obedience not only works well on the battlefield—it is mission critical.

But a military leadership approach is based on responding to a crisis, acting quickly and decisively to overcome an issue via a command. In a military crisis, it's standard and often necessary for soldiers to follow leaders without question. But, in civilian life, it no longer translates as a means of leading employees because the requirements of the situation and motivations of the people involved are entirely different. Nevertheless, command-and-control-type dominance prevails in the working world, remaining a blind spot for many companies. A business-focused efficiency and effectiveness strategy doesn't lead to the type of culture you need to create in today's world.

The Fallout

What were some of the consequences of applying scientific management and other business-centric theories? First, command-and-control management stripped away the creativity or individuality of workers by standardizing processes while timing each person as they worked. Because old paradigms die hard, it's not surprising similar constraints are put on employees delivering customer experience in contact centers.

The technology used employee-based metrics like average time to answer and average handle time built on company-oriented, old paradigm efficiency- and effectiveness-based metrics.

> ### Blind Spot
>
> A command-and-control management approach is appropriate in military operations but doesn't energize employee's motivation and passion.

It's no wonder attrition among contact center agents is among the highest of all job functions. Unfortunately, beyond technology, attrition is one of the most costly aspects of running a customer experience organization.[4] Why spend money on replacing employees when leaders could choose to invest in fostering a unique, employee-focused culture using employee-focused technology? You'd have people lined up with noses pressed against the door, just waiting to get in and apply.

While the workplace has changed a lot since Taylor's time, similarities remain. Employees are expected to conform to specific acceptable ways of working—some of which aren't within their control. As we saw in previous chapters, sometimes they are grouped into an averaged employee persona, where companies use routing software to match the averaged customer with the averaged employee. The result: customers are not routed to employees best suited for that particular customer.

Welcome to the World of Flabby Compliance

We've gone from a world operating without standard processes to scientific management and over-standardizing and over-measuring employees, taking the humanity and personal creativity out of work. What's left are rigid, inflexible corporate cultures full of employee dissatisfaction. We are at a historical turning point in corporate cultures, where it's critical to create individual, personalized experiences for employees and customers in parallel.

As we saw with patterns of customer disrespect in Chapter 3, if we take a bird's eye view of management theories and their application, we can see a similar pattern of employee disrespect. From the early titans of industry to Taylor and all who came after him, they didn't necessarily create those practices to disrespect the employee; at that time, the focus was business-centric operational mode. What didn't factor into the equation in that business-centric paradigm was how employees felt about the work they did. Leaders hadn't connected emotional intelligence, motivation, or pride in one's work to how well employees performed or how prosperous a business could be.

The following excerpt was written by best-selling author William H. Whyte, who conducted extensive interviews with CEOs of major corporations, and in 1956, published his findings in a book called *The Organization Man*. His content perfectly depicts the by-product of inadvertently applying scientific management-type theories without walking in the employee's shoes and designing empathy-based work experiences:

America is now peopled very largely by the Organizational Men. They are the middle-class Americans who have left home, spiritually as well as physically, to take the vows of the organizational life. They not only work for the Organization; they belong to it. Each one of them stands at the center of a deep conflict in American values.

Business has institutionalized itself to the point of resembling the bureaucracies it deplores and asked of its growing armies of employees a total lifelong loyalty.

Perpetuating the Yes-man culture, it has gotten what it asked for: Flabby compliance. That is the revenge of the "company-oriented" man who chants, "Love that System," while biting their tongue with their real feelings. Some executives sense there is something wrong somewhere. They dreamt of bold, imaginative enterprises and instead have a corps of bureaucrats . . . [5]

Company-focused cultures imposed rigid constraints on this "organizational man" without regard to their ideas, creativity, and passion.

Without empathy, we are left with hollow corporate cultures and employee discontent. It's what led to the labor unions in the United States around the country's birth (the late 1770s), their origins being traced back to the eighteenth-century Industrial Revolution in Europe. Companies waste employees' creativity and compassion by having them follow rote protocol. Employees don't leave companies. They leave managers who rule by the tired old ways of command-and-control management.

Empathy Drives Performance

HeartMath has spent over 30 years providing scientific research showing how employee discontent manifests itself physically, driving the emptiest to search for work that creates coherence between the work to be done and the work experience.

Traditionally, researchers have approached the study of communication pathways between the head and heart from a rather one-sided perspective. Scientists previously focused on the heart's responses to the brain's commands. The thinking was the brain is the primary driver, but current science has revealed it's the heart, or how people feel, that drives their thoughts, actions, and motivations to do their best or become complacent and merely show up to collect a paycheck.

HeartMath's research shows that communication between the heart and brain is a dynamic, ongoing, two-way dialogue, continuously influencing the other's function. Their research has shown that the heart communicates to the brain in four major ways:

- Neurologically (through the transmission of nerve impulses)

- Biochemically (via hormones and neurotransmitters)
- Biophysically (through pressure waves)
- Energetically (through electromagnetic field interactions)

For instance, the research shows it takes eight hours for an employee to recover from being yelled at, which is typical in a command-and-control, "my way or the highway" culture (Figure 7.1).[6] Additionally, the messages the heart sends to the brain are recognized as key to our ability to perform at our best. So, while empathy may seem like fluffy stuff to some people, science and data show it affects our ability to perform and drives focus, creativity, and stress, which all affect innovation and business performance.

Figure 7.1 Command-and-control and "my way or the highway" cultures affect job performance.

The focus on the thinking versus feeling in corporate settings is exemplified in this quote from corporate poet David Whyte:

> *We leave 60 percent of ourselves in the car bringing into work an empty shell of ourselves, yet we complain that "they" are like "that."*[7]

According to Whyte, "we are them." We are each individually responsible for the culture at work. As the mind is abstracted from the heart, employees close themselves off. As management closes off these metaphorical "air vents of creativity and passion, employees gasp for air." And yet, because management is stuck in old paradigms about leadership and employee experience, they keep closing off the next vent and the next one and the next one. Companies are suffocating on these old management paradigms, leaving humanity out of work. How can we change it? By completely rethinking how we hire, train, and organize the employee experience—by shifting the paradigm.

Politics and Psychological Safety

In transformation initiatives, new people are often brought into the organization, roles change, and the desire to please the boss is strong. Employees are so desperate for approval that what's good for the company, customers, or employees gets put aside, and political agendas reign. But, of course, none of this is good for progress, innovation, or disruption (Figure 7.2).

> ### Blind Spot
>
> During a transformation, without a formal, measurable organizational change program focused on behavior change, politics and divisive behaviors become the norm.

"This really is an innovative approach, but I'm afraid we can't consider it. It's never been done before."

Figure 7.2 Corporate politics and the lack of psychological safety limit everyone's progress.

During corporate disruptions and change, we've observed that these kinds of behaviors typically operate below the surface of the senior leadership team's awareness. Problems are compounded when a project doesn't have an official, measurable organizational change management program to detect and manage behaviors and outcomes. It's best to start these programs before change initiatives begin.

It's up to leaders to set the tone, put a stop to divisive behaviors, and create a workplace that is—as Amy Edmondson, author of *The Fearless Organization*, would term it—psychologically safe.[8] It helps when employees at all levels believe in the new, true north because change doesn't occur by pronouncements or official programs. It takes place slowly inside each of us by the choices we make. As Brad Blanton said in his book *Radical Honesty*:

> *It isn't so much that people are afraid of change or attached to the old ways, but it is the place in between we fear . . . It's like being in between trapezes. It's Linus when his blanket is in the dryer . . . There is nothing to hold on to . . .*[9]

Leaders need to create collaborative cultures where employees feel the psychological safety needed to embark on this new journey together to the extent they will go the extra mile to ensure each other's success. The culture cannot be one where feedback is seen as rejection. Instead, there is an openness to view things differently and help others see situations from different viewpoints. Otherwise, the "Not Invented Here" syndrome dominates the culture, conversations, and results (Figure 7.3).

> **Blind Spot**
>
> For innovation to flourish, psychological safety must be a cornerstone of corporate culture.

"Before we start this round of wide-open brainstorming, I'd just like to remind you that all ideas that are not mine must be rejected."

Figure 7.3 Cultures without an open mindset are doomed to the "Not Invented Here" syndrome.

Find Your Force Multipliers

Your company is only as strong as your team. And each team has its fair share of "bomb throwers" and force multipliers—both are important to identify. The term "force multiplier" is pretty much what it sounds like. In military terms, a force multiplier increases the effect of the existing

> **Blind Spot**
>
> Companies must cultivate and reward change agents as the force multipliers to propel exponential disruption.

forces: it ascribes greater value to the same number of assets. This brings new math principles into play, where 1+1 provides a value much higher than 2. A force multiplier is also a factor that dramatically increases or "multiplies" the efficacy of an item or group—in this case, your whole company. In Chapter 1, we showed how empathy is the most significant force multiplier for businesses, driving innovation and improving everyone's experiences with a company (Figure 1.4). Here, we're talking about the people on your team.

Where force multipliers add the grease so things move smoothly, bomb throwers are the sand in the gears. Remember, we're not suggesting that employees shouldn't give dissenting opinions when they disagree. As leaders, it is helpful when people point out what's not working along with ideas to solve the dilemma. Sometimes leaders will ask for several solutions, but we believe that employees should do their homework, weigh the options, and have a rationale behind why one solution is best. This new paradigm requires agile decision-making where leaders trust that employees' input is their best work—too many options lead to mediocrity.

For change agents to operate at their top capacity, it's up to leaders to create an atmosphere where they feel psychologically safe to express out-of-the-box ideas and help them determine what their unique contribution to the organization can be. Change agents often move from various departments or "homerooms" to pods depending on where they are needed and the organization's changes. They help the organization navigate the old way of doing things while bringing in the new. Change agents can get people excited, but if your employees don't have the right skills, it can be difficult to make the changes your business needs. Assessing current and future skills is key to the organization change education plan, as we'll see in Chapter 11.

Beware of Groupthink

While lack of alignment in a team is never ideal, groupthink is also a detriment to successful transformations. It can create a sense of misplaced confidence in solutions resulting from a

> **Blind Spot**
>
> Lack of alignment and groupthink destroy the opportunity for successful transformations.

homogenous team's shared thinking. Group members feel reassured that they've found "the solution" because everyone tacitly agrees, but shared assumptions often stifle innovation.

As we saw earlier, Kodak missed an opportunity to transform their customer experience by failing to embrace innovation. Kodak isn't alone in this. Other companies can serve as cautionary tales about missed opportunities, ranging from DEC to Microsoft. Let's look at an example of how the insularity of groupthink can go very wrong.

General Magic's Failed Groupthink

General Magic, a stealth off-shoot of Apple, is a company many people don't even know existed, but its effect on our lives has been lasting. The 2018 documentary *General Magic* is a captivating history lesson looking into an American software and electronics company in the 1990s.[10] The employees of General Magic imagined an extraordinary future of personal computing and set out to develop what is now the core of the modern smartphone, smartwatch, and music players.

> **Blind Spot**
>
> Unvaried, undiversified groups mistakenly feel buoyed by their shared agreement, confident that their limited views are the solution resulting in groupthink.

General Magic's goal was to deliver personal computing products focused on the customer experience. The team was staffed with a gifted and masterful group including the future White House chief technology officer Megan Smith, future Android cocreator Andy Rubin, future eBay founder Pierre Omidyar, and future iPod and iPhone co-designer Tony Fadell.

To put General Magic's brilliance into perspective, try imagining a world without smartphones. Back in the 1990s, the digital telecommunications industry and the web as we now know it didn't exist. But Marc Porat, one of the cofounders of General Magic, not only saw a future where that all existed, he also imagined the products and the first-of-a-kind partnerships like the ones between Sony and AT&T to deliver on an unparalleled vision.

Steve Jobs had been fired from Apple, and John Sculley, the new CEO, was looking for a legacy project. Sculley was captivated by Porat's ideas. Because the innovation was so mind-blowing compared to anything previously tackled at Apple, it was treated as a spin-off. The core team comprised the original Macintosh project veterans, including Andy Hertzfeld, Bill Atkinson, and Joanna Hoffman. And the team didn't suffer from a lack of funding like many start-ups. In fact, along with the funding from Apple, they raised $96 million in the IPO and a total of $200 million from 16 different investors.[11] The vision for this project was so clear that the company opened on the stock market before even having a finished product.

Porat documented his brilliant vision of personal technology's future and the experiences customers could have when interacting with it in his now famous doctoral thesis, "Information Economy" (Figure 7.4). The thesis not only contained hundreds of detailed drawings, many of which we know today as smartphones, activity trackers, and smartwatches, but it also predicted the transition from a manufacturing-based US economy to an information-based economy (Figure 7.5).

As Porat spoke about the mission before them at General Magic and the customer's experience of the technology, he said:

> *We are creating a tiny computer, a phone, a very personal object . . . It must be beautiful. It must offer the kind of personal satisfaction that a fine piece of jewelry brings. It will have a perceived value even when it's not being used ... Once you use it, you won't be able to live without it.*[12]

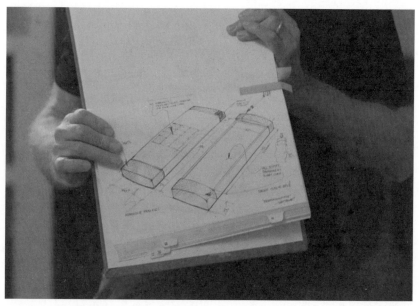

Figure 7.4 Marc Porat's big red sketchbook.
Source: Marc Porat

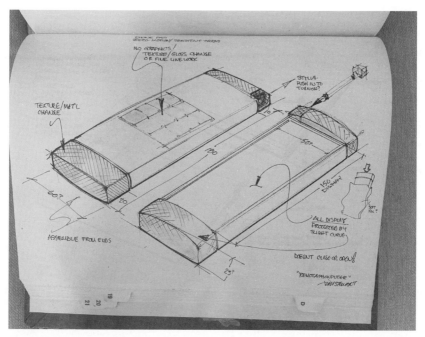

Figure 7.5 Concept pictures of an early smartphone from Marc Porat's sketchbook.
Source: Marc Porat

While Porat was very accurate about the future of personal computing devices, the company, by their own admission in the *General Magic* documentary, was so focused on the customer's product experience that the company couldn't ship a viable product and ended up in bankruptcy.

What went wrong? General Magic wanted to be a different kind of company, driven by purpose and mission. Veering from the traditional type of company structure, they didn't focus on efficiency or effective

> **Blind Spot**
>
> Developing products, services, and experiences without customer feedback results in insulated decisions that can't possibly meet market demands.

capabilities like having product managers and project schedules. And because the product was shrouded in secrecy until its big reveal, General Magic hadn't received customer feedback before releasing their product into the market.

However, in sharing what they learned through this experience, the General Magic team has contributed much to the business world. We can see that without a constant customer feedback loop in the product development process, it's impossible to build customer-centric products and experiences. Often, companies engrossed in insular discussions focus on features or other groupthink priorities that lead to analysis paralysis and indecision.

The General Magic team learned they spent too much time brainstorming ideas instead of the practicalities of producing a deliverable. They focused on creating empathic experiences for the customer, like developing emoji-type figures to make the devices more relatable (Figure 7.5). While their customer-centric, empathy-based premise was spot on, they ran out of time—and investors forced the launch of a less than fully functioning product. While the emoji-type figures were novel and important to the customer experience, the team spent too much time on the ornamental aspect of the customer experience and not enough time on elements that would result in a solid, fully functioning product that could deliver on the customer experience Porat envisioned.

> **Blind Spot**
>
> Artificially focusing on the novelty aspects of customer experience results in products, services, and experiences unable to deliver on a loyalty-galvanizing customer experiences.

What else can we learn from this example? It's not enough to focus only on the novelty aspect of providing empathic customer experiences. Today, a company must prepare a concrete plan to combine and scale new ways to deliver customer/employee-focused effectiveness and efficiency through the lens of empathy. When a company sees their products and services through the customer/employee lens, priorities and decisions change. In General Magic's example, they tinkered with features and never got a minimal viable product out the door. While the North Star triad of empathy, trust, and loyalty is vital, a company can't only focus on the customer experience at the cost of shipping a product or delivering a service. There must be tangible value added to deliver on C&E-centric efficiency, effectiveness, and empathy—in the product and the experiences it delivers.

What can you take away from General Magic's ordeal to try and deliver customer-centric experiences? Companies must rethink experiences and create synergy between the customers', employees', and company's point of view while accomplishing the "job to be done" for them all.

Create Lasting Change

Lasting change and diverse teams are worth the effort it takes to create and nurture them. But it takes skilled leaders to know and learn how to navigate this type of change. In Chapter 11, we'll provide skills that leaders often miss during these transformation periods. Many forget that leading a transformation is vastly different from overseeing the day-to-day maintenance of the status quo

> ### Blind Spot
>
> Leaders don't realize they adjust to a new way of doing business in corporate transformations faster than employees because they haven't assessed the level of cultural transformation readiness.

and that transformative processes are frequently met with resistance from employees. Reluctance toward change often occurs because leaders fail to:

- Realize they move through change much faster than employees; while executives are far down the path, employees delay adoption and progress if psychological safety and the right motivations are absent
- Deploy an assessment to determine the level of readiness and risk for a change initiative at a departmental, team, or pod level
- Create a sense of urgency by showing employees how the change will benefit them and articulate a massive transformative purpose (MTP) that employees can emotionally buy into
- Identify the change agents in the organization (at all levels) and empower them to enroll others in the new direction of the company
- Allocate resources for an organizational change management plan to drive accountability, mindset, and behavior change and to hit key business milestones while keeping morale high
- Execute a full-scale, continuous communication and education plan to include progress updates and results and to provide rewards and recognition for those supporting the change
- Understand that browbeating employees with what to do is ineffective because it takes eight hours or more to recover physically and psychologically

Remember, happy employees make happy customers. Approach employees' resistance with empathy—make it a point to understand the reasons behind your team's opposition, and then act in a way that demonstrates their concerns are heard. Understanding and appreciating the employees' point of view will go a long way in creating lasting change.

Chapter Seven

TAKEAWAYS

- The consequences of applying scientific management-type, business-only focused paradigms of efficiency and effectiveness theories are a loss to humanity, productivity, and innovation in the workplace.

- Groupthink is dangerous for a company culture because critical business decisions are often stuck in analysis paralysis and lack customer feedback to determine what can drive better products, services, and experiences.

- Empathy-based cultures drive better employee and customer interactions, innovation, and business value.

" Innovation works when people from different disciplines and backgrounds come together to create new possibilities that none of them could have imagined on their own.

—Amy C. Edmondson

EXPERIENCES AS A SERVICE: THE GREAT DIFFERENTIATOR

We looked at the urgency to improve experiences and make changes accordingly. The next question is: How do we think differently about business? As we saw in Chapter 4, Joe Pine and James Gilmore identified experiences as a crucial step to generate economic value for companies.[1] However, most companies still provide products and services

> **Blind Spot**
>
> Businesses are still focused on providing products and services and haven't figured out how to scale highly personalized, contextually relevant experiences that provide customers a more empathic experience.

without evolving their offerings to experiences. This next step in economic value creation is about delivering highly personalized, contextually relevant, empathetic customer and employee experiences at scale using exponential technologies. The ability to create remarkable C&E-centric companies is what we call Experience as a Service[SM] or Empathy in Action.

The bottom line is that businesses are no longer B2C or B2B or B2B2C. In an experience economy—it all boils down to B2E2C, where *E* stands for empathy. Companies need to deliberately design engaging, empathic customer experiences, with the same attention to design-thinking they give to product or user experience design (often referred to as UX, including the feelings and emotions users experience when interacting with a product[2]).

Let's look at how economic value has evolved from products and services to experiences by reviewing the classic birthday cake example from Pine and Gilmore's work. There was a time when families baked birthday cakes from scratch, and ingredients cost less than a dollar. Boxed cake mixes brought in the next phase of economic value. Families paid a few dollars for Betty Crocker or Duncan Hines' premixed dry ingredients or premade products for convenience.

Following the product-based economy was the service economy. Families were willing to pay for the convenience of ordering a cake from a bakery or grocery store. At $10 to $15 or more, store-bought cakes cost nearly 10 times as much as the packaged ingredients. But it was worth the extra money to save time.

In the 1990s, when time was even more of a premium, families started handing over the birthday party to companies like Chuck E. Cheese or the Discovery Zone for the convenience of easily creating memorable events for their children. Parents didn't have to do any planning, shopping, cooking, cleaning, or brainstorming entertainment options—even the cake was often included in the price of the party. Today, we see these ideas taking on new forms. During COVID-19,[3] companies that hosted parties in person offered stay-at-home, virtual, customized parties with entertaining performers and activities for friends and family, all via Zoom, Google Meet, or Teams.[4]

From clothes to cars to sneakers, we live in a world where people are willing to pay for experiences that meet their individual needs. Think about the spot-on product recommendations you get from Amazon, or that "up next" YouTube video you just have to watch, or how Netflix revolutionized the movie and online entertainment industries by understanding your previous choices and providing you with suggestions on what to watch next.

> **Blind Spot**
>
> Mass-produced customer experiences are created by matching an averaged employee and customer persona instead of personalizing every customer/employee experience at scale.

This evolution shows that successful companies will be the ones willing to disrupt their processes to focus on innovative solutions for customers and employees. They understand what customers and employees want and need and create new experiences that deliver on those needs. They are shifting their business model to align with current marketplace demands and conditions, and adapting to unforeseen market disruptions like those experienced in the economy by global pandemics like COVID-19.

Transforming from Services to Experiences

The difficulty for many companies is realizing what business they are in and knowing their defensible space. If they have a commodity mindset, a company making pedometers might think they provide a way to keep track of someone's exercise instead of realizing they are a lifestyle brand, contributing to their customers'

> **Blind Spot**
>
> Bad profits result from businesses that put profit over creating great customer/employee experiences.

health and well-being. Or, a transportation/distribution company might think they are in the business of transporting people and goods when in reality, they are a partner in keeping families clothed and fed. That's the difference between having a business-focused as opposed to a customer-focused strategy and purpose.

The challenge for businesses is to realize where their company is on the scale, from providing raw ingredients to highly personalized, empathic experiences. Unless a company wants to be in a commoditized business—which doesn't offer the margins today of experience-oriented companies—they will become part of the disappearing marketplace of companies that couldn't evolve. (There's an assessment in our closing remarks if you want to know where your business stands.)

This next wave in the economy is to design and deliver highly personalized, contextually relevant experiences that emphasize empathy at scale. By using empathy to innovate, companies can listen to their customers' current concerns, comments, and reviews. They can then use this input to transform their business model to offer customers what they need and want before their competitors do, and sometimes, even before customers know they want it.

Pine and Gilmore provide a unique example of taking a standard service and turning it into an experience. In the old television show *Taxi*, Iggy, a driver, decided to differentiate the transportation experience. To create remarkable and memorable experiences, Iggy offered sandwiches and drinks, acted as a tour guide during rides, and even sang favorite Frank Sinatra songs. Iggy was empathic to his customers—he wasn't just in a compassion mindset. Instead of just getting his customers from point A to point B, he created a distinct economic offering based on listening, understanding, predicting, and acting. Iggy learned what his customers wanted and created a differentiated, exceptional experience.

Iggy's cab experience was far more valuable than just a ride. Customers felt seen, acknowledged, important, and special. When they reached their destination, they were willing to pay extra to go around the block again and they left bigger tips. Using this example, how can you transform your products and services into empathy-based customer experiences?

With the evolution of themed restaurants like Planet Hollywood, House of Blues, or the Hard Rock Cafe, the food is just a prop to deliver what has become known as "eatertainment." Stores like Cabela's, REI, and Niketown draw customers in by offering fascinating displays, great activities, and events (also known as "shoppertainment" or "entertailing"). Amusement parks like Disneyland and Disney World

> **Blind Spot**
>
> Employee motivation is often misinterpreted. Empathy allows managers to pinpoint specific issues to ensure an employee is thriving in their position.

have been doing this for decades. And virtual and augmented reality are turning interactive and multiplayer games into immersive entertainment and retail experiences. These experiences are based on customer-centric empathy.

Seeing the Future Now: Experience as a Service

Research shows nearly 50 percent of consumers feel more connected to companies that remember them, and 66 percent are willing to share data in exchange for a more effortless experience. Customers are demanding more empathetic experiences while wanting more control over who's using their data and what they are doing with it.[5] While customers demand convenience and privacy, employees want their "future of work" needs met. Among the things employees want are control over their schedules, the ability to work remotely, and a better quality of work life. How do we accomplish this? Let's see . . .

Great Experiences as a Differentiator

Customer experiences are dynamic; they revolve around the interaction between the company and a customer. Prior economic offerings, products, and services weren't inherently personal. However, experiences need to be made personal to create engagement on emotional, physical, and intellectual levels. The following sections contain examples and case studies of businesses that have created pioneering, empathic customer and employee experiences that drive trust and loyalty. These brands are taking the inputs from the Empathy in Action Flywheel (Figure 1.4) and making them actionable.

Be My Eyes

Over 2.2 billion people are living with visual impairments worldwide.[6] While some are born with visual impairments, the vast majority experience vision loss with age. Regardless, adapting to a world that isn't designed for you can be difficult, to say the least. Technology has helped, though, and one of the greatest tools helping people with sight struggles today was invented by someone who shares those struggles.

The Be My Eyes brand story started in 2012 with Hans Jørgen Wiberg, a visually impaired Danish furniture craftsman. While volunteering at the Danish Association of the Blind and confronting his own vision loss, Wiberg recognized that the tasks blind or low-vision people often needed assistance with were quite quick and easy to solve. Around the same time, he began using video calls to connect with family and friends who, to his surprise, could 'be his eyes' through his smartphone camera without much effort. He wondered: Would total strangers assist individuals like me in this way, instead of having to rely on friends and family to answer the call?

Hans Jørgen began sharing the idea—first on the TEDx stage and then at a Danish start-up event where he met Christian Erfurt. Christian quit his job on the spot to help start the company, and today, he is the CEO of Be My Eyes. In 2015, when the Be My Eyes app was released, the team did not know if anyone would sign up. That's where the universal power of empathy kicked in.

Within 24 hours of launch and with no marketing, more than 10,000 people volunteered to help the blind see. The app was growing faster than anyone could have imagined, entirely by word of mouth. Within a few weeks, they were assisting people in more than 30 languages. Today, Be My Eyes has more than five million people assisting blind and low-vision users in 185 languages, making it the biggest "micro-volunteering" community ever. The app has won numerous awards—high honors from Apple, Google, the Webbys, Helen Keller Services, the National Federation of the Blind, and others. Most notably, Be My Eyes received the coveted Apple Design Award for Social Impact in 2021.

Be My Eyes brought its mission to the market in 2018, opening the platform for companies to join. Customer experience teams could now build a profile on the beloved app and take Be My Eyes calls on specific topics related to their company. For their hundreds of thousands of sight-impaired users, all of whom receive this sight support for free, Be My Eyes has become their one-stop shop for fast, easy, expert visual support.

Be My Eyes is a great example of tech plus human connection—a clear example of Empathy in Action. Today, companies can provide Be My Eyes support through a contact center experience-as-a-service platform integration. And many corporations have pledged their employees as volunteers, giving sighted individuals a glimpse into the lives and barriers encountered by visually impaired customers, job seekers, and employees. The company's motto is "see the world together," and the mutual exchange of eyesight and insight in the name of greater access for all is undeniably a win-win.

Starbucks

There's no doubt Starbucks has successfully personalized the coffee bean experience. While it charges far more than the beans cost, customers continue to patronize it because of unique experiences provided such as free Wi-Fi and a place to meet with others. And then came COVID-19. With such extreme external market conditions as the pandemic brought, Starbucks had to pivot its customer strategy—fast.

Starbucks transitioned from indoor spaces where people gathered to outdoor areas where people could enjoy favorite beverages and engage socially, but at a distance.

Even before the pandemic, Starbucks invested in mobile ordering and pickups as a calculated contrast to a cozy spot to work outside the office or hang out with friends. Thinking from a customer's mindset, the company doubled down on convenient coffee buying, but in new ways. The entire digital order and pickup strategy, slated for rollout between 2023 and 2025, was fast-tracked to 2020 because of COVID-19.[7]

Starbucks also accelerated new digital capabilities and real estate deals. It went from 30 percent of locations having drive-throughs to 60 percent. Expanding curbside pickup options, the company negotiated more parking spots at many of its locations.[8] Customers could use the smartphone app to order ahead and be assigned a parking spot, so the coffee was brought right to the customer's car window—a strategy similar to Lowe's, The Home Depot, Costco, and other retailers' curbside pickups.

Walmart

Another example company producing relevant experiences is Walmart, which in the summer of 2020 turned some of its parking lots into drive-in movie theaters and hosted its first Camp by Walmart. Using the Walmart app, families accessed 50 activities, from arts and crafts to fitness and other free activities. Camp experts and celebrities led the sessions, including a makeup tutorial with actress Drew Barrymore, camp challenges with actor Neil Patrick Harris, and mental and physical activities run by basketball star LeBron James with help from his I Promise School educators.

Janey Whiteside, Walmart's chief customer officer, said, "With the pandemic, summer hadn't really felt like summer yet, and I know I heard every day, 'Mom, I'm bored!' Through our digital means and vast footprint of stores, we brought some summer fun to families across the country. We know Walmart plays a role in our communities that extends far beyond getting them necessary supplies, and we see that now more than ever."[9]

Walmart transformed 160 of its parking lots into drive-in theaters in a partnership with Tribeca Enterprises, including hit movies and special appearances from filmmakers and celebrities. Ahead of each screening, families were able to order online and have concessions delivered to their vehicles.[10]

Lowe's

This Fortune 500 home improvement retailer is innovating customers' experiences through exponential technologies, including artificial intelligence, robotics, virtual reality, and additive manufacturing. Lowe's Innovation Labs has turned innovative possibilities and out-of-the-box thinking into reality.[11]

One of its first projects, the Holoroom, lets customers design their remodel on an iPad and then view it in an immersive virtual reality experience, right down to the wood grain on cabinets, using Oculus Rift or Google Cardboard. Lowe's has also developed robots that speak multiple languages and help employees with inventory tracking and customer service.

In addition, Lowe's teamed up with Made in Space, the company behind the world's first zero-G 3D printer, to launch the first commercial manufacturing facility on the International Space Station. Together, the companies developed the Additive Manufacturing Facility, an advanced, permanent 3D printer for use by NASA, researchers, educational organizations, and commercial customers.[12]

Kyle Nel, previously the executive director of Lowe's Innovation Labs and now the president of Singularity Labs, explained, "Whether you have a home in Louisville, Kentucky, or your home is the International Space Station, you have a lot of the same needs to fix something, replace broken pieces, often needing highly customized parts."[13]

While Lowe's is the first retailer in space, the partnership also brings together two parties, making each more creative and disruptive than either ever could be alone. The advantage for the space station? It doesn't have to receive replacement parts via rockets. Instead, it can recreate the broken part on the space station with a 3D printer using a visual file.

The advantage for Lowe's? Additive manufacturing is substantially changing how home improvement is done and how people design things or get them repaired. Having a 3D printer on location allows, for instance, an obsolete part to be 3D printed, changing not only the customers' experience but also their reliance on Lowe's home improvement services.

Casper

The mattress company Casper does two core things: it creates a physical product and establishes experiences around those products.[14] The founders—frustrated by an industry with commissioned salespeople, weak return policies, and indistinguishable products except in price—asked themselves, "How can we create an incredible experience that's as good as when you buy an iPhone?"

As a company dedicated to sleep, Casper launched *Van Winkle's*, an online publication about the science and culture of sleep. It also hosted an annual sleep symposium. And to make sleepless nights a little less lonely, Casper created a free chatbot, Insomnobot3000, specifically for insomniacs.[15] Using AI, the company's new bot holds conversations with people still awake in the wee hours. Occasionally, the bot initiates these late-night chats, making the interactions feel less like a one-way street. Casper can collect mobile numbers and send insomniacs promotional offers and discounts for their comfortable mattresses. This innovative service pulled in $100 million in sales for Casper within the first year of launching the chatbot.[16]

Grupo of Colombia

Grupo Bancolombia is a full-service financial institution providing a broad range of financial products and services for individuals and corporate clients in Colombia, Panama, Guatemala, and El Salvador. In 2020, a tough year for the whole world, Bancolombia reaffirmed the purpose of promoting sustainable economic development to achieve everyone's well-being.

Juan Carlos Mora, CEO of the company since 2016, has been aware of the relevance of the bank being part of a group of sustainable and conscious companies with an actual concern about the future they are building and making a positive impact on society and the environment. Then, taking the lessons learned from the pandemic, Mr. Mora declared 2021 the year of empathy. He sees that empathy can arise when people genuinely and honestly understand, feel, and care to see the world from the viewpoint of others. Mora explains further:

Empathy is what makes us want to help one another; it connects us for the greater good; it makes us feel valuable and allows us to fulfill our purpose. While we don't have to live another's experience, being empathic is the action of putting ourselves in another's shoes and asking ourselves, "How would we feel if that were happening to us? What is the best thing we can do in this situation? How can we really help?" We all want to feel understood, accepted, and, above all, worthy, even in situations we possibly can't solve.

In this evolution, Bancolombia's team started with an internal change program focused on their reason for being in business and serving their customers. The first point was remembering that each employee is first a person, then a banker—that's why they deeply listened and connected to their problems while looking for new ways to solve the issues they faced so they could fulfill their promise to provide superior experiences.

And with that human connection, employees created a "chain of empathy"—a new way to understand and practice the concept, challenging colleagues to make commitments to be more empathetic and, overall, Bancolombia evolved its brand to a new level and created a more collaborative and productive work environment by integrating new knowledge and competencies to generate greater value for not just for the company, but also for its employees, customers, and society.

Consequently, Bancolombia understands empathy as an intention that connects and inspires its purpose, its culture, and the delivery of close, reliable, timely, and easy customer experiences. So, it put itself in the shoes of its customers to understand their needs and how the company could serve them.

It means listening to understand and taking charge of realities in order to seek and deliver accurate, timely, and flexible solutions and guidelines. Also, this includes respectful and friendly treatment with close, simple, and conscious communication, establishing clear conditions to ensure a relationship of trust and transparency.

In other words, empathy enables the bank's employees to design end-to-end customer-centered experiences and develop agile, simple, and self-manageable processes; all to be closer to clients, strengthening their trust with clear and transparent conversations as well as relevant and easy to use solutions.

To sum up, empathy has become a competitive advantage that allows the bank to create a people-centered team with great organizational capabilities: an expert and deep knowledge of more than 20 million customers among individuals, businesses, and corporates, a broad portfolio of financial and nonfinancial services to meet customer's needs, a wide distribution chain, relationships with customers strengthened by its capabilities and partners, and a leading brand that generates trust.

And, most importantly, an organization centered on people with a clear conviction of its role to promote sustainable economic development that generates positive impact on society and well-being.

TechStyle Fashion Group

Innovation is always in fashion, particularly for membership-based, digital brands like Fabletics, Savage X Fenty, JustFab, ShoeDazzle, and FabKids. And TechStyle Fashion Group, the global, integrated operations and services provider behind these brands, is helping reimagine the fashion industry. By leveraging data science, machine learning, and predictive analytics, all powered by its proprietary, end-to-end tech platform, TechStyle Fashion Group enables fashion brands to deliver an unrivaled level of personalization, value, and satisfaction in the industry.

Global Member Services, a department of TechStyle Fashion Group, reviewed its member experiences and found many members of the brands it supports were making the same type of simple transactional requests. It seemed unnecessary to make members wait in a queue to go to a live agent for these requests. And at the same time, employees were experiencing frustration, repeatedly answering the same "simple" questions.

To reduce member and employee frustration, they began using a high-velocity member experience innovation platform to enhance personalized member experiences. By using exponential technologies within the cloud platform, like AI-enriched data to listen, understand, and predict the intent of the request, it could divide order requests into four main intents: skip, cancel, WISMO (where is my order), and update profile info. Answering the simple transactional requests using self-service (AI-voice and chatbots) meant members got what they needed with less time, effort, and hassle and employees were freed up to use their skills to solve more complex problems requiring their help.

This was a better experience for the members, the employees, and also for the company. Members raved about the new experiences on social media, spreading positive word of mouth about the brand. Global Member Services and the brands it supports realized the importance of using exponential technologies (AI/cloud) to not fall behind. At the same time, it became more member- and employee-centric, exceeding its five million members' expectations worldwide.

When COVID-19 hit, most companies faced the sudden challenge of enabling employees to work from home without disrupting service to members. However, Global Member Services and TechStyle Fashion Group—due to their cloud-based CX platform—were able to quickly implement disaster recovery strategies, empowering over 1,000 employees globally to safely work in remote environments. It enabled its workforce with the appropriate work-from-home tools, i.e., stable internet access, at-home office space, and more. Some employees were even able to work from a local hotel during the pandemic's lockdown, providing employees a safe and comfortable work environment while delivering the best possible member experience.

Cross-Brand Empathy-Centric Experiences

Customer/employee-centric software does take the right step toward customer empathy, but it doesn't completely solve the end-to-end or cross-brand customer experience. There are many scenarios where a customer's experience improves with the brand's active participation, solidifying customer loyalty. Cross-brand empathy means companies utilize open innovation platforms and application programming interfaces to enable a wide variety of service providers and businesses to develop unique combinations that deliver increasingly relevant experiences to customers. What if a customer's airlines, hotels, and rental car companies all collaborated on their behalf? Let's see how cross-brand experiences could be put into practice.

Vacation Travel Customer Experience

Oftentimes, a brand ends up on the wrong side of a customer experience, even though everything it has done was spot-on. Take, for instance, Sherrie and her family. They planned a trip to their vacation villa; it's their first time going, so the whole family is very excited. Sherrie works with the resort contact center to finalize all her plans, and everything is in order. However, without cross-brand integration, the resort has no insight into what happens to Sherrie and her family before she lands at the property.

In this case, the Uber driver they use to get to the airport is new and doesn't know about the new drop-off rules. As a result, they take a wrong turn, get stuck in traffic, and miss the plane. The family gets rebooked on the next flight, but the plane gets stuck on the tarmac, delaying the flight. Sherrie does her best to keep the kids entertained during the long flight, knowing that people around her are irritated. She tries to contact the resort, but the contact center call queue is long, and she's asked to put her phone away for takeoff. In the air, Sherrie tries to alert the resort via text and email, but the plane's Wi-Fi is not working, and she can't get through. By the time they land, the kids are cranky, tired, and hungry.

When they finally meet their resort concierge, they are exhausted. Getting to the resort was just horrible, and by the time they get there, the family is in such a bad mood that nothing the resort does can make Sherrie and her family happy. Is it the resort's fault? No, it couldn't control what happened with other brands as the family was en route to the resort.

Suppose the resort had insights into the family's experiences: the staff could have greeted the weary travelers differently (maybe even at the airport), perhaps doing something special for them that would melt away the day's mishaps. If the family knew they would be greeted with such care, no matter the setbacks along the way, how much more likely would they be to book with that resort again? And if each individual brand involved in the experience had insight into the customer's journey, how might they also make up for the mishaps? When we talk about companies having your back, this is what we mean—this is Empathy in Action.

Car and Home Customer Experience

You can see a cross-brand experience in action with the partnership between Lexus and Alexa. Let's say you are driving home after shopping. It's cold and getting dark. You want to turn on your home's lights, turn up the thermostat, and check the security system. Using only your voice, you can easily access thousands of the same functions you get with Alexa at home. This list might include turning on home appliances, listening to audiobooks, streaming Amazon Music, making to-do lists, checking the weather, and getting news updates. In addition to offering added in-vehicle convenience, Alexa can sync to your car's navigation system or provide on-the-go recommendations for shopping, hotels, and restaurants via traffic apps like Waze.

What Are the Cross-Brand Hurdles?

While cross-brand scenarios are exciting, there are some significant considerations and hurdles to overcome. Issues surrounding ongoing regulations for data sharing, privacy, and protection must be resolved so customers can control their data using a permission-based transient data model. In addition, companies that customers patronize would all need to use the cloud, as the ability to share this type of customer data can't be achieved easily with legacy, on-premise databases and systems. And brands would need to see the wisdom and possibilities in sharing data across brands.

Many companies have built their loyalty programs based on customer data and might be reluctant to share it. Credit card companies (and other brokers) may see the benefits of helping the customer have better cross-brand experiences because they aren't in direct competition with the brands the customer patronizes. But to provide these experiences, it will take industry-wide vendor and brand collaboration focused on creating the best services for the customer. It's yet another call to action for the experience industry.

Evolve, Adapt, Prepare . . . or Die

Creating empathetic experiences for customers and building the support infrastructure to deliver them takes time to evolve, adapt, and prepare, which is why companies need to start the process immediately (or yesterday). Achieving high levels of innovation as in the examples requires an empathetic company culture where employees actively participate in delivering the next evolution of the customer experience instead of maintaining the status quo. As we'll see in the following chapters, part of that employee buy-in comes from companies providing the tools, technologies, and access to data and insights in real time, allowing employees to deliver excellent customer experiences.

The bottom line? As with the commoditized products of yesteryear, the personalized, empathetic experience economy will grow, as economist Joseph Schumpeter stated, "through the gales of creative destruction."[17] Business disruption will make irrelevant those who stick to the diminishing returns of products and services. The concept of customer experiences goes far beyond theaters and theme parks. As the above examples show, it's something that every customer expects, and in which every company, large and small, must excel.

TAKEAWAYS

- Over time, customer expectations have evolved from products and services to experiences.

- The next step for businesses is to create experiences that are deeply infused with empathy at every step.

- The most successful businesses will be those that can offer experiences as a service.

TONY'S
LEADERSHIP CORNER

Blind spot: Being introspective

George Floyd was murdered on Monday, May 25, 2020. It became a lightning rod that sparked worldwide protests and a global movement.

This tragic event happened around my one-year anniversary as CEO of Genesys. At that time, we were a global company with employees in more than 100 countries, but we did not have a formal diversity, equity, and inclusion program. We were (and are) an ethical and compliant company, but we did not take public stances on social issues. We were a private company and opinions on controversial issues remained just that: private.

The film clips shown repeatedly on the news that Monday were visually disturbing. A police officer's knee on George Floyd's neck for 8 minutes and 46 seconds. "I can't breathe." It felt cowardly as a leader to stay silent on the sidelines.

As the intensity of the situation intensified, I wrestled with whether to speak to our employees or not. If I did not, I would be maintaining the status quo; a safe choice. If I did, there would be no turning back in taking a stand as a company on important social and political issues.

I decided to send an email to our employees expressing my support for them to peacefully protest and reiterating that we, as a company, did not condone violence. I wasn't solving for activism. I was creating a better place to work.

The outpouring of relief and support from our employees from that single email opened a door I could not have imagined. A few days later, we hosted an all-employee event where employees of color were invited to share their experiences in an open forum—and the rest of us listened. It was seminal, a turning point for our company culture. We named our first global diversity, equity, and inclusion officer in June. We now have a half dozen employee inclusion groups and monthly DEI talks for all employees. And we've expanded our efforts to sustainability, which is creating a strong company, a better society, and a better planet. We have much to learn and a lot of work ahead of us, but we are already a more open and trusted place for our employees to have these important discussions.

Leadership is not just about numbers and key performance indicators. It's about how you show up. The CEO owns the culture, and it requires introspection. It takes a lot of life experiences and to get outside your own head to see another view. The ability to empathize—to listen, understand, take action—is what enables leaders to have a greater impact on the world.

" Most people will forget
what you said; they will
forget what you did;
but people will never
forget how you made
them feel.

—Maya Angelou

EXPERIENCES AS A SERVICE FOR CUSTOMERS AND EMPLOYEES

Making Your Business Personal: Leveraging the Power of Norm

In the popular TV sitcom *Cheers*, a character named Norm Peterson was greeted with a chorus of "Norm!" whenever he entered his favorite bar. Millions of people watching the show related to its tagline: "You wanna go where everybody knows your name!" As American mythologist, writer, and lecturer Joseph Campbell explained in his many works that studied the human condition, humans have a deep need for a sense of belonging and to feel seen, heard, and understood.

What if companies leveraged this power, using the same principle to personalize customers' experiences as they navigate a website or reach out to a customer experience team? Instead of using technology that sacrifices the customer experience, they could use it to offer the most important differentiating factor in modern business—to create a sense of belonging by delivering personalized customer/employee experiences in real time and at scale. It's true inclusivity at its best.

It's a skill we can learn from Sam Malone, the bartender on *Cheers*, who listened to and understood Norm's preferences, needs, and desires. Sam could act on that information, and by remaining empathetic, he continuously learned more about his favorite customer. In so doing, Sam could provide Norm with precisely the experience he wanted. In return, Norm rewarded the bar with his unfaltering loyalty.

Revolution in the Evolution

Providing these *Cheers*-type experiences furnishes the sort of financial leverage we looked at in Chapter 4. Using the empathy-based financial input approach as seen in the Empathy in Action Flywheel (Figure 1.4) helps leaders increase the company's top and bottom lines by increasing EBBV, CLV, and ELV, all while reducing costs. Hindsight allows us to see patterns that might otherwise have remained invisible. By comparing where we've been to our customers' needs today and in the future (Figure 9.1), we have a new perspective on how companies can deliver loyalty-driving customer/employee experiences.

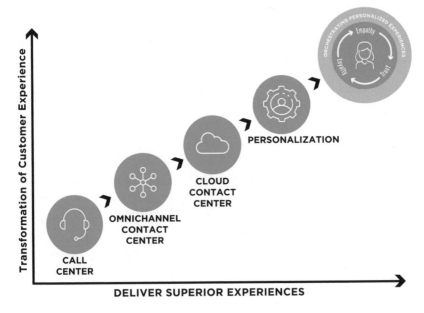

Figure 9.1 Evolution of call centers to experience centers.

What's left? Leaders must shift their mindset out of business-centric, cost-cutting modes of operation. Leaders must dedicate themselves to understanding exponential, loyalty-galvanizing strategies, technologies, and platforms—which include powerful orchestration or routing capabilities—to deliver C&E-centric, exponential business growth.

Empathy in Action Customer Experience

The experience revolution has afforded us the ability to create unparalleled orchestrations of exponential technology capable of delivering experiences as a service like the ones Sam provided Norm in *Cheers*. To build the experiences-as-a-service strategy, we used the Empathy Pillars framework introduced in Chapter 5 (Figure 9.2):

- Listen
- Understand + Predict
- Act
- Learn

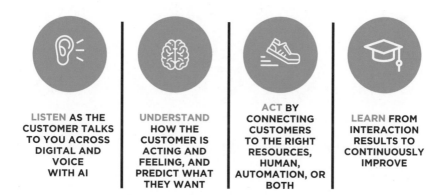

| **LISTEN AS THE CUSTOMER TALKS TO YOU ACROSS DIGITAL AND VOICE WITH AI** | **UNDERSTAND HOW THE CUSTOMER IS ACTING AND FEELING, AND PREDICT WHAT THEY WANT** | **ACT BY CONNECTING CUSTOMERS TO THE RIGHT RESOURCES, HUMAN, AUTOMATION, OR BOTH** | **LEARN FROM INTERACTION RESULTS TO CONTINUOUSLY IMPROVE** |

Figure 9.2 The Empathy Pillars framework.

As we explored in earlier chapters, personalized experiences form the core of an empathic business approach and garner empathy, trust, and loyalty in both customers and employees. The outer layers of the approach represent categories of technology that can be used to deliver those experiences (see the Empathy in Action Flywheel process in Figure 1.4).

You might be looking at Figure 9.3 and wondering, "How do I get from the outside ring of technology to delivering empathy, trust, and loyalty?" By using the four Empathy Pillars as guiding principles to light the path to delivering remarkable experiences.

Just like an orchestra needs a music maestro to deliver its magnificent harmonies, companies need a technology maestro to conduct and orchestrate the AI-enriched data in the omnichannel customer-employee experience. These maestros needn't be human elements, either. When companies use platforms specifically designed to orchestrate experiences, they follow in the footsteps of music masters. The platforms know when to bring in the right "instruments" to deliver personalized experiences resulting in empathy, trust, and loyalty. Choosing and implementing these types of platforms is key to how experiences are delivered.

Figure 9.3 Experience as a Service technologies.

To see the world through the customer's eyes, personalizing the customer's "job to be done," companies can begin by "listening" at scale, harnessing the power of data across enterprise, digital, and voice channels. As an authenticated customer, companies can gather information about who the customer is, where they've been, and what they have done (see Step 1 in Figure 9.4).

Using the power of AI to enrich the data and orchestrate the experience, the company gains a nuanced and unique understanding of customer sentiment, intent, and context and is better able to predict the best way to help them (Step 2).

With that predictive information in hand, companies are empowered to act through omnichannel engagements (Step 3), surfacing the right content and resources (automated, self-service, AI chat, voicebots, or the right employee) for a successful customer-based outcome.

Step 4 of the process takes an organization beyond individual interactions (Figure 9.5). Using the power of AL and ML (computational analysis), hundreds of millions, if not billions, of interactions are continuously evaluated, enabling the company to look for failure patterns and then iterate, pivot, and learn in real time and improve all customers' experiences and outcomes. This is a major shift from static business intelligence reports of the past to a dynamic capability to understand what is happening in your business at any moment in time.

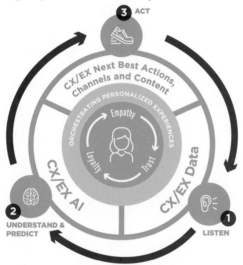

Figure 9.4 First three steps in empathy-centric experiences.

Figure 9.5 Fourth step in empathy-centric experiences.

Empathy in Action becomes tangible when a company can consistently see the world through customers' eyes. Figure 9.6 demonstrates why, when one's focus is B-centric, you really can't see who the customer is and what their needs are or anticipate and deliver a better experience from their point of view. With little context, a company can't tell much about who they are serving. But moving from left to right in Figure 9.6, we see that our vision becomes more precise with the ability to derive more context. With the full customer-centric context, this aperture allows us to focus on the customer's needs. We learn that this customer is a mom who just had her third child, her husband recently passed away, and she needs help with a life insurance policy to ensure she has funds to keep her house.

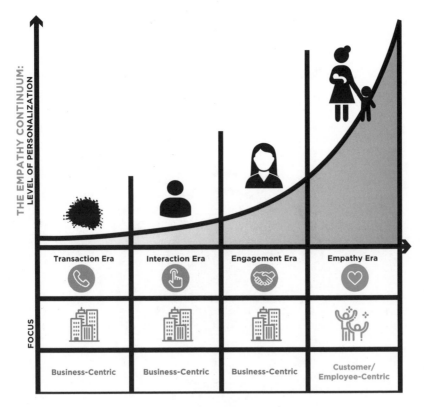

Figure 9.6 Using a C&E-centric lens, who the customer is and what they need becomes clearer.

When we start seeing our customers as human beings, our attitude shifts; we treat others like they matter instead of a number in a queue. And they do matter. When a company develops a C&E-centric focus, they have a clear picture that focuses on the best way to provide meaningful experiences to that customer in that specific moment. VIP experiences for all, at scale.

Let's review using Figure 9.7. Using this CX/EX paradigm, a company can "listen" to what a customer has been saying, "understand" their context, "predict" (qualify and clarify) the customer's sentiment and intent, and then determine who should "act" and deliver the needed information, answers, or solutions at the exact moment the customer needs it and on the channel best suited to their personal preferences. The business can then "learn" from all the experiences they have provided, thereby engaging in a self-propelled cycle of improvement.

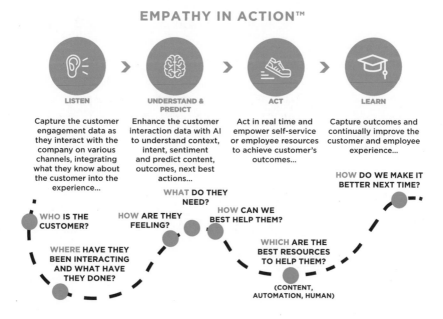

Figure 9.7 Empathy in Action: The empathic customer experience.

Bringing it All Together: Orchestrating Systems of Empathy

The key to a truly revolutionary disruption is not only your company's novel use of exponential technologies, but also the unprecedented orchestration of these tools to deliver the kind of loyalty-earning, EBBV-enhancing experiences described in Chapter 4. Empathy at scale requires an orchestration engine to choreograph all the customer/employee-related technologies—and therefore, employee and customer experiences—with the end goal of having these four systems of technology working together seamlessly:

- Systems of Listening
- Systems of Understanding & Prediction
- Systems of Action
- Systems of Learning

Systems of listening include capabilities for tracking various customer event data. Examples of this event data include when a customer navigates a website, pushes an IVR button, or receives input from IoT (Internet of Things) devices. Systems of understanding and prediction include the capabilities to segment, cluster, and enrich the customer event data with AI so as to understand and predict potential outcomes. These predictions provide the input to take action via the systems of action, providing relevant content and the right resources to help the customer.

Context and intended outcome are core aspects of these systems' capabilities, as they allow action sequences to route users toward the best resource, such as an AI-powered chat or voice bot, or an on-call employee. They also orchestrate the back-end process to provide the right content on the right channel, all without additional effort from either the customer or real-life employees.

Systems of learning are largely reflective and they include capabilities related to pinpointing the "voice" of the customer and the employee and then applying it to improve the experience and resulting business outcomes using machine learning or computational analysis.

Empathy in Action requires orchestrating the CX/EX-as-a-Service-technology platform along with components within the company's existing IT infrastructure. These can include all other CX/EX-related technologies across different sources and departments, such as marketing, sales, e-commerce, and back-office systems. Finally, you must integrate external databases, technologies, and applications already being utilized by your company. This orchestration "engine" brings all relevant information into the various Systems of Empathy™ and delivers a customer/employee experience.

Losing Heart: What a Lack of CX/EX Empathy Looks Like in Practice

If I log in to a company's website I've purchased from before and it greets me with a "Welcome back, Natalie," that's a great "Norm" moment. It's validating that they know my name and are happy to see me again.

As I navigate the site, looking to buy a product—and by my navigation path, I'm giving them insight into what I'm interested in—I find the paint I'm looking for and put it in my shopping cart (each action I take is recorded as an "event"). At this point, I'm wondering if the paint contains an anti-mildew ingredient. If the company is paying attention, they can see that my shopping cart activity has paused.

Guess what happens next? Nothing. And therein lies the problem many companies have with truly personalizing CX.

Going back to the Norm example, it's as though he's sitting on the barstool, staring at an empty glass of beer. Would the staff just let him sit there? For how long? As Norm, with my actions, I'm declaring, "I'd like a beer!" but the staff is ignoring me. In my paint example, the company doesn't engage me, so I type my question into their website search bar: "Is X paint anti-mildew?" Now I'm explicitly sharing my concerns and questions with the company. I'm directed to the FAQ, which provides information they think I might want, but it's not personalized toward what I need.

Then I spot a typical "Chat with Us" button, and I hope my resolution is right around the corner. I'm wary, though, because I've used such chat features before. But I'm here, so I click. Instead of knowing who I am and understanding my question, I'm presented with a form to fill out: they want my name, email address, and question. It's a dead-end because the site is not enabled to understand what I am looking for. I need real-time, tailored advice. This is common mistake number two, and it can completely derail the entire CX experience.

This is like Norm tapping the bartender on the shoulder, only to be asked, "Who are you?" and "What do you want?"

In my case, I wonder, "Why are you asking me when you know I'm signed in as Natalie?" The chat form should greet me by name, and because you can see what's in my shopping cart and that I typed "anti-mildew" in the FAQs, the chatbot should ask if I need more help with that. The experience? Customers are frustrated and left with the feeling that the company missed the mark.

Without another option in sight, I go ahead and add my information to the form. I am connected to a person who asks, "How can I help you?" They don't have any context of what I have been doing. I type, "Does this paint contain an anti-mildew agent?" They ask, "Which paint are you looking at?" At this point, the company has wasted my time and I must repeat everything I've already said. I'm ready to walk. I have no confidence that this company cares about me, wants to help me, or can provide the answers I need and want. It's easier for me to simply perform a Google search for anti-mildew paints and choose whatever options show up there than to dedicate myself to this particular seller. They've lost out on a potentially lucrative customer. I'm in search of a business that does create the personalized experience I'm craving, and they'll be the ones to secure my lifelong loyalty and continued purchases.

In Norm's case, he would probably hang his head and walk out of the bar, never to return. That's not the experience you want for your customers. I, like Norm, leave and go where they know who I am and what I need.

Unfortunately, this overall experience is extremely common. Customers are forced to repeat themselves over and over again because the technology being used by companies can't listen to their input, understand their needs, or take action to reduce their effort and provide an exceptional experience. This leads to customer frustration, abandoned journeys (bounce rates are a strong indicator of this phenomenon), and lost revenue. It's a big problem for companies trying to compete and differentiate themselves from the other retailers and service providers out there.

Powering Loyalty for the Long-Term: When Customers Experience Empathy in Action

Now let's look at an experience designed using the Empathy Pillars and the Systems of Empathy Experience Orchestration™ mentioned earlier. This time, as I move through the paint seller's website there are listening systems that monitor and track my activity data (Figures 9.7). Using integrated systems of understanding and prediction with this AI-enriched interaction data, the platform evaluates my intent and my shopping experience. It then uses the systems of action and leverages all of this data to proactively engage me with an AI bot to start a productive—and efficient—conversation. The big difference this time is that the bot is intelligent. It knows who I am, it knows the specific paint I want, and it's aware that I want to know about mildew prevention. Leveraging this, the bot retrieves information from its knowledge repositories and guides me to a self-service page that lists anti-mildew ingredients for this paint.

I like this company. They know me, they genuinely want to help me, and they quickly provide me the information I need. The experience makes me want to come back; there was no time wasted and little effort on my part. As I ask the chatbot about commercial accounts, it automatically transitions me to an employee. The ensuing conversation is seamless. The employee's unified desktop application provides them with my information, the journey I am on, and the conversations I've had with the bot. All of this information is laid out succinctly for them so they can focus on me. By providing the employee with my intent and context, it reduces the employee's cognitive burden and increases answer consistency. The employee knows I want to open a commercial account and helps me order the perfect paint for my new job site, providing me a discount based on the volume I'm purchasing.

The result? An incredibly easy, productive, and structured experience that is tailor-made for me, specifically. Like Norm, I am convinced that this is the place for me.

Predictive and Prescriptive Engagements

We need to dig a little deeper to understand some of the technological underpinnings behind amazing experiences like this one. The first factor enhancing EX and CX is that of predictive analytics, which uses ML and refers to the practice of extracting information from existing data to determine personalized patterns, predict future outcomes and behavioral trends intelligently, and trigger next-best actions on a consistent basis.

Prescriptive analytics uses reliable rules and functional optimization to orchestrate predictive models that maximize outcomes for each situation. These unique technologies drive improved decision logic, so platform decisions are more accurate as measured against business outcomes. Systems like this give insight into what a customer might need even before he or she tells you—or even consciously realizes that need themself. This is extremely powerful and has a profound impact on the way your customers view you.

From this process another arises. Predictive matching refers to a system whereby platforms learn patterns from historical and real-time data, then work with routing and orchestration technology to provide the ability to deliver a fine-grain match between the customer and the employee. This match enables an unprecedented ability for employees to offer every individual customer a VIP experience. They are able to do so with expertise and ease by being provided with the correct information to take care of specific issues, answer questions, complete sales, check on an order's shipping date, and more.

These customer/employee experiences are vital, as they form the human heart of all your other systems and processes.

Empathy in Action Employee Experiences

The future of work brings many new demands on companies, from remote working arrangements to new solutions for employees' work-life balance. Companies need to apply the Systems of Empathy orchestration not only to customer experience but also to the employee experience. Empathy-based employee experience technology provides sentiment and intent while also predicting how employees can best serve customers. But individual and team performance, whether in sports or in business, can be challenging to predict.

The movie *Moneyball* followed the Oakland Athletics baseball team and its general manager, Billy Beane. He went on to reinvent the game of baseball itself—and the related game of baseball team management. Billy used an analytical, evidence-based, and sabermetric approach to building and managing a competitive baseball team. You can think of Employee Experience Orchestration™ as the "moneyball" for your business' team management.

Traditionally speaking, companies have used workforce optimization (WFO) and workforce engagement management (WEM) technology to create employee experiences. These methods have been based on the old paradigms of business-centric efficiency and effectiveness. Workforce optimization focuses on the overall quality and efficiency of an operation, and workforce management technology focuses on effectively managing employees themselves.

A new category of employee experience technology is arising, however. The new employee workplace technology is based on AI-enabled workforce engagement management (AI-enabled WEM). Through the use of exponential technologies, empathy is integrated into the evolution and disruption of old WFO and WEM technologies. These new EX systems address the deeper needs of employees while aligning the company, staff, and customers with the shared goal of delivering excellent, stress-free experiences.

To see how this plays out, let's return to our previous example of buying paint.

CX/EX in Parallel

To deliver Empathy in Action, the employee experience must be orchestrated in parallel with the customer experience (Figure 9.8). We've seen how Experience as a Service tracks and simultaneously updates the customer experience so that, if the customer requires an employee's help, none of the engagement interactions on any of the platforms' channels are lost and the customer doesn't have to repeat themselves or explain what they have already done.

While Natalie was interacting on the paint company's website, behind the scenes, AI was listening, gathering her customer interaction data, and analyzing her behavior patterns. This information gets integrated into the EX platform to empower the employee experience. Based on AI-correlation analysis, the company can visualize both the customer and employee experience and intuitively predict the skills, knowledge, and capabilities best suited to serve each and every individual customer's interaction, giving every customer that coveted VIP experience.

All of that customer interaction data is collected and used to enhance predictive routing. This simply means that, when a customer needs to interact with a human, the company can match an employee to them based on the customer's historical and current intent and context. This is much more personalized than matching an average customer and employee persona group in the old paradigm technology approach discussed in Chapter 6. Deploying robotic process automation for simple tasks (filling in fields or gathering information from other systems) further reduces employee effort and increases consistency and reliability.

As the best customer-employee match is made, the employee can see in real time what the customer has done on the website, on the IVR, or on other channels, and they can see the full transcript provided from an AI-chatbot and its real-time interaction with the client.

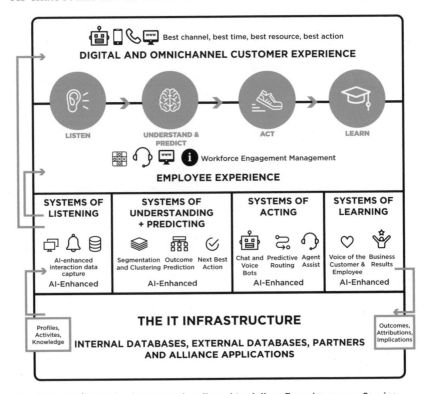

Figure 9.8 CX/EX technology must be aligned to deliver Experience as a Service.

When it's time to take action, the employee's experience is enriched with AI-based tools that automatically surface relevant, knowledge-based articles tailored for this specific request—and they can do this in seconds.

Whether your employee is sitting in a call center, a corporate branch, or working remotely as part of a virtual team, they can do all this. And gamification tools keep them engaged and connected. Once the customer-employee interaction is completed, the voice of the customer (VoC), the voice of the employee (VoE), and AI-interaction analytics investigate the best ways to improve future interactions for both employees and customers across all channels.

The orchestration system accomplishes the "job to be done" from the customer's and the employee's point of view, leaving them both feeling positive and cared for. It also leverages the power of experiences as a service by orchestrating exponential technology so that it drives customer and employee loyalty and associated metrics, thereby increasing CLV, ELV, and EBBV. The reduction in average handle time, contact transfers, and repeat customer/employee effort, for instance, can now be viewed and counted as across-the-board, loyalty-creating metrics. Not because the first contact resolution results in business-centric cost savings, but because the experience was better from both the customer's and employee's point of view.

The orchestration system also increases digital content utilization and self-service rates. Through context and intent qualification, the company identifies a lead, makes product recommendations, decreases the number of abandoned shopping carts, gains additional revenue and wallet share, and reduces customer churn—all arising from and contributing toward a better customer-employee experience. It's seamless.

This new EX empathy paradigm reduces employee effort and time spent, allowing employees to focus on what they are best at. In operating under the idea that no one is good at everything, and by matching employees with work they are good at (and providing them with the right information), employees can make sure that customers get assistance when and where it's needed. This increases employees' confidence, engagement, and retention rates, as they feel prepared for the work they have been personally selected to do to support the customer. Each successful interaction further builds their confidence and increases the retention of top talent. This is key because employee salaries are the most expensive aspect of providing good experiences. Everyone—the customer, the employee, and the company—benefits from an empathetic, technology-supported model.

Companies can use AI-based, data-rich employee profiles and expected customer demands to improve their ability to understand and predict employee forecasting, then shift scheduling so employees can have better work-life balance in accordance with their needs. At the same time, their data is used to illuminate coaching and training opportunities that will empower employee success and inform their profiles to better match an incoming customer request.

AI-Enhanced Workforce Engagement Management

When companies use design thinking to make employees the focus of their technology's process and functionality, teams can deliver experiences based on empathy rather than business-centric metrics that don't deliver the full picture. That's because AI-enhanced workforce engagement tools continuously improve over time, allowing companies to better understand how employees prefer to work and communicate. There needs to be a level of trust involved, too—employees know what will help them better than anyone else, and management needs to allow them to inform the process.

The outer ring in Figure 9.9 is how a company can address deeper levels of employee satisfaction by enabling employees to

- Improve their recruitment and onboarding process
- Incorporate their voice into how work gets done
- Provide empathy-centric metrics and recognition
- Deliver enhanced training and performance management

Evolution to AI-enabled Workforce Engagement

Figure 9.9 AI-based WEM increases employee satisfaction.

Under this model, performance is no longer some hidden process assessed on the whim of a manager; it is transparent, systematic, and fair. The AI-enabled WEM provides a transcription of all employees' interactions, including digital interactions, sentiment analysis, and scoring to get employees and managers on the same page. The role of a manager moves away from supervision to coaching. AI-enabled WEM also provides for the creation, management, and auto-assignment of learning modules. It provides a path for skill improvement and career advancement. Employees will understand what they can do to improve their performance and will have the tools to do so on their own terms, with their own insider perspective in mind.

AI-WEM Gamification

Employee analytics are an integral part of exponential technology-driven functionality, and gamification is a crucial AI-WEM element. Gamification leverages the natural human desire to compete. Gamified-WEM allows coworkers to challenge each other and compete in a friendly manner on specific metrics that promote empathy-based, customer-centric experiences. By tracking KPIs that align with customers, companies can use gamification to encourage employees to view customers as teammates that move them toward their goals.

Seventy-one percent of executives say that employee engagement is critical to their company's success.[1]

By knowing how they're performing individually, how they fare against their peers, and how they perform as a team, employees develop camaraderie with other team members. This leads to increased work satisfaction. With gamification, employees also compete with themselves to "keep up the rate of success." Just the incentive of "a few more points and I'll reach the next level" and the frequent recognition and feedback of, "You've learned a new skill!" or "You have reached a new level!" has an incredible effect on intrinsic motivation by encouraging them to outdo themselves, establish a new personal best, and "level up" their work, all while adding an element of fun to the tasks themselves.

AI-WEM Training and Performance

As technologies evolve and new generations of employees enter the workforce, companies need to rethink their "tried-and-true" methods for promoting employee engagement. With Generation Z and millennials forming a major part of the workforce, their personal values have shifted the dynamic between employees and companies. Traditional classroom training methods no longer keep employees engaged and excited, and often, it's not practical to have people attend in-person training. Companies must offer additional training options that fit into new, more flexible workforce demands.

When applied to training, gamification also helps motivate employees by showing them exactly how their training fits into the larger roles they will occupy and the improvement of performance within those roles. Companies can send training to workers' cell phones or provide them with more visual or video-based content instead of bland PDFs and Q&A documents.

By integrating employee performance management tools with operation and quality management data, companies can:

- Analyze and replicate the skills, knowledge, and attributes of top performers, and close the performance gap of their workforce through integrated performance management capabilities
- Increase speed to competency for new and existing employees and improve employee engagement, which provides better customer experiences and reduces costs
- Give employees personalized training plans, career mapping for future roles, and real feedback with the training team
- Augment skill-based routing with performance tools to ensure customers are directed toward the right employee
- Curate, tailor, and personalize training plans for each employee

AI-WEM Forecasting and Scheduling

Short-term forecasting tools use an advanced AI-driven, automated process that auto-detects outliers, performs mathematical fixes for missing data, and contains a library of state-of-the-art time-series scheduling techniques. The system quickly and automatically develops hundreds of thousands of individual forecasts and then returns them with the lowest number of errors. As a result, an AI-infused WEM can significantly improve the schedule-generation engine with considerably better solve times. Schedules can be developed 10 times faster. An advanced WEM system combines optimization modeling with simulation modeling to reduce the iteration required by most scheduling algorithms. It also integrates otherwise difficult data points, such as the scheduling preferences of individual employees.

Long-term and intraday forecasting and scheduling can be connected via the same advanced algorithms. These tools use advanced forecasting, optimization, and simulation techniques to create outcomes. Managers can also use these tools to conduct business unit forecasting and schedule for more extended periods of time.

What does all of this mean for businesses? For one thing, it increases the power of their empathy exponential by providing employees personalized work to meet their desired schedules, locations, and the type of work they excel at. By giving your employees autonomy while simultaneously ensuring that business KPIs can be hit, companies communicate more trust to their employees. This trust is naturally reflected in their interactions with each other and with customers.

IoT and Customer Experiences

The Internet of Things (IoT) extends the capabilities of the internet. It does this by using consumer devices (cars, watches, TVs, smartphones, appliances) as well as commercial machines (elevators, MRIs, inventory management systems) and factories which run on a digital, connected network wherein a large variety of devices can communicate and interact with one another.

Without IoT, if a product fails, the customer must contact support, explain what happened, schedule an appointment, and wait for the technician to be dispatched. Effective integration of IoT is an essential part of delivering empathy because, by using data flows from IoT devices with predictive analytics, what the customer needs can be predicted before they are even aware of the issue. They don't have to panic and go looking for help when something goes wrong—the device does this for them, whether it is a car, a washing machine, or even a power tool.

For example, an IoT sensor could circumvent all the extra steps above by alerting a customer about a part that is about to go bad in their car or appliance. In the automotive industry, Tesla is using IoT to proactively push patches and resolve electronic problems before they occur. IoT capabilities can also automatically notify a technician whenever a certain piece of equipment has failed. When they are dispatched, they already have the tools they need and can fix the problem in one trip.

IoT also provides an opportunity for sales to step in and match customers with relevant product solutions before they are forced to go looking for something. Say a washing machine is about to leak because the consumer is not using a suitable detergent. The IoT system can push a recommendation or a discounted offer to the customer, both solving their problem before it happens and potentially making a sale.

IoT can monitor machines and equipment in healthcare, smart cities, and manufacturing industries, and it can be a utility asset in power plants, water management, and chemical manufacturing. IoT can monitor everything from the power that commercial electrical panels energy use to the weak spots in a unified grid; if the devices find issues, they can deliver custom notifications to business owners and service technicians before things escalate.

IoT is even making the experience at sporting events better. Customers using mobile apps at venues like Boston's Fenway Park or London's Palladium can order seat-based food delivery and get automatic updates on when the lines at beer stands are short.[2]

Employee-Customer Engagement Pod Technology

We can learn a lot about leadership from Canada geese (Figure 9.10).

The flock shares and rotates leadership positions, communicating with each other to understand what is needed to help them navigate at any point in time. In fact, by flying in this formation, the group can gain a flying range up to 71 percent greater than if the birds flew solo.

Figure 9.10 Canada geese flying in formation.
Source: Getty

What if we put the customer opposite the lead bird (or employee)? That way, when the customer's needs change, the employee in the lead position dynamically shifts to the employee who is best suited to help the customer.

For example, a customer has a question about a specific offer and wants to speak to someone in marketing. If they need help getting the order status or fixing something after purchasing the product, they'll want to speak to order management and customer service, respectively (Figure 9.11). Under a dynamic model, the "point person" responding to the customer shifts in response the customer's needs and circumstance.

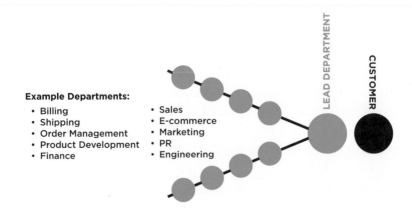

Example Departments:

- Billing
- Shipping
- Order Management
- Product Development
- Finance
- Sales
- E-commerce
- Marketing
- PR
- Engineering

LEAD DEPARTMENT

CUSTOMER

Figure 9.11 Switching leader roles based on real-time customer need.

With everyone in the organization participating as part of a centralized experience platform, all employees can follow the customer experience on any channel, and then respond to individual customers with empathetic, highly personalized customer interactions whenever their particular expertise is needed.

And because every employee has a view into the customer interaction, they all have context from previous interactions and can pick up right where the last employee left off. This provides a seamless experience for both the customer and all the employees that help the customer throughout their marketing, sales, and service journey.

Using this kind of integrated platform requires a complete cultural and organizational restructuring that takes the company from siloed departments to Customer-Centric Empathy Pods™. These pods seamlessly integrate customers, employees, and enterprise systems to create a collaborative workflow. For example, instead of only giving employees in the contact center access to the experience platform, every employee in the organization would have a seat at the table. Communication is greatly enhanced, as are problem-solving capabilities. After all, you have the right employee at the right time to solve a customer's issue.

Companies that take customer-employee experience seriously operate their cross-functional departments as a tightly integrated systematic pod, and in doing so, provide a real-time, holistic view of customer-employee interactions. This type of organizational structure, along with Experiences-as-a-Service technology platform, allows companies to truly act on behalf of the customer and deliver the relevant, real-time information needed to provide memorable experiences—regardless of the specific circumstances involved.

One example of these principles in action is the shift USAA made to their organization. Before the shift, the company's process of locating, negotiating, purchasing, financing, and insuring a purchased car were done through different people and departments at USAA.[3] USAA leaders realized that there was a better option. They began organizing their processes around the customer by placing employees from different product lines and functional groups into a unified customer team. As USAA rewired the organization's customer/employee experience pathways to suit this more cohesive model, they provided a seamless customer experience. And the expertise, once locked in silos, has become a powerful accelerant for innovating the brand's competitive potential as employees collaborate in new ways to serve the customer.

Why Exponential Technologies?

Why is AI/ML so integral to the new model? It's fairly straightforward: in the old paradigm, companies relied on the power of humans to try and meet increasing customer demands. This meant hiring more employees and using their human processing capacities (their brain) to listen, understand, act, and learn. When this got expensive, the industry came up with self-service options to reduce headcount or offshoring. But the old paradigm self-service capabilities (think of our dumb bot example) couldn't provide a high percentage of correct or useful answers. The result was a subpar experience for customers and employees alike.

However, with exponential technologies, we are augmenting human capability with the exponential computational power of AI/ML. This allows us to vastly exceed human capacities in providing more empathic experiences, resulting in new C&E-centric efficiencies, effectiveness, and empathy-oriented experiences that give customers what they need and want, often surprising them by being both prescient and prescriptive.

As you research AI/ML solutions, you'll want to look for an out-of-the-box, turnkey AI CE/EX tool so you can quickly integrate it into your existing corporate structure. An intuitive and user-friendly interface means you don't need a lot of technical resources. Built-in outcome prediction capabilities optimize logic toward KPIs like handle time or transfer rate—all while supporting existing business logic and processes. This makes it easier to analyze large amounts of data and extract key customer insights, empowering you to act in a way that truly enhances the CX/EX experience while simultaneously maximizing business benefits.

Being in the cloud is a critical, competitive advantage that relates directly to this model. It's only in the cloud that companies can be agile enough to easily orchestrate customer and employee data and integrate it with AI, and it's simpler for doing so via all the engagement channels available to deliver these better experiences. The cloud grants you the ability to provide access to APIs for many data sets (historical, behavioral, third party), data model standards, and source codes, thereby enabling more informed customer experiences. The cloud also provides for more rapid system development, faster integrations, and more opportunity for agile innovation and disruption.

There isn't a lot of configuration and customization necessary to tailor the cloud's software, so it ends up being less expensive to implement than on-premise technology—and the cloud enables automatic upgrades to be easily integrated over time.

CX/EX Analytics

To understand how well their business is delivering on its promise of great experiences, companies are investing in experience analytics. If you are focused on a specific path, you'll get an experience made up of individual and potentially disjointed touchpoints. When looking at the experience as a continuum, the overall effect is much more seamless.

To deliver empathic experiences, the customer-employee experience industry as a whole must graduate to the idea of end-to-end experiences with analytical visualization tools to capture, measure, analyze, and evaluate the quality and outcome of the customer and employee experience throughout all phases and interactions, and for all channels and activities.

The key is to use the experience platform system to provide analytical capabilities while anonymously stitching together the interaction data, and while providing an actionable visualization of the experience, then sharing them with other systems and departments as part of the integrated "pod" structure.

CX/EX Interactive Dashboards

Static reporting and manual spreadsheets are dead. Companies need interactive dashboards to serve up insights quickly—allowing them to understand the status of their customer experiences, provide critical insights, drill into exceptions, and promptly understand the root cause.

These dashboards enable the rapid dissemination of information as it relates to real-time, enhanced customer engagement experiences. Businesses need to quickly gain insights from visualizations and dashboards in multiple dimensions and mediums at the same time, such as those arising from mobile devices or augmented/virtual reality. With this type of system one can ask simple questions and choose actions from prescriptive option lists.

The Voice of the Customer and the Employee

We've all had experiences, whether at a coffee shop or while getting our car serviced, where genuine personalized experience made a difference. When businesses don't deliver on these genuine, personalized experiences, we notice it and express disappointment. That's the voice of the customer (VoC) and employee (VoE) in action.

Exponential technologies such as IoT, AI, and digital and social platforms gather billions of interactions daily for input into VoC and VoE. With the new pod organizational structure, CX/EX analytics, interactive dashboards, and VoC/VoE, companies have reliable feedback loops that fuel big data analytics engines. These engines then map behaviors and preferences into personalized customer/employee experiences.

If there's something that doesn't meet a customer's, employee's, or company's standards for providing an empathic experience, the VoC/VoE teams—along with the rest of the organization—are made aware and can take action to resolve it. Predictive modeling allows all teams to scale the voice of customers and employees and improve their ability to discover issues before they happen and make improvements proactively.

Next Steps

Comparing what we've done in the past to what exponential technologies can provide today, it's easy to see why previous eras in CX/EX can't compare. They simply can't deliver the same level of experience orchestration or provide outcomes so thoroughly focused on C&E-centric experiences (Figure 9.12).

NEW PARADIGM EXPERIENCES ARE DRIVEN BY FOCUSING ON THE CUSTOMER AND EMPLOYEE VS. BUSINESS-ONLY GOALS

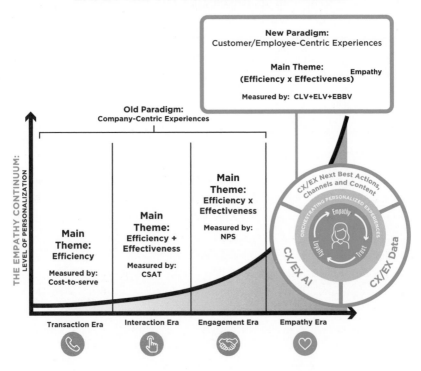

Figure 9.12 Experience orchestration provides more personalized, empathy-focused experiences.

This new empathy paradigm means interacting and engaging customers in ways that go beyond mere technology or budget decisions; these choices are human ones. You have just a few seconds to show empathy and establish trust once an interaction is initiated. Miss those seconds, and the spell is broken. That's why having real-time systems, the right employees, and correct data and insights are critical. Companies interested in leading the empathy economy must use the North Star triad of empathy, trust, and loyalty, and they must make changes to their organizational structures, processes, policies, and budgets accordingly. It requires a different type of cross-functional collaboration between customer experience professionals, the CIO, product managers, and IT to fully integrate context into the customer and employee experience.

In the next two chapters, we look at what it takes to deliver on experiences as a service from organizational and leadership perspectives.

TAKEAWAYS

- An empathy-driven customer and employee experience is based on four systems of experience orchestration: systems of listening, understanding and prediction, action, and learning.
- Each system of orchestration is made up of exponential technologies, including AI-enriched data and omnichannel interactions in the cloud.
- To deliver in the empathy economy, companies need to work with a data "composer" and "maestro" to orchestrate the technological Systems of Empathy to deliver on the ensuing customer/employee experience.

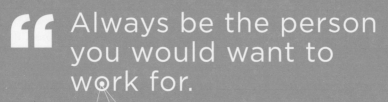

" Always be the person
you would want to
work for.

—Liz Brenner

REIMAGINING THE FUTURE OF WORK

Empathy-based cultural transformation goes much deeper than the reorganization or restructuring of roles, responsibilities, processes, and technology. It's also about invigorating and inspiring changes in an organization's cultural mindset and shared behaviors. There needs to be a shift in tone and perspective that ensures collaboration becomes completely natural for everyone involved—and when this mindset is adopted, results will follow automatically.

> **Blind Spot**
>
> Transformation isn't only about reorganizing, it's about inspiring changes in mindset and behaviors.

What Leaders Miss about EX

Successful change is a never-ending endeavor animated by true empathy. Again, it is only possible if the brand is dedicated to looking at things through the customer and the employee point of view.

In spite of this truth, leaders frequently continue to lead their organizations from a thoroughly business-centric point of view. They are often completely unaware of what customers go through to do business with their company. They haven't called their contact center, tried to buy something online, or experienced what it's like to use the chatbot to resolve an issue. If they did, they might find themselves in the same state as many customers—angry and either screaming into their phone or wanting to throw their laptop out the nearest window.

Many leaders also fail to realize what it is like for employees to do their jobs and be of service to customers. Without awareness of just how dysfunctional a company's culture is, leaders underestimate how difficult transformation will be. The results are most apparent when such leaders announce upcoming changes. Rather than feeling inspired, employees assume that the approaching change is just another initiative du jour. Disenchanted, they lay low to miss the crossfire and emotional chaos, turning the culture into a passive-aggressive swamp where nothing new gets accomplished. All of this means that the customer experience is doomed to fall short.

> ### Blind Spot
>
> Business-centric organizations miss how difficult is it for customers to do business with them and for employees to serve those customers.

According to the *Harvard Business Review*, emotional intelligence (EI) is the cornerstone of empowered, engaged, and energetic corporate cultures.[1] Nevertheless, research shows that companies worldwide are underestimating EI's value, and there is a growing disconnect—a cognitive dissonance between what executives are saying about the importance of company culture and what actually happens within a company.

The resulting employee turnover leads not only to ballooning recruitment costs, but also a whole host of talent management problems. The worst part is that low employee morale and turnover are completely avoidable if culture is a tangible leadership priority.

Just like there are bad profits from poor customer experiences, there are also bad profits from poor employee management practices. Some businesses still solve problems based on who happens to be the loudest, who acts like the biggest bully, or who is best at playing politics and preying on people's insecurities. It's time to recognize that management like this feeds directly into the painful phenomenon of bad employee cultures, and that it's long past time to stop allowing it.

Empathy-Centric Cultures

In a 15-year study involving interviews with over 20,000 managers, experts found better employee performance when management styles changed from a command-and-control approach to a more empathy-oriented approach (Figure 10.1). Empathic leaders exhibit qualities such as a collaborative mindset, cooperative work styles, strong communication skills, synergistic principles, devotion to connectedness, a desire to network across the organization, a tendency toward recognition of others' achievements, and a natural desire to celebrate those achievements whenever they happen.[2]

> **Blind Spot**
>
> Companies don't realize when we are empathetic, we can receive and process information better, causing measurable changes in our cognitive style and our problem-solving abilities.

These qualities don't need to be innate, either; they are more like skills than personality traits, and they can be developed over time. Empathic leadership, like all leadership, is more about determination and a growth mindset.

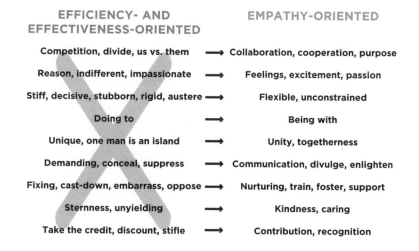

EFFICIENCY- AND EFFECTIVENESS-ORIENTED		EMPATHY-ORIENTED
Competition, divide, us vs. them	→	Collaboration, cooperation, purpose
Reason, indifferent, impassionate	→	Feelings, excitement, passion
Stiff, decisive, stubborn, rigid, austere	→	Flexible, unconstrained
Doing to	→	Being with
Unique, one man is an island	→	Unity, togetherness
Demanding, conceal, suppress	→	Communication, divulge, enlighten
Fixing, cast-down, embarrass, oppose	→	Nurturing, train, foster, support
Sternness, unyielding	→	Kindness, caring
Take the credit, discount, stifle	→	Contribution, recognition

Figure 10.1 Empathy-oriented characteristics of leaders and cultures.

Innovative Empathy-Oriented Cultures

Kevin Kruse, the author of *Employee Engagement 2.0*, found that cultures where employees are empathically engaged enjoy a positive domino effect as a result of their empathic environment:[3]

- Higher service, quality, and productivity leads to . . .
- Higher customer lifetime value, which leads to . . .
- Increased sales (repeat business and referrals), which leads to . . .
- Higher levels of profit, which leads to . . .
- Higher shareholder returns (i.e., stock price)

Empathy can help us innovate more quickly, which ultimately means we can sell more products, satisfy more customers, and generate greater revenues. With that in mind, you're probably wondering: What does a productive, empathetic workplace culture look like in practice?

In these environments, the atmosphere is truly collaborative. Listening skills are cherished, and everyone's input is both encouraged and respected. People are treated with dignity, and teams/pods are cohesive whenever they engage company strategies.

A positive workplace culture is a holistic one that allows communication to flow seamlessly from the top ranks down to the bottom ones—and vice versa. They are successful because they harness each and every unique mind in the organization rather than the few "loud" or highly visible ones. Meetings are full of "Aha!" moments and "Yes, and . . ." statements where people build on each other's ideas, and employees at all levels feel heard.

In practical terms, these cultures are expressions of the notion that a company's strategy is best informed by grassroot input from employees. Leaders themselves occupy a service-oriented role rather than an authoritarian one. They view their job as one of guidance, support, and ideation.

In these cultures, everyone wins—except the competition.

Innovating with Customers

Customers are another vital source of ideation and inspiration. One way to ideate with customers is through online communities or forums where customers can easily interact with others who have been in their shoes and provide prescriptions for solving problems and getting the most out of products and services.

Companies who choose to empathize with the human desire to be recognized often "gamify," providing customer point systems and "expert" or "guru" titles to empower users who receive high ratings

> ### Blind Spot
>
> Empathy applied to action results in the ability to innovate more quickly, sell more products, satisfy more customers and employees, and generate greater revenue.

from peers in response to the support they provide. This empathy-focused solution reduces operational costs by allowing customers to take on company roles, increases customer satisfaction, and provides the organization with firsthand insight into their products, processes, services, and experiences.

For context, let's use the example of a diaper bag company. The business has become well known because of the ease of use, practicality, and functionality of their bags. In a string of posts in their online community, a father expressed that he liked the diaper bag but was self-conscious about taking it out in public because the design style catered more to feminine preferences. Another dad suggests the company keep the bag's internal functionality but make the outside of the bag suit more masculine styles of dress. As other dads chime in to agree and provide design input, a whole new product line is born.

This is a great example of how a company which had never seen their product through male customers' eyes was able to listen to and understand the needs of this customer segment, and then take action. In this way, companies are continuously evolving and learning from customer feedback. When applied, results can become unique and best-selling products, services, and experiences.

Innovation Requires Diversity and Inclusion

Innovation is the extent to which creativity has been applied to action, resulting in new products, services, and experiences. If companies are going to create exceptional, customized, and personalized experiences, their cultures must live and breathe creativity. Creative expression empowers employees to better solve business challenges and generate new ideas. It is the raw material of brainstorming and innovative thinking—all of which fuel company growth.

Study after study shows that diversity directly drives innovation. At the same time, this well-documented research exposes how some executives are stuck in the blind spot of thinking that diversity, equity, and inclusion are issues of their hiring practice. One searing example of a blind spot was in the news fairly recently: In a leaked June 2020 memo, Wells Fargo CEO Charlie Scharf wrote, "While it might sound like an excuse, the unfortunate reality is that there is a very limited pool of black talent to recruit from."[4]

This statement provoked a firestorm of criticism from black employees, experts, and executives who pointed out that diversity, equity, and inclusion (DEI) isn't just a matter of typical hiring processes but also employee education, recruitment, and, most importantly, the training hiring managers receive in spotting hidden or unconscious biases in the hiring process.

Diversity, Equity, and Inclusion

The old definition of diversity as a synonym for mere representation is profoundly misguided, according to the authors of a *Harvard Business Review* article titled, "Diversity Doesn't Stick Without Inclusion."[5] As part of reimagining empathy, we need to understand that "diversity" and "inclusion" are not the same process. Without making sure that genuine inclusion is part of the diversity initiative, the benefits of diversity——such as innovation—are often lost. True inclusion demands that a company possess the cultural DNA

> **Blind Spot**
>
> Without making sure inclusion is part of a diversity initiative, the benefits like innovation and a more positive workplace are often lost.

of empathic leadership as well as empathic colleagues.

Diversity is being invited to the party.
Inclusion is being asked to dance.

–Vernā Myer

Diversity Equals Smarter Innovation

The endeavors of scholars like Scott Page (University of Michigan[6]), Jon Kleinberg (Cornell University[7]), Lu Hong[8], and Alex Pentland (MIT[9]) show how the dated practice of homogenized teams is being reversed because of the economic benefits a diverse workforce provides. These scholars' work reveals that the more diverse the workforce, the better the innovation, the decision-making, the problem-solving, and the final outcomes.

Financial results improve greatly within a more diverse workforce. A Coqual (formerly Center for Talent Innovation) study on diversity and innovation surveyed 1,800 professionals, looked at 40 case studies, interacted with numerous focus groups, and conducted interviews.[10] The reason for the study was that, while leaders could accept that employees might benefit from being in a diverse workforce, they found it difficult to prove or quantify this fact—especially when measuring how diversity affects a firm's ability to innovate. The study revealed that only 25 percent of companies surveyed had a population diverse enough to meet the requirements necessary for driving innovation.

The same research also showed how organizations with Empathy in Action have leaders who unlock the innovative capabilities in their employees (Figure 10.2 and 10.3). These leaders are inclusive. They ask for opinions, actively invite employees to share their thoughts, and reward them for participating. Without inclusion like this, the crucial connections that attract diverse talent, encourage participation, foster innovation, and lead to business growth simply don't happen.

> ### Blind Spot
>
> Many leaders are not familiar with the substantial amount of research revealing the economic benefits of diverse workforces.

	Leader exhibits NO inclusive behaviors	At companies WITH 2D diversity in leadership
Employees who report that their team...		
Embraces the input of a diverse array of members	40%	67%
Is not afraid to challenge the status quo	29%	50%
Is not afraid to fail	22%	43%
Takes risks	21%	40%

	At companies WITHOUT 2D diversity in leadership	At companies WITH 2D diversity in leadership
Employees who report that their ideas...		
Win endorsement from decision-makers	45%	63%
Get developed or prototyped	30%	48%
Get deployed into the marketplace	20%	35%
Employees who report that...		
Groupthink is a problem on their team	40%	25%
Leadership at the company does not perceive value in ideas they don't personally see a need for	62%	37%

Figure 10.2 Employees at companies with 2D diversity in leadership.
Source: Coqual[11]

When diversity and inclusion pay a high dividend, employees in publicly traded organizations with 2D in leadership are 70 percent more likely to report newly captured markets and are 45 percent more likely to improve market share than employees in publicly traded organizations without 2D diversity in leadership.[12] In the fast-paced business world of today, the risk of ignoring new ideas and missing new market opportunities represents the difference between survival and collapse.

	Leader has NO acquired diversity traits	Leader has at least three acquired diversity traits
Team members who report their leader...		
Ensures that everyone speaks up and gets heard	29%	63%
Makes it safe to risk proposing novel ideas	34%	74%
Empowers team members to make decisions	40%	82%
Takes advice and implements feedback	25%	64%
Shares credit for team success	27%	64%
	Leader exhibits NO inclusive behaviors	Leader exhibits at least three inclusive behaviors
Welcome and included in their team	51%	87%
Free to express their views and opinions	46%	87%
That their ideas are heard and recognized	37%	74%

Figure 10.3 Diverse leaders unlock the innovation potential of their workforce by taking advice and implementing feedback.
Source: Coqual[13]

Succeeding in this competitive marketplace means fostering a workplace where everyone is treated with dignity, respect, and worth, and where the culture indexes high on values like empathy and honesty.

In addition to the internal culture between employees, managers, and leaders, this type of human-oriented culture must extend to the culture between employees and customers.

Pod Diversity and Innovation Lift

Diversity leads directly to greater innovation and better business results. So how can leaders transform purely functional departments and roles to encourage the diverse perspectives needed? It can feel good to be in a group of people who agree firmly and quickly, who are okay with the status quo and don't put up any resistance to "the way things are done." It can feel more difficult to navigate unchartered waters with people who think very differently and aren't afraid to say so.

In a diverse group or pod that questions each other, disagrees, and debates in pursuit of customer-centric experiences, they go through a process where—at first—it may not seem they have found a solution at all. It's not the typical, rapid-fire storming, norming, and forming. Instead, pods use a distinctly different mindset, adding richness as they question and reflect on assumptions and challenge the status quo that others take for granted.

David Rock, cofounder and CEO of The Neuroleadership Institute, commissioned research that shows how the pod interaction challenges your brain to overcome its stale ways of thinking and sharpen its performance—if you are open to it.[14] This research indicates that diverse, nonhomogeneous teams/pods process information more carefully, keep team members' biases in check, and boost a company's innovation potential. Creating a customer/employee-centric culture can't be a platitude or a slogan; it must show up tangibly in how employees work, informing a unified approach that prioritizes customers' experiences over office politics or personal feelings.

Leaders must encourage individual employees to be assertive in expressing their needs and concerns and, at the same time, cultivate an understanding of how everyone in the pod can gain alignment so they can soar toward success as a unified "flock."

As Canada geese travel in their characteristic V-formation, the flock shares and rotates leadership, playing to individual strengths. Each goose understands exactly what they need to do to make the migration (experience) successful. Any company working to transform the way they do business must excel at creating powerful partnerships and alliances across and within functional departments, and with external resources as well. Pods offer a new way to think about structuring professional relationships as well as offering customer experience (as we saw in Chapter 9, Figure 9.11).

> **Blind Spot**
>
> When teams are diverse, they're better at questioning assumptions, challenging the status quo, overcoming stale ways of thinking, and sharpening performance.

You should be aware that the time it takes for a diverse team/pod to get synchronized can be longer than the norm, especially if this is not how you currently work together. Those new to working in pods may initially find problem-solving uncomfortable compared to working in homogeneous groups. But an effective pod strategy can mitigate the risk of conflict over time and set up a norm for truly having each other's back, so collaboration rings true even when it proves challenging.

When the pod has come to a consensus, they can fly in formation. In that perfectly aligned formation, everyone understands their position, their role, and how their role will change throughout the flight. In the end, everyone gets to celebrate their collective success. There is a special kind of beauty in working this way and determining a company's long-term success. When a pod gets to their shared destination, they will hardly believe they've done it—but they'll be able to rejoice in the success of allied transformation.

> **Blind Spot**
>
> Companies operating in silos or with blind hand-offs miss the intended purpose. Instead, they could reach unparalleled advantages by flying together in formation.

Without this pod or V-formation, the lead bird is flying in one direction and all the other birds are flying in different directions. The team doesn't end up at the intended destination together. This lack of alignment wastes precious time and energy in a world that is changing exponentially, and this ends up giving competitors the edge they need to overtake you.

Massive Transformative Purpose

As leaders cultivate an atmosphere where people are genuinely excited about the future, it helps employees to believe in the new direction their company is taking and begin to see how it will result in a bright, new, and shared future. It also gives them the courage to keep moving forward when they face hurdles. To support the pod's organizational collaboration, leaders must help people unite beyond their differences by coalescing around the pride they feel regarding what the company does, dedication toward what it strives to be, excitement about their new approaches, and a feeling of ownership toward its successes. Instead of a CEO-led initiative, it's a grassroots effort where all employees work together collectively to create a better company. They do this both by offering better CX/EX and by using shared values to contribute to a better world at large.

In empathy-oriented organizations, employees are motivated by something beyond a traditional mission or vision statement. The secret to this lies in a shared purpose. The founders of companies like TED, xPrize, Boston's Children's Hospital, and Google transform the world through their organizations because they began with a massive, inclusive transformational purpose. This is represented by the equation MTP^X (Table 10.1). The x stands for an impact exponential of 10, meaning these companies establish at least 10 times the impact of their peers.

Table 10.1 The MTP^X of exponential organizations.
Source: Singularity University[15]

Company	MTP^X
TED	"Ideas worth spreading"
Google	"Organize the world's information"
World Top 20 Project	"Educate every child on the planet"
Business Interviews	"We tell your story to the world"
XPRIZE	"To build a bridge to abundance for all"
Angels of Impact	"Women creating an inclusive and prosperous world for all"
Boston's Children's Hospital	"Until every child is well"
Tesla	"Accelerate the transition to sustainable transportation"
St. Margaret's School for Girls	"This is the school where girls who want to change the world become women who do"
INTERProteccion ExO Project	"Simply solving humanity's risks"
CarePay	"Connect people to quality healthcare"

The *M* stands for massive, meaning that audaciously big and aspirational goals are reached regardless of challenges that might stand in the way. The *T* stands for transformative, representing the collaborative asking of questions such as "What significant transformation to industry, community, or even the planet can we accomplish as an organization?"

Finally, the *P* of this equation stands for purpose. This is the "why" of an organization's goals and efforts. The concept of "your why" was coined by Simon Sinek, the best-selling author of *Start with Why: How Great Leaders Inspire Everyone to Take Action*. This all-important purpose is what "unites and inspires our hearts, minds, and actions."[16]

Before employees and leaders jump in wholeheartedly, they want to envision what the new world will look like and why they will be proud once the company reaches that destination. Organizations reach this moonshot destination when disruptive initiatives include a financial and emotional (motivational and inspirational) case for change. Having an MTP^X mindset becomes the emotional flywheel for why employees get behind change, forming a crucial aspect of the empathy-based culture input (Figure 1.4).

Again, an MTP^X motivator is not a mission or vision statement. An MTP^X is an organization's higher, deeper, and most aspirational purpose.[17] It is all about directing an organization's passion and "heart" toward something bigger than any one employee or department. This kind of purpose attracts the right

> **Blind Spot**
>
> Companies using generalized vision and mission statements miss the power that comes from developing a massive transformative purpose, providing an emotional flywheel for employees' engagement.

people and invests them in the mission to champion a new, better world, allowing you to recruit top talent and make radical changes such as the ones we are suggesting. Because all stakeholders (employees, partners, alliances, and more) are united around this purpose, it depoliticizes organizations and lessens the effect of interpersonal challenges. Anyone who does not align to the MTP^X will have a tough time within the organization and will soon find themselves swimming against the current. It may sound harsh, but such individuals will either adjust and align or "weed" themselves out.

Organizations turn into learning environments because the consensus mindset encourages everyone to constantly ask, "What can I do to help us achieve that MTP^X?"

The ideal MTP^X should be so sweeping, aspirational, and definitive that competitors cannot craft an MTP^X capable of surpassing it. The creation and use of an MTP^X results in a new breed of organizations called exponential organizations, or ExOs, a title coined by Salim Ismail.[18] Ismail has founded or operated seven early-stage companies. Under his leadership, his team has analyzed over 3,000 ideas and launched four major products. His last company, Angstro, was sold to Google and he is now the founding Executive Director of Singularity University, whose MTP^X is "To positively impact one billion people."

What is the key to Ismail's success? Each time they began an initiative, he and his team defined an MTP^X. Each employee had a clear vision of the larger purpose of their work, and each individual knew precisely how they were contributing to fulfilling their MTP^X.

Above all, it is purpose that unites and inspires Empathy in Action.

The Learning Organization

Part of how companies transform themselves from company centricity to customer/employee centricity is by becoming what Peter Senge, author of *The Fifth Discipline: The Art and Practice of the Learning Organization,* calls learning organizations. This evolution to an B2E or an empathy-centric approach requires a mindset of continuous improvement and depends on a thorough commitment

> **Blind Spot**
>
> In the absence of a customer-centric, empathic learning organization, companies repeat old practices and patterns.

to learning.[19] In the absence of learning, companies—and individuals—repeat old practices and patterns. Change remains cosmetic, and improvements are either lucky one-shots or short-lived bursts. In the end, this results in a stagnant growth rate and hurts the company's culture and business outcomes.

Empathy is a powerful force that fuels the learning process, enhancing our ability to receive and process information on a broader scale. Research on the neuroscience of empathy shows that we are more helpful and generous after an empathic encounter with someone else.[20] Putting ourselves in someone else's shoes creates measurable changes in our cognitive style, increasing our problem-solving mindset and modifying the approaches we take to solve problems, find answers, and go in new directions. This empathetic behavior motivates us to solve business challenges better by viewing them as human and collaborative journeys.

Handling Conflict and Uncertainty

Of course, establishing this level of unity won't necessarily be smooth sailing. By nature, human beings like routine, and we get accustomed to—and quite comfortable with—doing things the way we have always done them. Innovative organizations realize that any type of real change naturally creates conflict, both internally and externally. As humans, whenever we experience something new, modify a process, or try to learn a new way of working, we experience a certain level of anxiety. On top of that, people have differing opinions regarding what needs to be changed and why. If the company culture isn't grounded in learning and innovation isn't met with open arms, employees often resort to protecting their own "turf" rather than face challenges as a team. Conflicts themselves are not the only issue; problems also arise because of how the conflicts are handled.

> **Blind Spot**
>
> If business-centric organizations go through transformations without taking time to create a learning organization where innovation is part of the DNA, employee's resort to "turf" protecting.

Two illuminating research studies by communication experts Dr. Susan Ferris and Dr. Albert Mehrabian resulted in a general formula for how the mind creates meaning through communications.[21] They concluded that our interpretation of a message is 7 percent verbal, 38 percent vocal, and 55 percent visual—meaning a full 93 percent of communication is nonverbal in nature. What this indicates comes as a surprise to many leaders: positive communication outcomes depend more on the body language and tone of transformational conversations than actual dialogue. Whether leaders can affect those conversations is connected directly to their awareness of the political jousting, land grabs, and turf wars in the ranks below them, and it is informed by an understanding of how these ranks communicate with one another.

According to experts at the World Economic Forum, not only does empathy come with profound, science-backed mental and physical health benefits, but it also makes our work lives more enjoyable and productive. Empathy-based thinking helps us put information in context and pick up situational cues, which are essential when we seek to understand how things relate to one another either literally or figuratively.[22] Innovation, communication, and collaboration are all about connections. Empathy allows us to make those connections in the best and most effective manner.

Karla McLaren, author of *The Art of Empathy: A Complete Guide to Life's Most Essential Skill* and founder of empathyacademy.org, notes that nothing can derail a project or task at work quite like a misunderstanding. Using empathy as a tool for understanding others' emotions and motivations helps reduce conflicts and misunderstandings. McLaren says, "Many studies suggest that empathically skilled employees increase customer satisfaction, reduce stress and conflict, and help [other] employees and customers feel that they are valued, heard, and respected."[23]

Helen Riess, MD, is an associate professor of psychiatry at Harvard Medical School and has conducted groundbreaking research on leadership and communication. She explains:

> *"One of the biggest mistakes that leaders can make is to assume that a lack of productivity or a lack of engagement is due to [employees] not caring about the work, or lack[ing] understanding of] the importance of a job. By putting themselves in the employee's shoes, managers can pinpoint the employee's specific productivity issues and listen and understand to determine how to ensure the employee is thriving in their position."*[24]

Assumptions are rarely empathic in nature. They tend to hold us back, create conflict, and foster mistrust, and they ought to be avoided.

Dr. Reiss also talks about the importance of empathy when giving and receiving feedback at work, an important process which allows us to adjust and improve. She suggests that "one way to incorporate empathy into giving feedback is to start with a question like, 'How do you think things are going?' or 'How are things going for you?'" These questions allow others to open up about an area in which they're struggling and give the manager insights from the employee's point of view first. Instead of being punitive, managers can then work on solving the real issue at hand.

Figure 10.4 looks at five ways of working out conflict. A leader's job is to facilitate this natural tension and conflict of diverse points of view without sacrificing the benefits of this diversity. Depending on the company culture, there may be a primary mode of resolving issues. In an empathic culture, collaboration is the predominant method by which everyone works with one another and with customers.

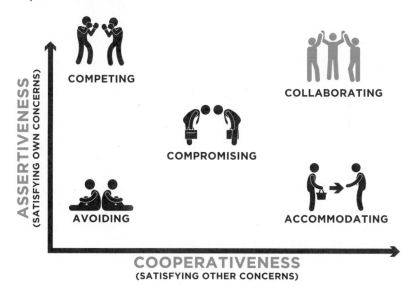

Figure 10.4 Five ways to approach conflict when transforming the CX/EX experience.

The level of organizational change required to integrate a customer/ employee point of view into a company's culture and operations requires a collaborative approach. For employees to feel included in this collaboration, a leader must promote individual employee's assertiveness in expressing their needs and concerns, and at the same time, encourage them to understand others' needs as well. In group dynamics, it's common for a pattern to emerge in which certain people always do the talking. What insightful leaders know is that some of the best ideas come from people who are less assertive about expressing their points of view. Quiet or shy employees may have the most profound, innovative insights to offer—they just need a little more encouragement to share them. It's key for leaders to make sure everyone participates in the conversation.

Cosmetic vs. Deep Change

It's vital for leaders to understand the difference between cosmetic and deep change. Deep change means you are examining your processes, your interactions with customers, your employee workflows, and work-life balance—all with the participation of employees at every level in the organization.

When we did this within our own organization, Natalie and I were able to learn a lot from the process. We started looking at the experiences we provide our potential, current, and past customers by using traditional methods like focus groups, surveys, and interviews. That gave our customer success group, sales teams, the senior leadership team, and others information to start making meaningful changes from the ground up. We listened carefully to everyone involved, regardless of their official title, salary, or the number of years they've spent with the company. Meaningful change makes the most of everyone's time and voice. Cosmetic changes waste time and result in customer/employee attrition by making them feel that they aren't being taken seriously. In some cases, cosmetic or shallow change is worse than no change at all.

We also looked at various aspects of our employees' experience. We sought brutally honest feedback from team members at all levels of the organization. One outcome arising from this feedback was the appointment of a global diversity, equity, and inclusion officer. Through collaborative and ongoing effort, we are building this initiative into the culture of our workplace and integrating it with the way we do business. As a result, the senior leadership team has been able to begin making changes to a culture that has been around for over three decades, and they can ensure that these changes are meaningful both to individuals and to the modern world.

Understanding the need for diversity and inclusion led us to build a global framework and governance model for our diversity, equity, and inclusion office and advisory council. This organized approach allowed us to quickly execute a few key initiatives, such as unconscious bias training and our Affinity Group operating model. It also provided the traction and momentum needed to move us toward a multiyear, sustainable set of strategies. We started by taking a long, hard look in the mirror and formalizing our process of self-examination to ensure leadership commitment and transparency about our hiring practices and employee demographics. Our goal is to ensure balance, equality, and opportunity across all aspects of our business. We aren't afraid to face our own demons in the process, and we know it's always a work in progress.

Another employee-informed initiative was the creation of our COVID-19 pandemic task force, which continually evaluates the status of the pandemic on a global level and makes decisions about how to keep our workforce safe. This involved instituting a work-from-home program for approximately 5,000 employees while still running and managing our business successfully.

We aren't telling you all this simply to toot our own horn. Our point isn't that we are a perfect company; on the contrary, our initiatives are examples of how listening to employees at all levels and allowing them to contribute results in organization-wide change throughout its root systems and branches. We needed this change because we aren't perfect, we want to continuously improve, and we have more to accomplish. Change can be messy, but in the end, it's worth it.

To meet this all-encompassing goal, we practice the systems of innovation; and by listening, understanding, taking action, and learning, we empower our strategic changes to revise the structure, resource allocation, metrics, and values of the organization as a whole.

Change Remorse

As you think about change, you'll also want to consider what we call "change remorse." This is a sensation that often arises when change was not well thought-out or was change for change's sake.

Let's put this into context. Suppose you and your team give intense consideration to what your organization needs, and you make the changes for the right reasons. You have collected data from customers and employees and know what the status of their experience is and where their pain points are. You have employees come forward with suggestions, ideas, and new approaches. You listen, understand, take the right actions, and you learn from it.

If this is what you have done, you are starting to engage in deep change.

The second part of this process is how you implement that change. When new initiatives are implemented in an empathic way, employees will know leadership heard, understood, and cared about their perspectives, and this will prevent change remorse from arising once the changes actually happen. Being listened to, understood, and acknowledged is part of what generates long-term, loyal employees.

If, however, you engaged in the right processes for listening and understanding but then chose to take actions which did not honor these steps, employees will feel betrayed, confused, and disillusioned by the changes that do occur as a result. These changes may contain aspects of innovation, but they won't last and they won't secure the respect or loyalty of your employees and customers.

Change itself isn't the goal of Empathy in Action—the standard needs to be much, much higher than that. There's a saying that "change without action is no change at all." We take it even further and posit that change without empathy is not worth acting on in the first place.

Change Agents and Change Saboteurs

Another aspect of deep change is supporting decisions once they are made. It can be difficult to get four people to agree on what movie to watch; it's even more difficult to get buy-in and agreement in the workplace when hundreds or thousands of people are involved.

At the same time, for disruption to yield results, employees need to support a change even if not everyone completely agrees with it. Sounds tricky, right? Let's take a closer look.

Part of the way Tony leads change as CEO is through an openness to suggestions. He also brings in fresh ideas on how to approach our business and our culture. Although a certain level of authority is necessary for leaders, Tony prioritizes collaboration and interpersonal communication in a way that goes beyond hierarchies. We listen to his ideas and the ideas of other employees, we discuss them, and we debate them. Within a team, we are given the chance to speak our mind, share our thoughts, and express our perspectives

> ### Blind Spot
>
> Alignment and agreement are different; leaders need to give employees the opportunity to voice their perspectives. After all the input is taken into consideration and a decision is made, everyone can fall into alignment.

from where we sit in the organization, giving insight about how change may impact us and our teams, employees, and customers. Careful consideration is given to the many different points of view before any changes are made.

However, Tony and the senior leadership team do ask that once all input has been taken into consideration and the change is made, that we all fly in formation—even when we don't all agree on the final decision. This is where alignment is different from agreement. Often, it comes down to employees' trust in the wisdom of the leadership team, which is earned when these leaders have taken employee and customer feedback into account.

Under the leadership of Tony and his team, we've found that we can only make and stick with tough choices if we as a culture don't give up or second-guess ourselves. As we go through a change, because we are listening and understanding the change's implications, we can iterate and pivot. But as we said, if there are changes, they are founded on contextualized data and authentic feedback.

Leaders that want everyone in agreement need to watch out for team members who are saying, "Sure, I support that," while internally shaking their heads and saying no. This quality is typical in passive-aggressive cultures where leadership doesn't encourage the open expression of views and feelings.

Even when almost everyone is aligned, change saboteurs can derail efforts. These negative players often bring up more excuses, revisiting what was discussed and already decided on by the pod's in-depth discussions. When the saboteurs don't express their thoughts openly, they turn the situation into mental excuses of why "it" (the change) won't work and ultimately, passive-aggressively sabotage positive change. This type of behavior is antithetical to building trust and moving forward.

> **Blind Spot**
>
> Passive-aggressive cultures often allow saboteurs to slow down the progress of a project by diverting others into additional cycles of indecision, derailing alignment.

Instead of promoting forward progress, saboteurs divert the team into additional cycles of discussion where they end up "beating a dead horse," further derailing the alignment. The team as a whole has already debated and agreed, but the saboteurs (consciously or unconsciously) take the team down the road of rehashing the situation over and over again. Sometimes they directly sabotage themselves and their team by telling them to ignore the new direction. This can happen when people are attached to an idea, take a political stance, or have a greater need to be right than to move the project or team forward. If people recognize this behavior in themselves, they must learn to let things go and realize there will be plenty of opportunities to share their ideas in future projects and participate with a growth mindset.

Change agents, on the other hand, are frequently the organization's internal cheerleaders who help the company navigate big changes. When saboteur behavior is allowed in an organization, the change agents get discouraged and often leave the organization to find a more supportive and effective environment. This means team leaders need to strive to get real feedback and gain an accurate view of the situation. When saboteurs are whispering against what's being done, team leaders need to take decisive action and tell them to knock it off. At the same time, it takes a brave soul to be honest with senior leaders and tell them this is going on. They may bring leftover baggage from a previous leader or company culture where telling the truth led to punitive measures.

It's only when they are able to let that baggage go and experience a different kind of culture that they become free to be open and honest. As a leader, it's up to you to make that a reality. Because our brains are wired to fear change and assume external forces are worse than they are, toxic dissent can quickly grow into a metastasizing counterforce, becoming a cancer within the organization. Chronic complainers, no-accountability finger-pointers, or learning-resistant laggards are culture killers and can cost an organization the opportunity to differentiate in a competitive market.

Sometimes, when a leader comes into a new situation, individuals or groups may long for the way things have always been done, maybe because it's comfortable and they don't have to learn something new. Only 20 percent of teams and individuals achieve their true potential because of these internal, hidden self-sabotaging behaviors, a statistic that author Shirzad Chamine explored in-depth in his book *Positive Intelligence*.[25]

> **Blind Spot**
>
> Only 20 percent of teams and individuals achieve their true potential because of internal, hidden, and self-sabotaging behaviors, limiting the overall success of the transformation to deliver business results.

It's the job of leaders to create open and honest cultures where people can speak freely without repercussions. At the same time, part of the agreement in this type of culture must be that, because employees have been allowed to provide input and have been respectfully listened to, once the pod has reached a consensus, they need to accept it even if they are not in complete agreement.

Real Change

Remember that change should never happen for the sake of some management checklist. All transformation must arise from the authentic, shared purpose of the organization, as it is this purpose which lends clarity to the mission as a whole. Ambiguity leaves employees confused. Communicating and being clear on why, what, and how changes are happening is key.

One of the things Tony does to communicate this purpose during times of great change is to not only send out an email message to employees, but also a personalized video where he communicates what's happening, provides the why behind it, and thanks the employees for the hard work they've already put in. Tony conducts events, like live town hall meetings, where thousands of employees join an online discussion about proposed changes and have the option to contribute to the conversation. With this empathetic approach, he can clearly make the new "ask."

What Tony has found is that taking the extra time to personalize messages with the why means a great deal to employees. After a town hall meeting, his inbox and the online community pages are often flooded with thank you's, ideas, suggestions, and comments. Earning that type of participation is part of how he's creating an open and honest culture where people feel safe to speak up and express themselves.

TAKEAWAYS

- Empathy-based transformation and leadership is not about traditional reorganization, but rather inspiring changes in behaviors so collaborative and natural that, when adopted, results follow.

- The triad of diversity, equity, and inclusion are the key to creating and retaining loyal employees and driving more innovative and financially successful companies.

- Defining a massive transformative purpose (MTP^X) should be so sweeping, aspirational, and definitive that it propels your company beyond your competition to new heights.

TONY'S
LEADERSHIP CORNER

Blind spot: Leveraging a crisis to define culture

Leading through the global COVID-19 pandemic was like being a wartime crisis leader. Our top priority was to keep our employees and families safe. Next was using our cloud technology to enable our customer service agents to work from home so they could continue to serve their customers through this devastating crisis.

During the first year of COVID, we were able to execute well on both fronts. We set up a global task force to create policies and programs to keep our employees safe and well. We gave our employees Fridays off in August, a mental health day in October, and paid time off between Christmas and New Year's Day. When we surveyed our employees nine months into the pandemic, 93 percent felt that they were being treated with empathy during this crisis. We honed our ability to host successful virtual events. We created programs to get our customers up and running on our flexible cloud products—sometimes in a matter of hours. This reinforced the mission we're on: to accelerate our transformation to the cloud and deliver incredible customer experiences. On top of it all, we delivered the best results in Genesys' 30-year history.

What is it about a crisis that so often brings greatness to bear? Your sense of purpose becomes clear. Your priorities become clear. Teamwork and collaboration become almost effortless.

When it's business as usual, i.e., without a crisis, the challenge for leaders is to create the same sense of clarity, urgency, and teamwork. The blind spot for leaders is to learn how to maintain a steady, predictable pace while holding on to a greater sense of purpose.

" A true natural servant automatically responds to any problem by listening first.

—Robert Greenleaf

Chapter Eleven

LEADING CHANGE: IT'S NOT BUSINESS AS USUAL

Leading in this customer/employee-centric era requires far more than ever before. Digital disruption is a forcing function for business evolution, causing unrest in the very nature of the roles that the CEO, senior leadership team, and board of directors play. They are accountable for delivering real financial results from corporate initiative investments and disruptions. They also have the most significant influence on initiatives' success.

Focusing on disruptive company growth requires something different of leaders, especially in this new era of exponential technologies, which leads us to the fourth input in the Empathy in Action Flywheel— empathy-based leadership (Figure 1.4). "The Business Impact of Change Management" article in *Graziadio Business Review*[1] serves as a reference for the long-standing proof that organizational change management empowers leaders with the skills to go beyond the status quo of leading day-to-day operations to heights previously unimaginable.

> ### Blind Spot
>
> Many leaders do not realize there is a difference between maintaining the status quo and leading a transformation, which positions them to new heights previously unimaginable.

Servant leadership theory suggests that the most influential leaders are in service to their stakeholders: employees, customers, partners, alliances, and others. This contrasts with the old command-and-control type of leadership, which strives to attain power over stakeholders. This distinction is key. Often leaders see the future clearly and want to make changes faster than the organization can absorb. But having patience can greatly impact whether employees become engaged and support the transformation. To give the process of change momentum, executives need a communication and education plan that motivates stakeholders to be excited about the change, celebrating progress with clear milestones providing the impetus to absorb, take action, and be inspired by the road ahead.

Empathy Leadership Principles

Open and Honest Communication

We've discussed how leading change requires a culture of psychological safety and open, honest communication where people candidly express ideas. Leaders must create cultures where ideas are taken into consideration and debated, reaching a consensus together. If someone disagrees, there are valid reasons for those disagreements to be heard and discussed. When colleagues appreciate other people's viewpoints and unabashedly welcome diverse opinions, innovation flourishes.

Leaders need to develop cultures where people feel free—without fear of repercussion—to say, "Yes, I hear you, but I don't agree with that direction, and I'd like you to consider X." Great leaders want to know differing opinions. As a pod debates the facts, with everyone hearing the pros and cons, together they can come to a new level of understanding that informs a new perspective.

> **Blind Spot**
>
> Many leaders are not comfortable with allowing employees to openly express their thoughts and ideas. The result is a culture of compliance that stifles transformation and innovation.

Leaders who don't allow employees to express their thoughts and ideas may end up with passive-aggressive behavior. As we've said, employees may be saying "yes" but internally shaking their heads "no." This behavior leads to cultures of compliance that stifle transformation and innovation.

Creating a Blameless Culture

As a leader, you may inadvertently inherit a passive-aggressive culture from a predecessor, so it's essential to be aware and create a new culture that rewards and celebrates communication. In a culture where blame is reinforced, people dissect ideas and processes to determine who is at fault, and real change never happens. Leaders will need to show their teams how a "blameless" culture works: pull people into the discussion and the change process, encourage participation, and listen actively. Companies that consistently blame individuals will continue to see mistakes because the blame-shifting takes precedence over learning for improvement.

Employees Are Skeptical of Change

We've discussed the importance of empathy—understanding things from the customer's and employee's point of view, but it also applies to leading change. When employees hear a new initiative is being launched, they may be skeptical because they have witnessed so many change initiatives go south. As a result, they don't take their leadership seriously enough to get behind yet another change—they're burned out on change.

> **Blind Spot**
>
> Because employees have seen so many change initiatives go south, they may be skeptical, burned-out, and often ignore them.

We've faced internal organizational inertia or resistance in our years of implementing new initiatives. While not a true road map for delivering organizational change, the best-selling book *Who Moved My Cheese?* by Spencer Johnson demonstrates that how people react to change differs, from those willing to go the extra mile to those who actively resist it. The book could be summed up by John C. Maxwell's quote:

Change is inevitable. Growth is optional.

It doesn't work to just say "we're going to change." Change must come from the hearts and minds of the employees.

Statistics on Transformation Failures

What's the upside of leading a company in implementing exponential technology to transform how it does business? Accenture's *Reworking the Revolution* report estimates that if businesses invested in exponential technologies like AI and human-machine collaboration at the same rate as top-performing companies, they could boost revenues by 38 percent by 2022 and raise employment levels by 10 percent.[2] Collectively, this would increase profits globally by $4.8 trillion

> ### Blind Spot
>
> There are telltale signs of why transformations fail, leading to hundreds of millions and billions of dollars in wasted resources. Many companies ignore the signs or remain unaware of their significance to the transformation's success.

over the same period. For the average S&P 500 company, this equates to $7.5 billion in revenue and an $880 million lift to profitability. Clearly, there are financial benefits to taking exponential technologies like AI, digital, and the cloud very seriously.

The downside of poorly led change? Just like we saw the writing on the wall with customer/employee initiatives, history provides telltale signs around organizational change that most companies and leaders ignore or are unaware of.[3] Not much has changed in the last 25 years, and it's a sobering read:

- In 1995, Kotter found only 30 percent of change programs were on time, on budget, and delivered the expected outcome.
- In 1998, Turner and Crawford showed that when implementing new software, 88 percent of executives believed that the organizational changes were right and that their organization could achieve them, but only 33 percent achieved partial or complete success when the project was implemented.
- The Standish Group showed little progress from 2012 to 2016 in organizational change management, with only an unacceptably low 34 percent improvement.
- In 2019, most organizations had a 70 percent organizational change failure rate.

Few business schools or leadership programs teach change management. We recommend providing change leaders with baseline training that builds their understanding of the change process and the leadership skills required to facilitate that process. Let's look at some of the fundamentals to get you started.

Why Change and Transformation Initiatives Fail

With Tony's experience in leading the growth of many companies like Skype and GoPro and the insights from Natalie's career as a management consultant as well as the opportunity to lead change in many organizations, we've compiled information to help you be a better change leader. The first three things to understand about leading change are:

1. **Change is inevitable; adoption is conditional**. Organizations must continually adapt, iterate, and pivot with all changes to remain competitive. However, we frequently overlook that when changes are made, they drive other changes, anticipated or not, especially with people. And managing people well during a change is key to its success.
2. **The stages of change are the same**. Whether making a change in your life or your organization, you must complete three stages of transition (Endings, Valley of Despair, and New Beginnings) for the change to be successful. The timing and the experiences may be different for each person, but the stages of change and the transition process are identical for everyone.
3. **Change fails for consistent reasons**. Since corporations began taking on change initiatives, research has shown the reasons they fail are invariably the same. The good news? Because the reasons for failure are consistent, there are proven ways to prevent wasted time, resources, and budget; to instead end up where you want so your organization can soar.

While every company is different, let's explore some of the pervasive, universal truths about corporate change. By observing and collecting empirical data from a variety of companies in other industries and countries, with different customer bases, different products or services, and unique cultures—all going through many kinds of change—this significant base of information provides you with a unique advantage and showcases the universal truths that apply to everyone leading change, regardless of industry or business type.

By no means do we want to imply that most leaders aren't committed to successful transformations. The first distinction new to many leaders is the difference between "being the leader or being involved the change" versus "being an actively engaged, adaptive, and empathetic leader of change." To mitigate risks, ensure the internal culture supports the change and employees feel included, and then act accordingly so business outcomes are obtained, the second type of engaged leadership is required.

> **Blind Spot**
>
> When leading a transformation initiative, there is a tremendous difference in the outcome when leaders are only involved vs. being an active, engaged, adaptive, and empathic leader of change.

Leading change means using new or different skills and capabilities. The result? You and your pods/teams will be better prepared to inspire change in your organization, and ultimately meet or exceed your planned return on investment—and we don't just mean the financial aspect. We also mean winning the hearts and minds of your employees, your customers, and all your stakeholders.

How Change Affects Employees

What people often miss about change is that it takes leaders doing things differently—like having an implicit schedule and plan implemented—for it to work on time and within scope and budget. In part, that's because new initiatives don't affect leaders in the same way as they do employees. The higher a leader is in an organization, the more quickly they move through the change; they can see the intended destination before others even know the race has begun. But it's also because employees' roles and what's required on a day-to-day basis after the change is quite different from theirs.

For example, when a new software system is implemented, leaders are seldom required to learn how to use the new systems or tools. But the new processes and technologies directly affect how employees get their work done, and they have a big, daily impact. Even if the new system is better and easier, employees and managers must learn a new way of doing business. Let's look at what leaders need to do differently when they lead change through the Seven Empathy Leadership Proven Practices™ (Table 11.1).

Seven Empathy Leadership Proven Practices

Table 11.1 The Seven Empathy Leadership Proven Practices for leading transformational change.[4]

7 Proven Practices for Leadership
Understand the Business Case for Change
Start with Your Executive Team: Make the Commitment, Move from *Involved* to *Engaged*
Engage *All* of Your Organization's Leaders and Prepare Them for the Journey
Build a Broad Understanding of the Change Process
Evaluate and Tailor the Change Effort
Develop Adaptive Leadership Skills and Capabilities
Create Change Leadership Plans

Proven Practice #1:
Understand the Business Case for Change

Leaders need to first hold facilitated "expectations workshops" for the executive team, followed by workshops for the broader leadership teams and employees, especially change agents. These workshops are critical not only for alignment but also because they provide opportunities to craft

Blind Spot

Leaders often move through a change faster than employees because what they do on a daily basis doesn't change. The changes in strategy, process, and technology directly affect the daily life of employees, requiring more time to learn new things and adjust to the changes.

and review the new narrative about why company disruption is essential. Without this exercise, employees may shrug their shoulders, appearing half-heartedly to support the change. Often, it's not that they don't support it, they just don't know how to articulate its value to those around them or effectively communicate the emotional and business reasons for change.

We suggest that the change narrative be something that can be a 30-second or two-, five-, or 20-minute elevator pitch in which all employees, bottom to top, are fluent in. Something that lends itself to a stand-and-deliver style where every employee becomes confident in delivering the brand's new direction as a narrative while speaking to customers. You will also want to set up a train-the-trainer initiative to have people who can teach and coach others in the company's MTP^X and change initiative narrative. Every employee should be able to authentically tell the story, along with the why, the what, and the how of your MTP^X—your North Star.

During the workshop process, it is normal and expected to see mixed or adverse reactions. There will likely be some pushback even in cultures with open and honest communication. What's great about this is, as you all go through the value understanding and narrative internalization workshops, you will be able to see changes in attitude before and after the workshops as well as throughout the project.

This gives you measurable indicators along the whole project to show how the level of adoption is increasing over time. The board of directors or investors like to see clear statistics as concrete evidence the company is transforming. With high employee adoption, you can demonstrably measure whether they are on board, taking the vision and turning it into reality.

With an MTP^X, you'll want to customize a meaningful case for change for various audiences, from

> **Blind Spot**
>
> Leaders often miss that just saying what the change initiative is isn't enough. Leaders must create a financial and emotional business case for change so compelling employees are inspired to get up every day and give it 100 percent.

the board of directors to middle managers to employees. Meaningful implies a strong financial case to support the change (i.e., the company will stay in business, rise to the top of their competitive field, create a new market category, drive higher revenues and profits, and provide better raises and benefits for employees).

Meaningful also includes measuring defined outcomes to provide value and impact for all stakeholders on an emotional level. Because individuals are expected to change their thinking, do something new, alter their behaviors or processes, and change how they do their jobs, leaders need to create a compelling reason for employees to personally embrace the need for the changes.

Part of making the business case for change personal is to find out what isn't working so well for employees. With this, you are in a better position to articulate and visualize the benefits of the new world. For example, compelling reasons might include the following:

- The new system is designed to deliver information in real time to help you help the customer.
- Mundane aspects of the job that you dread (resetting a password or answering the same basic questions) will be handled by automation so you can use your creative problem-solving skills to help customers with other issues.
- The work you will be doing after the change is something you excel at and enjoy.

Leaders Need to Create a Sense of Urgency

Employees may not be aware of the role of exponential technologies and how they drive the need to change or be displaced by competitors. No one wants to lose their job or have their company go under, but that's what is happening to companies that aren't implementing changes. Leaders, managers, and employees want to be proud of where they work and what the company stands for. Another way leading change is different is senior leaders must set the stage and assist everyone to see what's at stake, why the changes are needed, and how they benefit from them in the short run and the long run. It will set the company apart from the competition.

> **Blind Spot**
>
> Socializing the financial and emotional business benefits for employees, getting feedback, and making adjustments are key to appealing to employees' desire to support a change initiative.

Our intent is not to tell you how to build a business case for change, but rather to acknowledge that you may struggle with the other six proven practices for leading transformation without it. Suppose you cannot articulate why the change difference is vital to everyone in the organization and why there is a need to change now. In that case, you cannot advantageously engage your leaders or employees. Along with the MTP^X, socialize the financial and emotional business case for change, and establish a baseline for the quantitative and qualitative metrics. Measure the project against your specific business case for change. Those measures become part of the one-on-one meetings with employees and managers as well as part of the employee performance evaluation process. What gets measured becomes the culture.

Proven Practice #2:
Move from Involved to Engaged Leadership

It's nearly impossible to lead an organization through any successful disruption without alignment. They may not all agree on the final course, but they need to be aligned. This situation often is best facilitated by an external change firm before the company embarks on large-scale disruption, and will result in far better results than bringing someone in to "fix" the lack of alignment and reduce politics. Otherwise, employees spend their time on politics instead of the real work that's necessary and never easy.

Suppose your executive team approves the strategic choices and the financial support of any considerable business improvement initiative at the beginning of a transformation. Doesn't this mean they are engaged and sponsoring the project? Not necessarily, an executive team that only provides the budget and approves the project is a true red flag and common pitfall that steers projects off course. These assumptions indicate leaders who are "active" but not truly "engaged" in the change effort. Research shows that while key individuals may believe they are providing enough attention for a project's success by being involved, it is the leadership engagement behaviors that drive bottom-line success.

> **Blind Spot**
>
> Leaders need to exhibit the behavior changes they seek in employees when the company is going through a transformation.

Some common attributes and behaviors that signal either cursory involvement or genuine engagement in the change process include:

- Accountability/ownership
- Communication—frequent, two-way, and at all levels

- Frequent and consistent engagement during the change process

As the sponsor of your organization's change initiative, you also need to work with your executive team to set the expectations for their engagement. Do this by building the project goals into the change initiative's project plan and everyone's performance plans, holding each other accountable. Most importantly, you need to demonstrate the behaviors you actively seek. You may want to find a coach to help you monitor your performance against your own goals. Lastly, be sure that the executive team is engaged in the following sections' recommendations and are working side-by-side with the organization's change leaders and change agents.

Proven Practice #3:
Engage Your Organization's Leaders

Leading change is different in that you have to accept that 80 percent of any group will resist change. The other 20 percent will get behind the change effort (these are your change agents) and pull along the other 80 percent if the process is well managed. As you take steps toward ensuring active engagement in a transformational process, an early and critical stage is identifying the change leaders in your organization. Often, companies think the organization's executives are the only change initiative leaders. However, change agents take on many forms and exist on many levels within an organization.

The "Waterfall Effect" in Leadership

The waterfall effect in leadership describes the chain of influence in the organization. Who are your natural "relationship influencers" and how do you identify them? They are your formal or informal influencers of change. You can use the work style assessments in Chapter 12 to identify them. They tend to have DISC profiles that are high in interpersonal skills and have a high tolerance for risk, seeing change as an opportunity instead of a threat.

When you choose your change leadership team, include people from all levels and positions in the organization. Preparing leaders for their role in transformation means ensuring they learn how to work with the change, not against it. To lead change, a leader needs to understand it and their role in implementing it.

Another critical aspect is understanding the level of effort required for success. When you or your external change facilitators bring your change leaders/agents onboard, you need to set their expectations appropriately. You and the executive team must stress:

- This is an active role
- It's not an easy role
- Their level of participation will increase over time

Figure 11.1 shows how a change leader's role and its importance continue to increase over the project's lifetime. This also means change leaders must let go of some of their normal responsibilities and tasks to give this new role the time and attention required.

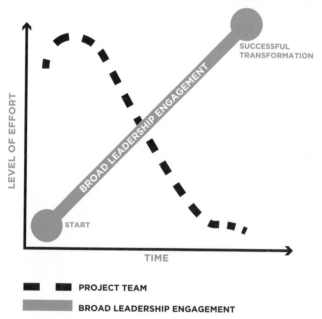

Figure 11.1 A change leader's role increases over the life of the project.[5]

Proven Practice #4:
Build a Broad Understanding of the Change Process

Critical to your success is educating your stakeholders on the science of change. It is essential for everyone in the organization to understand how people process change; how we internalize and move through the three stages of change. With this education, all employees can recognize their behaviors and understand why they are feeling unrest, internal turmoil, and uncertainty—all normal feelings that shouldn't be discarded. With a solid foundation on the science of change, they will recognize the signs and stages of resistance that all organizations and people go through.

The three high-level principles to bottom-line, successful change initiatives include:

- Organizational and personal transitions
- The stages of change
- The ROI (return on investment) of change

Organizational and Personal Transitions

One of the old paradigms in organizational change management was only the organization goes through the change, deemphasizing the personal aspect. Corporate leaders who aren't comfortable dealing with—or even speaking about the three natural transitions people go through on a personal level—often take this approach. This is typically because they haven't received any organizational change management (OCM) education.

An organization is a combination of strategy, people, processes, and technology. Only one dimension of those can resist change—the people, and at a personal level. Leading change must include an empathic organizational change education program that focuses on understanding not only the transitions at a collective level, but also on the transitions we need to move through on a personal level to be instrumental in reaching new goals for ourselves and the organization (Figure 11.2). We don't want to be the reason the initiative is hung up, but without this awareness, this is often the case. This slows down our success as well as the organization.

> **Blind Spot**
>
> Leaders need to provide support and guidance to employees as they move through the transition process in a change initiative.

ORGANIZATIONAL CHANGE MANAGEMENT PROCESS

Figure 11.2 **Both corporate and personal transitions must be part of OCM training.**

The Stages of Transition

Understanding the transition process is a must for change leaders. Often, leaders assume everyone has bought into the change. But the research shows that leading people through change requires leaders to take accountability to move their teams through the three transitions before the change can produce the intended result.

Figure 11.3 breaks down the personal transitions into three distinct phases. Each individual must traverse these three phases:

> **Blind Spot**
>
> Change doesn't happen overnight. There are three distinct phases: Endings, the Valley of Despair, and New Beginnings, all of which must be traversed successfully.

- **Endings:** People have to let go of the way things used to be. Recall the saying, "You can't steal second base with your foot on first."
- **Valley of Despair/Transitions:** Even after people have let go of their old ways, they often find themselves unable to start anew. This occurs when they enter into the in-between state, which can be riddled with uncer-

tainty and confusion. Although the Valley of Despair is uncomfortable, it's where the real transformation takes place as they move from the old ways to the new. Change leaders should play a key role in helping their teams to recognize when they are in this phase. This is where many projects get stuck, and the longer they are stuck, the less is accomplished toward the initiative and the more politics, jousting, and negative inertia ensue. This delay costs the company time, money, competitive advantage, and market share.

- **New Beginnings:** Individuals reach this stage only after working their way through the earlier phases. At this point, an individual will accept the "new world" and their role in it. Real behavioral change will occur. Without that behavior change, bottom-line results can't take place. So, not educating people on these phases and that they will have these feelings to one degree or another means you may not ever get beyond the Valley of Despair. This is why there are so many transformation project failures.

INDIVIDUAL CHANGE: PHASES OF TRANSITION

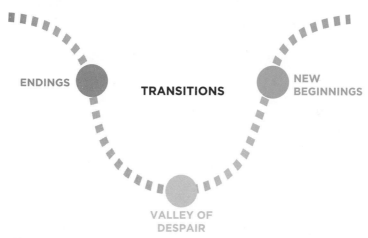

ENDINGS **TRANSITIONS** NEW BEGINNINGS

VALLEY OF DESPAIR

Figure 11.3 Personal transition phases that individuals go through during a change project.

The trouble is, most leaders imagine that the transition process is automatic—that it merely occurs because the leadership team made an announcement in the annual kick-off meeting and it's repeated in the company's monthly newsletter. But that's not enough to change people's behaviors. Change and transition are two separate and distinct aspects of transformation, yet leaders often treat them the same.

Change is the external things people can see, like a different policy, practice, or system. A transition is the internal, psychological reorientation that people go through before the change can produce the intended result. It's also essential for change leaders to understand that transitions typically happen more slowly than change. This reality must be considered when developing an initiative's schedule, time line, scope, and budget. And none of this can be done without a formal educational change management program as part of the initiative.

> *Until all of us have made it, none of us have made it.*
> – Rosemary Brown, United Nations Human Rights Fellow

The ROI of Change: Managing Change and Transformation Well

While the stages of change are the same, the time line of the three stages of transition and their organizational impact differ from one organization or project to another. One variable could be the size of the change project (i.e., an enterprise-wide software implementation is a larger undertaking than updating the software on desktops in a contact center). But regardless of the size of the change, research shows the crucial challenge is the reaction of individuals impacted by the change.

> **Blind Spot**
>
> The return on investment of a change initiative depends on the organization and individual employees' abilities to navigate through the three stages of change; it requires more from leadership than most understand.

Most leaders may not realize that the return on investment of the change initiative depends on the individual's and team's ability to successfully get through the three stages of transition. The need to help educate people on the change transitions is one of the most critical reasons leaders shift their leadership style and approach to include empathy. With an engaged/empathic leadership style and its corresponding skills, companies can obtain greater economic value faster by effectively developing, deploying, and aligning employees to the initiative. Most leadership teams have not been trained to facilitate their people moving through the transition—this is all the more reason to invest in an external firm's help with the organizational change management education program.

Why does moving through the transition greatly affect the ROI? Figure 11.4 shows the link between financial impact (business performance/productivity) versus the project time line, and stages of change in a project. The depth (loss of productivity) and width (increased time line) of the transition phases are directly proportional to how well leaders handle the change. If leaders do a poor job of leading change (the dotted line), the Valley of Despair will widen and deepen, resulting in the project running over budget, scope, and/or schedule.

THE IMPACT OF THE VALLEY OF DESPAIR

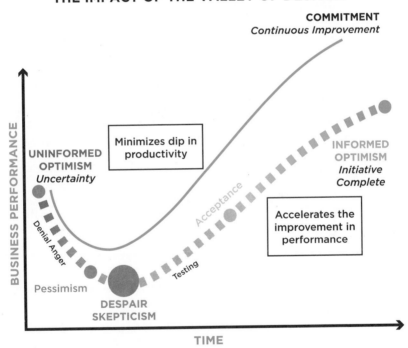

Figure 11.4 Organizational Valley of Despair and its effect on business performance over time.

Research shows when change leaders skillfully lead employees through the transition phases, it directly impacts the initiative's ROI.[6] Therefore, change leaders should understand how these two key dimensions—performance and time—intimately relate to an initiative's positive outcomes, thereby impacting whether a business case will be realized and exceeded.

Proven Practice #5:
Evaluate and Tailor the Change Effort

To obtain an ROI on a project, you'll want to use some sort of diagnostic tool to evaluate the risk level against the variables affecting the change initiative. For instance, here are seven variables in a typical risk diagnostic transformation project tool:

Blind Spot

Many leaders don't realize they need to conduct an organizational change readiness and risk assessment to measure the degree of alignment across various groups. This guides communication and education planning to reach the intended outcomes.

1. Level of risk if the stakeholder group does not adopt the change
2. Impact to the stakeholder group if they do not adopt the change
3. Skill gaps of employees between current and future state
4. Size, number, and diversity of locations of the stakeholder group
5. Level of anticipated resistance/adoption to the change effort
6. Number of change initiatives being implemented to the stakeholder group in a similar time frame
7. Degree of education on the science of successful change and transformation projects

With this type of assessment, leaders and teams can better discern how to tailor the plan to ensure reaching the business goals and the project's intended ROI. Research also shows conducting informational interviews is key to gaining insight and perspectives on evaluating the current state of a change effort.[7] We know people want to be heard, seen, and acknowledged. Conducting interviews and analyzing them will enable you to prioritize which departments are in most need of organizational change management training. It will also allow the change leaders in each department to adapt their leadership style to better meet their specific group's needs. Additionally, an assessment demonstrates an understanding of the current world and what it will take to transform to the new world.

Another pivotal point in tailoring change plans around diverse groups is acknowledging the critical differences between the values, behaviors, and priorities in functional business units. With that understanding, as you move into a pod structure, you will have this baseline information from each group. Then, as you interact with the pod members, you can use it to elicit constructive and thriving discussions resulting in the best performance and not get stuck because of lack of alignment. How you are organized will also affect how you measure success. In addition, there is extensive research on generational differences in the workforce and how they process and accept change.[8] These differences are key to your approach.

It's also crucial to understand how the project will impact the employee experience and evaluate who will experience the change. Success means understanding whose work experience will change, the degree of change, the transition process, and making sure they have gone through organizational change training to help adapt to the new world.

Finally, this analysis can direct your change leaders to better analyze the type of skills required for their teams/pods to be truly successful in the new world. Exponential technologies are rapidly changing the future of work. Throughout history, whether it's a transition from handpicking cotton in the fields to the invention of the cotton gin or the use today of AI to automate routine tasks, revolutions in technology change the future of work and frequently create a scarcity mindset—people fear they will be unemployable. Often, when new tools or processes are implemented, it's assumed that the current roles and skills will be enough to successfully support employees in transitioning to their new roles. In reality, the role, the skill sets, and capabilities all need to be closely evaluated for the future state so that leaders can provide the appropriate level of training, reskilling, and skill-building for their employees, teams, and pods. And with an

> **Blind Spot**
>
> Just like any project, a change initiative should have a project plan with distinctive phases in which specific goals are set to evolve culture, education, communication, mindset, and behavior changes to reach the intended business outcomes.

optimistic perspective to appreciate the transition to the new world, employees are fully prepared to deliver on the promise of the new vision.

Proven Practice #6:
Develop Adaptive Leadership Skills and Capabilities

To become an empathic leader is to adopt a leadership style that is highly people-oriented and empathy-centric. This means stepping away from more authoritative "telling" styles that many managers are comfortable with and instead "asking" to elicit discussions leading to alignment. It also means stepping beyond the management of tasks and getting into the business of leading personal transitions. Table 11.2 provides a high-level summary of empathic/adaptive and nonempathic/nonadaptive leadership styles.

Table 11.2 Empathic, adaptive vs. nonempathic, nonadaptive leadership styles.

Nonempathic, Nonadaptive Leadership Traits	Empathic, Adaptive, Engaged Leadership Traits
Command and Control Leader	People-oriented, Loyalty-based leader
Competition, Divide, Us vs. Them	Collaboration, Cooperation
Reason, Indifferent, Impassionate	Feeling, Excitement, Passion
Stiff, Decisive, Stubborn, Rigid, Austere	Flexible, Unconstrained
Doing to	Being with
Unique, One Man is an Island	Unity, Togetherness
Demanding, Concealing, Suppressing	Communication, Divulge, Enlighten
Fixing, Cast-down, Embarrass, Oppose	Nurturing, Training, Fostering, Supportive
Sternness, Unyielding	Kindness, Caring
Take the Credit, Discounting, Stifling	Contribution, Recognition

While there are many components for the approach to adaptive, empathic leadership, here are several to consider:

- **Create Dialogue:** One of the primary contributors to a leader's failure to enable change is their communication style. Using a EEOC-approved work style assessment like DISC (see Chapter 12) allows a leader or manager to tailor the conversation to an individual's style, while keeping in mind how they themselves communicate and adapt to change.

- **Actively Manage Conflict:** An effective leader understands that change naturally creates conflict. The ability to handle conflict will directly affect a leader's success in leading change. This can be done if collaboration is the method of conflict resolution (Figure 10.4).
- **Understand the Strengths and Weaknesses of Change Leaders:** Change leaders have been chosen because of their ability to help the organization make the planned transition. Each leader, however, comes with unique strengths and weaknesses. To be a robust, adaptive leader, these strengths and weaknesses need to be understood. Work style assessments (DISC) allow leaders and employees to identify these and provide a structured avenue to work together.

Proven Practice #7:
Create Change Leadership Plans

Though most projects have official plans, leaders often don't realize the importance of creating an organizational change project plan with clear deliverables and business outcomes. Leaders need this plan to manage the various parts of organizational change and to include a communication plan that lays out the anticipated changes and their impact.

Table 11.3 An example of leadership engagement plan stages for transformational change.

Project Stages	Leadership Roles and Tasks
Mobilization	• Articulating the Business Case for Change • Defining Change Leader Role • Setting Expectations • Teaching Organizational Change Management Concepts
Define	• Reemphasizing the Business Case for Change • Defining Leadership Commitment Standards
Design	• Anticipating Impacts • Effectively Managing Resistance
Development	• Preparing Your Team for Change • Mitigating Issues
Deployment	• Evaluating Deployment Readiness of Your Organization • Dealing with Resistance
Transition	• Evaluating Transitions • Measuring Stickiness • Measuring the Business Results

Just like any other project plan, change initiative project plans need to have phases with key milestones set for each phase (Table 11.3). The transformation leadership team must have the strength to stay the course and not move to the next phase before key milestones are accomplished.

We recommend creating the change management project plans with senior leaders during the expectation-setting workshops. This allows change leaders to exchange ideas and voice their concerns in a productive and safe environment. By developing change project plans around the concepts provided in Table 11.3, you will be well on your way toward reaching the business goals of the change initiative. Once the overall plan is created, it needs to be communicated and discussed at every company level, so everyone is flying in formation as one team.

Putting It All Together

In the next chapter, we'll help you start the change discussion in your company. We'll look at the motivation and mechanics to drive change across your people, processes, strategy, leadership, and technology. You'll see how to take control of digital transformation projects and ultimately emerge with a truly customer/employee-centric organization.

TAKEAWAYS

- Change leadership requires a different mindset and skills than managing your organization day to day.

- Leaders need to acknowledge the process employees go through when a transformation initiative is announced and must become an engaged, empathic leader, providing the organization with formal education on the science of change, transitions, and alignment with the organizational change project plan.

- The amount of time and focused energy empathetic leaders will spend with employees and on the project increases as the transformation initiative progresses. The ROI is highly dependent on the majority of the organization moving through the transition state of change and the phases of the project plan.

TONY'S
LEADERSHIP CORNER

Blind spot: The gem in the signal

When I joined Genesys in May 2019, the company was doing well. Genesys was a $1 billion-plus company that was a market leader in the CX industry. The company was preparing for its cloud future, having acquired Interactive Intelligence, a cloud computing company, and AltoCloud, a cloud-based customer journey analytics company. The culture was friendly. People were very collegiate and seemed to genuinely like one another.

In my first few weeks as CEO, I went on a global tour to get a pulse of the organization. I had employee meetings in Indianapolis, Raleigh, and Galway (where we have major sites), then several countries in Europe. I started picking up a signal that perhaps there was some tension beneath all the niceness.

At the end of my second tour, I visited Frankfurt and was asked to meet with one of our high potentials; someone described as "a killer account executive." Naturally, I expected to meet a positive person. Instead, he was very negative. As I listened to him, the signal that I had been picking up was manifested in a moment. The message: the handoffs between our internal organizations are weak, and there is always finger-pointing.

One of my core principles has always been customer centricity. How can you be great with customers if the internal handoffs don't work?

The gem in the signal was what sparked "One Genesys," our cultural mantra for flying in formation as a single team. From then on, I set a clear expectation with my leadership that the days of individual heroes were over. We were going to win as a team. We implemented a structure known as pods, where product, sales, and marketing worked cross-functionally to support customers versus operating in siloes. The answer wasn't the pods themselves; it was Genesys. It's great to be friendly, but it's much more important to have teams working in harmony toward a common purpose and goal.

" One of the most important lessons about crossing the chasm is that the task ultimately requires achieving an unusual degree of company unity during the crossing period.

—Geoffrey Moore

Chapter Twelve

THE EMPATHY TRANSFORMATION

Imagine the following scenario. There is a large assembly of your customers. Some of them have questions about your products. Others want to buy your product but need more information. Some have questions about how your product compares to your competitors' products. Others are experiencing a problem and are upset. Some have feedback about your product and want to return something. And then others just want you to listen like you mean it.

If a meeting like this were taking place at your company,

> **Blind Spot**
>
> Customer interactions and feedback are a gold mine for learning why customers are interested in your brand and buy your products, providing insights to better run your business.

how would you handle it? Who would you ask to address the group? The vice president of sales or product marketing or someone from the C-level? What special message would you create to address their questions, concerns, and issues?

These "meetings" happen every day via your customers' interactions. Typically, customers reach out because they are either upset or angry. The opportunity? Massively shift cost center inquiries into golden assets, inspiring loyalty and creating products, services, and experiences with significant competitive differentiation. This chapter focuses on a perspective, a process, and questions to begin your transformation discussions.

Are You Ready to Commit?

Through years of working with organizations going through change, we found companies generally fall into five levels of organizational commitment to empathetic customer/ employee experiences (Figure 12.1). The outcomes and results of a customer/ employee experience transformation are directly proportional to the organization's commitment to change. Few companies

> **Blind Spot**
>
> Few companies truly commit to transformation that results in business outcomes.

are truly ready to bridge the gap between mediocre commitment and embracing the challenge of introducing full Empathy in Action. However, the higher the level of commitment, the greater the return on the investment.

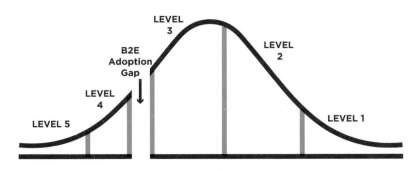

EMPATHY COMMITMENT CONTINUUM

Figure 12.1 Empathy initiative commitment continuum.

As we work with organizations, we see companies distributed across the various levels of empathy commitment (Table 12.1), resembling Geoffrey Moore's technology adoption curve. The area under the curve represents the distribution of companies at each commitment level.

Few companies are genuinely focused on empathic, personalized customer and employee experiences and can also score high in every aspect of the five capabilities—strategy, people, processes, leadership, and technology. For change to stick, you must differentiate your company in the marketplace, to your stakeholders, and to Wall Street by increasing your level of commitment to transforming your company—from the old business-centric paradigm to the customer/employee-centric paradigm.

Table 12.1 The characteristics of the five levels of organizational commitment.

Level of Adoption	Customer/Employee-Focused Characteristics
LEVEL 5	• Culture is future-forward, disruption-oriented • Customer/employee experience is in their DNA • Optimize all 4 capabilities of strategy, people, process, and exponential technology • "All in" attitude • Started the transformation • Working in a pod structure with full alignment
LEVEL 4	• Culture is positive, supportive, and innovation-oriented • Customer/employee experience is part of how they think • Optimizing 2 of the 4 capabilities of strategy, people, process, or exponential technology • Positive attitude • Planning the transformation • Moving from traditional departments to pods; moving from agreement to alignment
LEVEL 3	• Culture is structured • Starting to consider customer/employee experience • Optimizing 1 of the 4 capabilities of strategy, people, process, or linear technology • Neutral attitude • Transformation us part of next year's plan • No changes to the organizational structure or operating modes
LEVEL 2	• Culture is rigid • Customer/employee experience is outdated, but not on the road map • Not optimizing any of the 4 capabilities of strategy, people, process, or linear technology • Transformation is 3-5 years out • Hierarchical organization structure with many rules and policies that must be followed
LEVEL 1	• Culture is mired in politics and inertia • Customer/employee experience is not something that is top of mind • Using all linear technologies; processes strategy the same • Don't feel a transformation is necessary • Don't think information in this book can be applied to their organization • Organization doesn't feel stuck, satisfied with everything as is

Does Your Organization OODA?

Besides the level of a company's commitment, another aspect that drives successful change is a process for continuous, measurable improvement, a process to quickly iterate and pivot. We referred to this process in the Empathy in Action Flywheel in Chapter 1 (Figure 1.4). A novel way to look at that process comes from the former military strategist, colonel, fighter pilot, and management strategist John Boyd.[1] The business world found his framework particularly helpful for creating change agility.

As a fighter pilot, Boyd had to quickly make real-time decisions. Those decisions were a matter of life and death for himself and the pilots he trained. The process Boyd created is called the OODA Loop and consists of four steps: observe, orient, decide, and act. When business strategists apply this repeatable process, they can enhance innovation, generate new ideas, and make changes to thrive and grow in an uncertain and competitive world.

Employees and pods need a process to analyze the business and deliver change. Using a process like the OODA Loop is similar to what W. Edwards Deming—a professor, author, and management consultant known as the "Father of Quality"—suggested when companies wanted to incorporate customer/employee feedback into a business.[2] Deming observed that while some companies collect data and feedback, rarely does that information get to the right department, pod, or person who could use it. If it does get to the right destination, there often aren't any systems or processes to use that insight to make changes and improvements. As your company embarks on becoming customer/employee-centric, there will be many things your pods will need to discuss and change. The OODA Loop provides a framework for those discussions and how to approach the changes required. A key question is: Can we go through the OODA Loop process faster than our competitors, providing a time advantage? Here's what you want to do for each step:

- **Observe**: Using your systems and technology, observe, listen, monitor, and collect data on what employees and customers know, think, and feel about how you provide experiences. (Use your systems of listening, understanding, predicting, acting, and learning from Chapter 9.)

- **Orient:** Benchmark, orient, and compare ideal experiences to your current customer and employee experiences to those of your competitors. (Use the Experience Index in Chapter 4.)
- **Decide:** Determine your gaps in providing those ideal experiences based on the business KPIs and outcomes you want to improve. (Use the Empathy Assessment™ from our closing remarks.)
- **Act:** Make changes to your people, strategy, processes, leadership, and technology to deliver better experiences and continually learn from them to improve. (Use your organizational change management project plan and measurement system from Chapter 11.)

Why is using a process to make agile decisions so important? Consider the two companies in Figure 12.2. Company 2 is much slower to analyze, synthesize, and act on customer and employee data, feedback, sentiment, and actions, much less learn from any of it.

Because Company 1 moves through the OODA steps faster than Company 2, they can improve customer/employee experiences faster. This means they can drive more customer/employee lifetime value (CLV/ELV) and EBBV at a higher rate, increasing their revenue, profits, and margins. Now ask your team: "How fast do we OODA compared to our competitors? And what can we do to change our current mindset to improve our OODA process?"

> **Blind Spot**
>
> Companies don't realize their competition is already listening, understanding and predicting, acting, and learning from their customer/employee interactions, providing them with unprecedented business advantages.

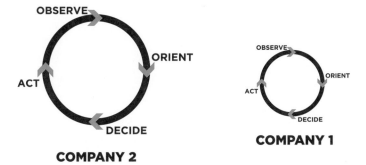

COMPANY 2

COMPANY 1

Figure 12.2 Comparing two companies' ability to make changes that will differentiate them.

In military operations, the OODA Loop takes place in seconds. In corporations, it's much slower. However, successful companies don't rigidly stick to the year's plan. Instead, they use the OODA Loop process as part of their culture to develop an agile attitude of iterating and pivoting to improve the customer and employee experience, ideally while their competitor is still observing their last action.

> **Blind Spot**
>
> Companies that don't stick to a rigid strategic plan but use a process to continually iterate and pivot are more likely to surpass their competition.

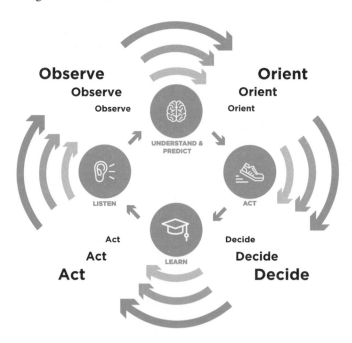

Figure 12.3 The OODA Loop with the Systems of Empathy on repeat.

And it's not just about doing this once. The ability to iterate and pivot regularly (forming continuous OODA Loops) is part of what makes agile, exponential companies so much more successful (Figure 12.3). You will want to use the results of your last actions as the next set of observations to reorient, making your next decisions even better. As a leader, your job is to help your organization become proficient—and faster than your competitors—in the following:

- Observe the ever-changing market conditions, customer/
  employee expectations, and current experiences
- Orient and benchmark these experiences
- Decide on what to change
- Act to change, improve, and outmaneuver the competition

Course Correct with OODA

Another reason why customer/employee experience is critical now more than ever: word of mouth. The authors of *The Cluetrain Manifesto* predicted that technology would allow customers to communicate directly with each other and talk back to companies online when dissatisfied, enabling everyone to see negative interactions.[3] We've reached that point. Companies need to consider the experience of live customers in a real-time, mobile web world. Waiting a day, a week, or a month can take a customer experience issue—spread by social and digital channels—and turn it into a PR nightmare, perhaps unintentionally showing the world how little customer/employee experience means to your company.

> ### Blind Spot
>
> Digital and social platforms allow customers to talk to each other directly, and they trust other's reviews more than corporate messaging.

Customers find ways to fight back against companies delivering poor customer experiences. Consider the story behind the song "United Breaks Guitars."[4] When band leader Dave Carroll was forced to check his guitar for a United Airlines flight, baggage handlers broke it. And when Carroll sought help, he was denied. So Dave and his band created a music video about the poor customer experience. The video got over 20 million YouTube views. Within four days of the song going online, the gathering thunderclouds of bad PR caused United Airlines' stock price to suffer a mid-flight stall; it plunged by a reported 10 percent and cost shareholders $180 million.[5] When customers reach a boiling point and use digital channels to make their voices heard, it damages the brand's reputation. There's no time like the present to make this a priority. It's critical in this digital world to have a process like OODA to correct experiences and validate we're on track.

Every employee needs to be involved in the OODA process to generate the company's success in using it. Setting an OODA Loop process and strategy posits customer/employee experiences as a key to innovation, change, and competitive advantage. Why? Because experiences can be the reality check for PR brand promises, key marketing messages, product capabilities, and sale promises. They can also provide feedback to back-office functions like billing, engineering, manufacturing, and shipping. This is your opportunity to drive innovation and change in your business by transforming your customers' and employees' experience before bad word of mouth spreads and is unrecoverable.

Begin Where You Are

When evaluating your empathy capabilities, you'll need guidelines to determine where you are on the empathy scale to score your organization. As you look at the experiences, you want to understand whether you have empowered your team to maximize empathy.

The Fast-Forward Empathy Transformation Questions™ are designed to help invigorate the dialogue about your capabilities. Use them as a reference point to develop questions for your company's transformation, gain executive buy-in, build stakeholder consensus, streamline processes, hire the right employees, select the enabling technologies, identify quick wins, and optimize your road map for innovation in customer and employee experience. You can also ensure changes translate into customer/employee retention and loyalty while reducing costs and increasing revenue by moving from B-centric to C&E-centric.

For some, going from linear technology systems into the world of exponential technologies like AI and cloud may seem daunting. For others, it might sound exciting. You have to begin where you are. The first step on the journey toward establishing empathetic business practices is evaluating your organization's brand promise, strategy, leadership, culture, processes, and technology. Use the questions below to guide your discussions to the North Star triad of empathy, trust, and loyalty.

Fast-Forward Empathy Transformation Questions

The Brand Promise

As your marketing and branding departments develop a brand promise, examine what your company stands for. What types of experiences, on the customer and the employee side, do you want to be known for? How do employees deliver your brand promise through their actions, from sales and marketing to customer service and product development? Are these daily actions consistent? Do they advance the new paradigms you are marching toward? What needs to be revisited using the OODA Loop and organizational change management plan to ensure everyone is aligned?

The Leadership

We've looked at the empirical data from many project failures among companies trying to embrace change. Leaders must change their approach in executing the schedule and plan envisioned to take companies to the next level. What needs to shift? Orchestrating a project to a successful outcome requires employees and their leaders to take the following steps:

- Assess the readiness and capability of employees to change the way they do their work.
- Gain management's support to supply the needed training, financing, a realistic time line, and scope of work.
- Create a communication plan around the time line and changes to the technology, business model, training, and workflow processes, and schedule regular communications with the whole company.
- Outline the current processes that the technology supports and map the changes to the process and new business models. Don't reconfigure the technology to match outdated processes; instead, realize many processes will have to change.
- Develop an implementation plan and schedule to realistically transition legacy systems to the new systems, running the old systems in parallel for a period to assure a seamless transition.
- Foster a "lessons learned" process so that once the new system is running, improvements and updates can be made seamlessly and employees can be trained on the changes.

Leaders also need the courage to recognize when things are off course, honesty, and when correction is needed, decisiveness to act on input even if the data you'd like isn't present. That's how you become a force multiplier for your company, your employees, and most importantly, your customers.

The Strategy

The loyalty-centric strategy identifies customers the company intends to serve and articulates the desired empathetic, personalized experiences to be delivered. Here are some questions for your customer/employee experience strategy:

- Are we strategically aligning our people (culture), processes, and technologies to deliver the best possible employee experiences, resulting in the best possible customer experiences?
- Are we making customer experience a priority by evaluating our current state and comparing it to customer and employee feedback and best practices to deliver on the art of the possible?
- Are we committing enough resources to make empathy a company-wide effort so customer experience becomes part of our DNA and our brand (and each employee) exudes high-level dedication to the customer/employee experience?

The Process

The process is how things get done by people and technology. If a process has too many steps or is too cumbersome, employees and customers find workarounds, creating inconsistent employee and customer experiences. How well has your organization orchestrated C&E-centric processes to deliver empathetic, personalized customer experiences from their point of view? Here are some process conversation starters:

- Have we laid out all the steps for various customer journeys in our business process mapping?
- Have we mapped out all the steps in how employees serve customers?
- Have we evaluated whether all the steps are necessary?
- Do we have redundancies or steps that no longer make sense?
- Do we have more than one group of employees doing the same thing?
- Are our people, teams, departments, partners, alliances, and more collaborating as pods?

- Do we know when it's best to use AI-driven bots versus human interactions for serving customers?
- Are we empowering both employees and bots with exponential technology to provide great customer experiences?
- Have we looked at our service levels and internal and external processes to produce realistic goals for creating empathetic experiences?

The Technology

Leaders often think of customer/employee experience as just a technology decision: buy the right system and the company's issues will magically disappear. In this fast-paced world, technology allows us to scale consistent, personalized, repeatable, and seamless experiences that show customers and employees empathy. However, while exponential technologies like AI, machine learning, IoT, and the cloud are key to enabling empathetic customer/employee experiences at scale, technology is not the starting point. Let's look at some questions to ask your team as they think about how to transform and deliver great experiences.

- Do we understand the specific business objectives behind each part of the technology matrix?
- Can all the technologies—new and legacy—work and communicate with each other across the entire customer/employee experience and provide the context necessary for a holistic, personalized, empathetic experience?
- Which legacy systems can we keep and what needs to go to effectively deliver consistent, scalable, empathetic customer/employee experiences?
- Are we orchestrating all technologies through one AI/ML engine to utilize customer and employee data across all channels to deliver highly personalized, contextually relevant experiences at scale?
- How can we integrate the new technology and get it up and running to show initial results?
- How will we optimize the new technology to deliver on the business outcomes?

The People/Culture

As we've looked at employee culture and leadership capabilities, we can see everything begins and ends with people. Your human capital talent initiatives include:

- Organization's corporate culture and an MTP^X
- Leadership practices to lead individual and business transformation

- Organizational structure and transitions to a pod operating structure
- Collaboration and conflict resolution methods
- Employee skills, reskilling, and new capabilities training for the new world
- Performance measurement approaches to measure and encourage the transformation
- Change management readiness, risks, and execution strategy, education, and communication

Here are some conversation starters around your human capital and talent processes:

- Are our employees' opinions part of our customer/employee experience strategy?
- How do we gather that information, assess it, assimilate it, and use it in taking the next steps?
- Do we have systems to continuously monitor/measure what employees know, think, and feel about their work and the employee and customer experience?
- Are our customers' points of view included in our customer/employee experience strategy?
- Do we have systems to continuously monitor/measure what customers know, think, need, want, and feel?
- What behaviors are most important for gaining and keeping customers?
- Do we know what drives those behaviors?
- Have we allocated resources, time, and budget for leading the people involved in transforming our customer/employee experience?
- How are we training leaders to shepherd change instead of maintaining the status quo?
- How are we preparing our employees to lead and carry out change?
- How do we gather all this information, assess it, assimilate it, and integrate it into actionable processes?
- How do we make continuous, measurable changes to the right things?

Maximizing CLV and Minimizing Employee Attrition

Why are people so key? Let's first compare the lifetime value of two customers and the company's they buy from.

For Company 1, the customer spends:

- 1st year – $50
- 2nd – $100

- 3rd – $150

For a total of $300 per year per customer.

For Company 2, the customer spends:
- 1st year – $50
- 2nd – $25
- 3rd – $0

For a total of $75 per year per customer

Let's assume the total customer lifetime value for one customer is $300 for Company 1 and $75 for Company 2. Company 1 moves through the OODA process faster than Company 2 (Figure 12.3). They are quick to listen, understand, act, and learn because their employees and customers are top priorities and as a result customers spend more with Company 1.

Let's look at the customer lifetime value for all customers over three years. Let's say both companies have 100,000 customers. At the end of three years (Table 12.2)

Company 1 CLV= 100,000 customers × $300 = $30M
Company 2 CLV = 100,000 customers × $75 = $7.5M

Table 12.2 Comparison of the CLV of two companies.

Customer Lifetime Value	Company 2 – Slower OODA	Company 1 – Faster OODA
CLV Year 1	$5M	$5M
CLV Year 2	$2.5M	$10M
CLV Year 3	$0M	$15M
Total CLV	$7.5M	$30M

Which company would you rather own, work for, or buy from? Repeat business comes from providing what the customer wants and needs. Your revenue comes from customers, and the best way to increase your CLV is by offering better experiences that elicit repeat business.

The Cost of Employee Attrition

According to the Bureau of National Affairs, US businesses lose around $11 billion annually due to employee turnover.[6] With recruiting costs running approximately 1.5 times an annual salary, the ability to engage and retain valuable employees has a significant impact on an organization's bottom line.[7] Globally, voluntary staff turnover accounts for over a trillion dollars every year in recruitment, hiring, training, and productivity costs.

Research has found that highly engaged employees are twice as likely to be top performers—and miss 20 percent fewer workdays.[8] They exceed expectations in performance reviews and are more supportive of organizational change initiatives. Firms with an engaged workforce experienced 26 percent higher employee productivity and lower turnover risk. These firms also can more easily attract top talent.

What about business results? Companies with high levels of employee engagement see 2.3 percent to 3.8 percent greater stock returns annually than competitors, and 13 percent higher total returns to shareholders over five years. By increasing investments in employee engagement by 10 percent, firms can yield $2,400 per employee in increased profit.[9] These statistics confirm the synergistic combination of empathy-based cultures to create compelling work experiences.

Now let's repeat the exercise but look at how experiences affect employee attrition costs. Again, Company 1 advances through the OODA Loop faster than Company 2—listening, understanding, acting, and learning at a swift rate because employees and customers come first. Let's look at company attrition costs; both companies have 10,000 employees.

In the first year Company 1 has an attrition rate of 3 percent per year, and Company 2 has a 10 percent attrition rate per year. The cost to replace an employee is about $50,000 (assuming the salary is around $30,000 and it costs about 1.5 times the salary to replace an employee.)

Company 1's Attrition Costs Calculation in Year 1:
10,000 employees x .03 attrition rate = 300 employees
300 employees x $50,000 = $15,000,000 spent on attrition in year 1

Company 2's Attrition Costs Calculation in Year 1:
10,000 employees x .10 attrition rate = 1,000 employees
1,000 employees x $50,000 = $50,000,000 spent on attrition in year 1

Now let's say that Company 1 is using the OODA Loop and the empathy pillars, which reduces their attrition rate in years 2 and 3 to 1.5 percent. But Company 2 does not improve at all.

Company 1's Attrition Costs Calculation in Years 2 and 3:
10,000 employees x .015 attrition rate = 150 employees
150 employees x $50,000 = $7,500,000 spent on attrition in years 2 & 3

Company 2's Attrition Costs Calculation in Years 2 and 3:
10,000 employees x .10 attrition rate = 1,000 employees
1,000 employees x $50,000 = $50,000,000 spent on attrition in years 2 & 3

Table 12.3 Comparing the cost of attrition for two companies.

Employee Attrition Cost	Company 2 – Slower OODA	Company 1 – Faster OODA
Attrition Year 1	$50M	$15M
Attrition Year 2	$50M	$7.5M
Attrition Year 3	$50M	$7.5M
Total Attrition costs	$150M	$30M

At the end of three years, Table 12.3:
Company 1 Attrition Costs =
$15,000,000 + $7,500,000 + 7,500,000 = $30M

Company 2 Attrition Costs =
$50,000,000 + $50,000,000 + $50,000,000 = $150M

Now if we look at CLV and attrition costs, we can see Company 1 is earning $30 million in revenue and spending $30 million in attrition.

Company 2 is earning $7.5 million in revenue and spending $150 million in attrition.

The best way to reduce attrition costs and increase your employee lifetime value is by offering better experiences that elicit better work experiences. Why spend the money on attrition when you could spend it on improving your customer and employee experiences, thereby increasing your revenue and reducing costs? Both CLV and attrition costs should be incorporated into company metrics to balance revenue, profits, and margins.

Business Work Styles

One way to improve the employee experience is to understand various work styles. As we work together, we intuitively pick up on clues about people's preferred way to interact. If you know a colleague likes punctuality, you make every effort to be on time. We might notice some people like structure while others don't. Some like to work alone; some don't.

When companies don't provide structured processes to understand each other's work styles, they often use a shot-in-the-dark approach. And employees vote with their feet because they do not feel appreciated or respected. Whether employees feel appreciated and respected has everything to do with how you interact with them based on their style— and that's where work style assessments come into play.

One system that provides excellent insight into work style preferences is the DISC system, which describes human behavior in various situations.

- D is for how you respond to challenges
- I for how you influence others
- S for preferred pace
- C for how you respond to rules and procedures

Our uniqueness as individuals comes through in a distinct mix of behaviors. These attributes are not bad or good; they just are who we are. By tuning in to each other's behavior styles, you gain a deeper appreciation, perspective, and understanding of one another. By communicating on each other's frequency, you are more likely to be heard, acknowledged, and understood; interactions become more meaningful and work more satisfying.

Figure 12.4 shows the profile of a boss and employee's work styles. The styles are opposite, which can create conflict if we're unaware. But diversity in work styles can also be the reason behind a team's success.

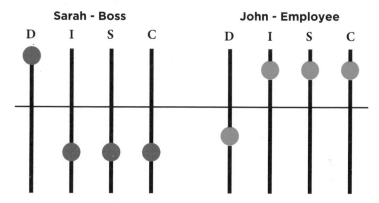

Figure 12.4 Work style profiles of a boss and an employee.

Boss Sarah gives employee John an assignment to research all the various companies they are considering buying from. Sarah's expectations of John are based on her work style and include that . . .

- The work will be done quickly (high D)
- The employee will provide a bulleted, short presentation with a few facts (high D)
- The solutions will be significantly out of the box, with the latest and most advanced capabilities (low C)
- They won't have much to discuss when reviewing the study's outcome and choices—the boss is just looking for an answer (low I)

Several weeks go by, and Sarah wonders where the report is, thinking she could have done it faster herself. She goes to John's office and requests the report. Because of his work style, John needs socialization time before plunging into an explanation, but he can see Sarah is frustrated.

John tries to improve the situation by explaining in detail how he's contacted vendors, received their brochures, and read them at home, scrutinizing the options. John doesn't understand why Sarah is frustrated—while the research isn't fully complete, his process has been thorough. He decides to give Sarah the information he's collected so far, four binders full of data, but Sarah is still frustrated.

John feels unappreciated and demotivated. He thinks, "Why bother working so hard when Sarah is never happy with anything I do?" Sarah thinks, "Why don't people just do what I ask? I'll ask Georgia; she'll do what I want." What Sarah doesn't see is that because Georgia has the same work style as her (high D), she will work quickly but won't be as complete, and they could miss essential information.

What happened on a behavioral level? If John and Sarah had understood each other's behavioral profiles, John would have never . . .

- Taken so long to get Sarah an initial review (high D and low S like fast turnaround)
- Given her four binders of data (high D wants a short synopsis)
- Told Sarah the long story about how he did his work (low I and high D get straight to the point)

With the example, you can see how not understanding each other's behavioral work styles can create conflict, slow down work and productivity, stretch out the schedule, and increase costs. You can also see that if John and Sarah, aware of their differences, had adapted and set expectations up front, they both could have felt confident about the work being done and gotten to the best solution faster, both feeling empowered to continue doing their best.

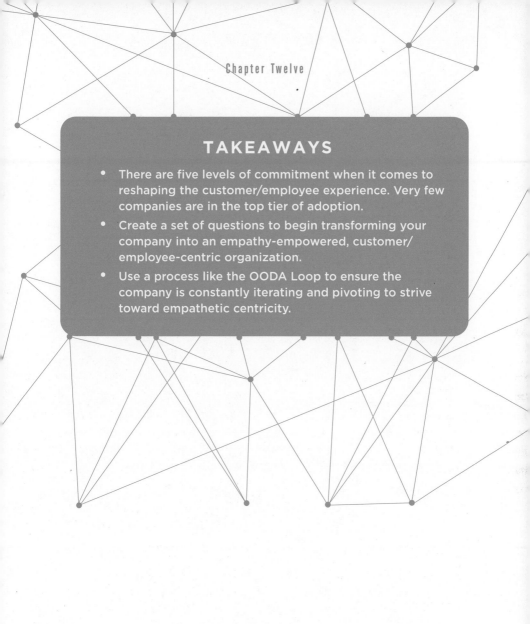

TAKEAWAYS

- There are five levels of commitment when it comes to reshaping the customer/employee experience. Very few companies are in the top tier of adoption.

- Create a set of questions to begin transforming your company into an empathy-empowered, customer/ employee-centric organization.

- Use a process like the OODA Loop to ensure the company is constantly iterating and pivoting to strive toward empathetic centricity.

" It's good to have
an end to a journey
toward; but it's the
journey that matters,
in the end.

—Ernest Hemingway

IGNITING A CUSTOMER AND EMPLOYEE RESPECT MOVEMENT

The foundation of empathy lies in the ability to see things through someone else's eyes. It is the conscious decision to focus on the needs of another person from their point of view, not yours. For a business, it means that all of its people, processes, strategies, leadership, and technologies are aligned around its customers' and employees' point of view—not the company's.

It means the business has recognized the need to put employees and customers first, not only in theory but in practice. And it is on its way to changing the paradigm within its own company; from one of narrow company centricity to one that champions putting customers and employees first as the most profitable action it can take.

Before we talk about the customer and employee respect movement, we provided an assessment to help you and your organization better understand how you take the concepts in this book and apply them to your business—i.e., convert them into Empathy in Action and become part of a bigger paradigm shift in business.

How Does Your Company Score on the Empathy in Action Adoption Curve?

To help companies understand where they stand on the adoption of Experience-as-a-Service and empathy, you can access our assessment at **www.genesys.com/assessment.** There, you will receive an initial score that indicates where your company lands on the Empathy in Action Adoption Curve, along with scores for each of your Systems of Empathy and ideas to help your organization evolve (Figure C.1).

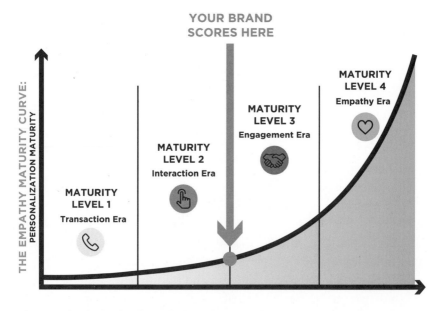

Figure C.1 Example of an Empathy in Action assessment score.

This assessment evaluates your ability to deliver experiences as a service and empathy from both the customer's and the employee's points of view (Figure C.2).

This tool is intended to gauge how well your company uses the Empathy Pillars and systems we discussed in Chapter 9 and provide you with a personalized gap analysis, enabling you to know what you need to **listen** to across customers' channels interactions. It will also evaluate whether, as you listen, you can **understand** and **predict** what the customer wants and needs. Finally, it will help determine whether you have the context necessary to take the best course of **action** to satisfy that need.

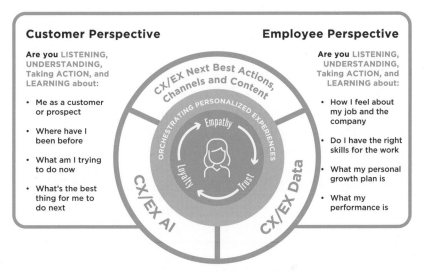

Figure C.2 Assessing abilities from the employee's and customer's point of view.

In parallel with improving your organization's ability to listen, understand and predict, act, and **learn** from customer interactions, our assessment also looks at how you empower your employees. This is done by evaluating the same four Empathy Pillars—and your ability to deliver on them—this time from the employee point of view. By spotting the gaps and then equipping employees with needed context and understanding, they are then empowered to provide an improved, more empathic experience to their customers. And they'll be more confident and motivated, enjoy their work more, and feel like they're making a difference.

The assessment also looks at CX/EX leadership, people/culture, strategy, brand promise, processes, and your use of personalized, people-focused exponential technologies.

Maturity of Empathy in Action

We've created a maturity model to help you put a framework around where you are and what you need to do to reach the next level of Experience as a Service. We take our four CX/EX eras in Chapter 5 and correlate them to a traditional maturity model, consisting of four stages, or eras: transactions, interactions, engagements, and empathy.

As you look at your current capabilities, consider the damage you may have done to your empathic capabilities if major blind spots are present in your company (Figure C.3). Throughout the book, we highlighted typical blind spots as well as some more public examples of how being business-centric can become a major detriment to employees and customers.

Traditional ways of handling the customer and employee experience (i.e., focusing on business-centric efficiency and effectiveness) result in a deficit for that same experience, leaving the company at a clear disadvantage—especially when compared to those that started on this journey long ago, and who are now marching forward with a sense of CX/EX purpose and passion.

The blind spots we've explored range from low customer lifetime value to poor, noncustomer/employee-centric decisions. All of these result in poor profits and missed opportunities for innovation. Not correcting your blind spots leaves your company in the dust, far behind your more agile competition. They hurt your brand reputation, cost you in employee and customer attrition, and often mean going out of business.

Stubborn companies, so attached to the way things are, bleed money in the long-term by effectually sending their customers and employees to competitors by delivering bad experiences. In most cases, the experience these recalcitrant businesses provide is so bad that it can't garner anything resembling trust or loyalty; instead, it propels defection along with public contention and dissension by word of mouth, both in person and on digital channels.

Is this what you want for your company?

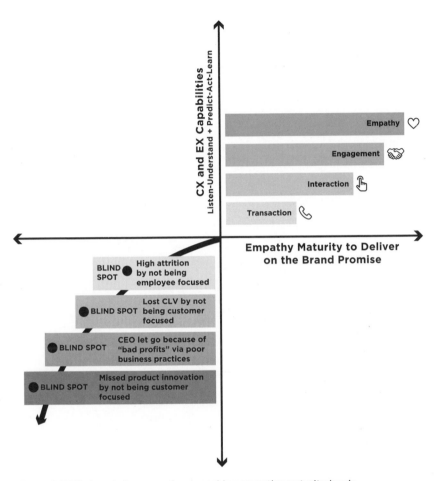

Figure C.3 Blind spots keep you from reaching empathy maturity levels.

When we place the old, business-centric efficiency and effectiveness paradigms alongside the new, empathy-based ones, we can see clearly how transitioning to the new paradigm digs the company out of the old ways that push customers and employees away (Figure C.4). And as we move up on the maturity capabilities spectrum by using the lens of empathy to reevaluate efficiency and effectiveness, the true payoff becomes a reality.

We can then begin to develop relationships with our customers and our employees that result in empathy, trust, and loyalty for the long-term.

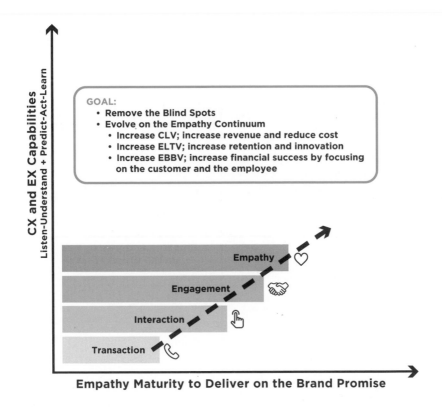

Empathy Maturity to Deliver on the Brand Promise

Figure C.4 Moving up the continuum of highly personalized, empathetic experiences happens by removing blind spots and increasing capabilities.

Regardless of the size or industry, all companies can provide empathetic, mission-critical customer and employee experiences. And since customer/employee experience is a key differentiator, a small competitor that is more agile and has lower operating costs can quickly knock a larger company off their game. Customer/employee experience tools and capabilities no longer require large capital expenditures. This shouldn't come as a surprise, since this book is full of examples that demonstrate the many ways exponential technologies reduce costs while providing dramatically improved capabilities over time.

What we have learned is that the brands who make customer/ employee experience their differentiator have better financial results, simply because they are focusing on the true value of the customer, the employee, and the perspectives of each. Every time a customer or an employee has a standout experience with a company, it sets the bar higher for the next experience. And, as we've discussed, expectations are only going to increase. With the number of customer interactions growing at an astonishing pace in this digital age, it's no wonder some organizations are struggling to keep up.

Think about the last time you reached out to a company. What was that experience like? When looking through the lens of the customer, most people wonder, "What was that company thinking? That experience was horrible!" Yet it's as if we get amnesia once we arrive at work, and we forget how much we dislike bad customer and employee experiences.

We can't allow that status quo amnesia to exist. Nobody wants cringe-worthy experiences. We've all been on the receiving end of bad experiences, and we know how frustrating they are on a personal level. Now we need to take that knowledge from personal experience and apply it at work so we don't damage the company's value and reputation. Research even shows customer effort is 40 percent more accurate at predicting customer loyalty than customer satisfaction.[1]

When you make customers feel remembered, heard, and understood, you build brand affinity and loyalty. And when you build a company culture that employees are proud to be part of, they take up the company banner and advocate on your behalf.

More than anything, it's this level of loyalty that drives us toward true success in business and in life.

Fueling the CX/EX Respect Movement

On a personal level, the movement toward empathy should encourage all of us to think differently. Take a moment to listen to the people around you—don't jump to conclusions. In writing this book, we took the time to reflect on the ways our human differences make all of our interactions, work outcomes, and lives better across the board.

As a customer, expect empathy from the companies you do business with. Even better, demand it from them. If you aren't receiving it, it's time to let them know that it is not okay. You can do this by spreading the word and connecting with other unhappy customers. Imagine for a moment what could happen if customers collectively stood together and challenged companies that disrespect, demean, or fail to empathize with the people they serve. What effect would this have on how all companies treat customers?

This book is more than a guide. It's a call to action urging everyone to take a stand, demand more, and live by the conviction that your hard-earned dollars deserve respect.

It's a timely reminder of the power and influence you have as a customer. If you don't buy from a business, they can't stay in business. It's a simple equation. No customers, no business. We are serious. Stop putting up with bad experiences. If you allow companies to think it's okay, they won't ever change. But if they suddenly start losing revenue and customers are honest about why they are leaving, few executives would want to be responsible for going out of business because they didn't take your experiences into consideration. Especially now, with blind spots revealed and paths cleared to customer and employee respect.

Don't think we've forgotten the other half of the equation. If you work for a company that doesn't respect employees, say something. Make yourself heard. Work with them to see what can be done. And if you are in one of those "not invented here" cultures, consider other options for work. Otherwise, it will eat at your soul. You deserve better.

Again, without employees to serve customers, businesses simply can't stay in business. It's up to each and every one of us to drive real change through the choices we make in our everyday lives.

Igniting CX/EX Respect in Your Company's Culture

Do you understand what it's like to do business with you? Empathy is the first step on your journey toward disruption. Go on your website, call your contact center, deal with your chatbot, wait in your IVR. Go incognito, if necessary, and fully inhabit the customer and employee experience as a customer or employee. Put yourself in their shoes.

You might get shifted around from agent to supervisor to manager and still not get your issue resolved. Maybe you'll realize how frustrated, demoralized, and held back your own employees feel. There's no guarantee that this kind of empathy will be pleasant to learn. Sometimes it's painful or even embarrassing to realize how your organization's blind spots have affected its operations. You may begin to understand what your customer goes through, and you might realize why they don't like interacting, contacting, or buying from you.

But while these negative experiences might be difficult to endure, they are also necessary. They are an act of courage that tells the world that you are more than a figurehead—whatever your title, you are a leader, and you take your customers, your employees, and your company seriously enough to do whatever it takes to improve, transform, and thrive in this new, unbounded era of empathy.

This means slowing down to go fast. It means taking the time to listen to and evaluate your customer experiences from the root. It means using tools like our assessment to truly understand why those experiences, both the employee's and the customer's, aren't all that they can be. Use the information in this book to start the process of giving your customers and employees the experience they want and deserve. Don't ask for their loyalty—earn it. In respecting them, you put yourself in the company of those iconic brands we know and love. They stand out because they prioritize us and treat us well, no matter our question, problem, or issue.

It takes a village to succeed. Partner with companies who specialize in enabling the kind of transformational success you've read about in this book. Collaborate with them and build capabilities that make it possible for you to provide customer and employee experiences that boost your profits. Allow your teams and partners to join you in building brand loyalty by inspiring the best qualities of human interaction and celebrating our innate desire to connect through changes to your business' culture. And remember: strategy is not enough. You'll need the brand promise, leadership, strategy, processes, exponential technology, and people/culture to scale personalized Empathy in Action.

Look for technologies developed on a foundation of design-thinking—with empathy as the first principle. The technologies and processes you choose must be capable of orchestrating personalized experiences by incorporating customer/employee-based problem-solving (effectiveness) in a timely manner (efficiency). They must allow you to provide amazing human interactions with the right context and understanding to get it right the first time.

These aren't merely business values. These are human values. And we still believe that human values power the best experiences and the best possible realities for us all. We are all more than customers, and we are all more than employees—we're people first. It's time to make customer and employee experiences truly personal.

TAKEAWAYS

- Make personalized Empathy in Action your top goal.

- Start now.

- Never stop.

ABOUT THE AUTHORS

Tony Bates

Tony is the chairman and chief executive officer of Genesys®. He leads the company's strategy, direction, and operations in more than 100 countries and oversees a global team of more than 5,000 employees.

Tony has decades of experience steering business-to-business and business-to-consumer companies through major market transitions and rapid scaling. A passionate technologist at heart, Tony began his career in network operations and internet infrastructure, teaching himself to code during his daily train commute. He swiftly gained the business acumen to advance into trusted executive roles at some of the world's most respected global SaaS companies.

His career highlights include leading the Service Provider business at Cisco, growing its Enterprise and Commercial division to more than $20 billion in annual revenue. He also served as CEO of Skype, where he was responsible for expanding the business to over 170 million connected users. Once Skype was acquired by Microsoft, Tony became president, where he was responsible for unified communications before serving as executive vice president of business development and developers.

In addition to his role at Genesys, Tony continues to serve on the board of directors at both VMware and eBay.

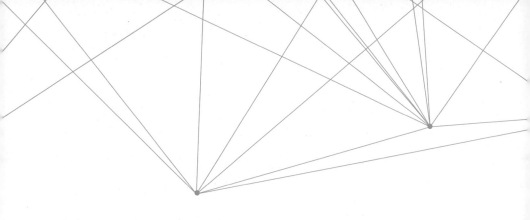

Dr. Natalie Petouhoff

Natalie is a senior customer experience strategist and business consultant at Genesys®. Her career spans many years in technology and customer and employee experience, holding positions in and consulting at companies including Salesforce, Hulu, Marriott, General Motors, General Electric, Sony Pictures Entertainment, Weber Shandwick, Forrester Research, PWC Consulting, Hughes Electronics, Pepsi, Verizon, Best Buy, Procter & Gamble, Chevrolet, and Electrolux.

Her PhD in Material Science and Engineering from the University of California and years as a "rocket scientist" provide her with the left-brain skills to strategically analyze how things work and redesign the world for a better future.

In her endeavors, Natalie has focused on the interplay between the evolution of technology and who we are as humans. From her early days as an engineer, she remains a true believer in "what is good for employees and customers is ultimately what is also good for companies." As a speaker and participant at Singularity University, she's captivated by the rapid advancement and impact of exponential technologies and how they are reshaping our lives and businesses.

Natalie's current passion is shifting outdated paradigms by juxtaposing current beliefs with seemingly contradictory ones to reveal insights to drive the future of work, customer's experiences, businesses, and humanity forward. She believes we can imbue technology with our hopes and dreams for a future focused on bettering humanity. We just need to understand what we are optimizing for and why.

> **"** Make personalized
> Empathy in Action
> your top goal.
> Start now.
> Never stop.

—Tony Bates & Dr. Natalie Petouhoff

ACKNOWLEDGMENTS

We thank our families for their unending patience and support:

Tony's family: Cori, Matt, David, Claire, and Ethan

Natalie's family: Tanya, Mike, Nick, Anna, Alex, Nick, Justin, Michael, Lynn, Sarah, Aunt Olga, Leonard, Tushka, City Kitty, and Angel

We thank the people who shaped and influenced our professional gravitas:

Tony's career: Steve Ballmer, John Chambers, Vint Cerf, John Donahoe, Egon Durban, Graeme Fraser, Pat Gelsinger, Dave Goldberg, Tom Herbst, Daniel Karrenberg, Ed Kozel, Terpstra Pierre Lamond, Michael Marks, Shantanu Narayen, Brian Ruder, John Seymour (for believing in me in the beginning), Marten Terpstra, Roland Trice, Mike Volpi, and Tarim Wasim

Natalie's career: David Armano, Marc Benioff, Sandy Carter, Jay Baer, Jeanne Bliss, Judith Coley, Alex Danyon, Sanjay Dholakia, Barbara Gonzalez, Charlie Isaacs, Wendy Lea, Erica Lehman, Kate Leggett, Charlene Li, Sheryl Kingstone, Beverly Macy, Amy Mildren, Charles Miller, Renata Muerez, David Myron, Art Norman, Sharon O'Neill, Dimitris S. Papageorgiou, Jan Ryan, Beth Montag-Schmaltz, Jenny Sussin, John Taschek, and Lois Townsend

We thank all of our colleagues at Genesys and industry thought leaders for the work they do every day and their efforts toward the book:

Adam Ackerman, Faheem Ahmed, Dan Arra, Margaret Baumgartner, Claire Beatty, Chris Becker, Martha Blanco, TJ Blanchflower, Merijn te Booij, Lara Booth, Daylan Burlison, Shannon Cannizzaro, Andrea Chin, Joseph Ciuffo, John E. Clark, Jessica Coburn, Judith Coley, Ginger Conlon, Julieta Conconi, Sergio Coretti, Scott Cravotta, Matthew Cunningham, Giuliano Da Silva, Adriana Defina, Janelle Dickerson, Janelle Dieken, William Dummett, Yasser El-Haggan, Matt Fangman, Andrea Friio, Peter Graf, Charlie Godfrey, Paul Greenberg, Barbara Gonzalez, Ricardo Saltz Gulko, Denise Hamilton, Chris Helzerman, Trish Hearn, Mark Henderson, John Hernandez, Rob Hilsen, Jill Hundley, Brad James, Odessa Jenkins, Olivier Jouve, Maggie Kelley, Joyce Kim, Zane Knight, Sarah Koniniec, Tejus Korde, Jeannette Larsen, Kellsey Lequick, David Liddicoat, Chrissy Linzy, ML Maco, Eva Majercsik, Elcenora Martinez, Bridgette McAdoo, Benji McDonald, Christie Minns, Daniel Morales, Brittany Mullen, Paige Mummert, Becca Mayers, Alice Nagle, Jason Napieralski, Toni Newton, Jack Nichols, Emily Olin, Rick Olson, Barry O'Sullivan, Pierluigi Pace, Leslie Paterson, Keith Pearce, Valentina Postelnicu, Arjun Ramchandran, Michele Remsing, Jim Rene, Tricia Reynolds, Johanna Rogers, Steven Rust, Melanie Salvatierra, Angela Santarossa, Cameron Smith, Joe Smyth, Prashanth Sreetharan, Mark Stanley, Andy Stuckey, Brian Swartz, Adrian Swinscoe, Eric Thomas, Andrea Trozak, Gina Tyree, Lanette Valles, Lisa Varni, Tibor Vass, Marcee Wardell, Alan Webber, Rutger Wilschut, Simon Wright, and James Xiao

And we thank our publisher and editors for their tireless dedication to making this become the best book possible:

Jessica Angerstein, Chhavi Arya, Rohit Bhargava, Kameron Bryant-Sergejev, Judith Coley, Shreya Jain, Nancy Kirwan, Marnie McMahon, Emily Montague, and Herb Schaffner

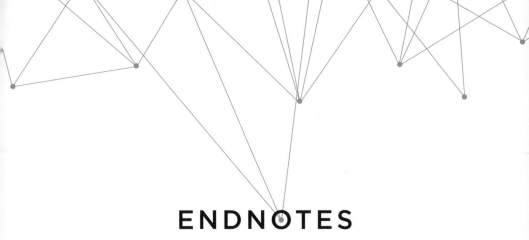

ENDNOTES

Introduction

1. Satya Narayanan, "Changing the Way We Work, Live, Play and Learn as a Team," *Cisco Blogs* (blog), October 4, 2018, https://blogs.cisco.com/wearecisco/changing-the-way-we-work-live-play-and-learn-as-a-team.

2. Farhad Manjoo, "Jurassic Web: The Internet of 1996 Is Almost Unrecognizable Compared with What We Have Today," *Slate Magazine*, February 24, 2009, https://slate.com/technology/2009/02/the-unrecognizable-internet-of-1996.html.

3. "Internet Users to Exceed 2 Billion by the End of 2010," *BBC News,* October 19, 2010, https://www.bbc.com/news/technology-11576486.

4. "Internet 2010 in Numbers," Solarwinds Pingdom, January 12, 2011, https://www.pingdom.com/blog/internet-2010-in-numbers/.

5. Joseph Johnson, "Global Digital Population as of January 2021," Statista, April 7, 2021, https://www.statista.com/statistics/617136/digital-population-worldwide/.

6. S. O'Dea, "Number of Smartphones Sold to End Users Worldwide from 2007 to 2021," Statista, March 31, 2021, https://www.statista.com/statistics/263437/global-smartphone-sales-to-end-users-since-2007/.

7. Ibid.

8. "GoPro Announces Fourth Quarter and Full Year 2015 Results," GoPro (Press Release and Media), February 3, 2016, https://investor.gopro.com/press-releases/press-release-details/2016/GoPro-Announces-Fourth-Quarter-and-Full-Year-2015-Results/default.aspx.

9. "Personalization & Empathy in Customer Experience: Multinational Consumer Survey" (Genesys, June 2020), https://www.genesys.com/report/the-connected-customer-experience.

10. Ibid.

11. John Kotter, "Leading Change: Why Transformation Efforts Fail," *Harvard Business Review,* May-June 1995 Issue, https://hbr.org/1995/05/leading-change-why-transformation-efforts-fail-2.

Chapter One

1. Tom Puthiyamadam and José Reyes, "Experience Is Everything: Here's How to Get It Right" (PwC, 2018), https://www.pwc.com/us/en/zz-test/assets/pwc-consumer-intelligence-series-customer-experience.pdf#page=9.

2. "2020 Global Customer Experience Benchmarking Report. The Connected

Customer: Delivering an Effortless Experience" (NTT Ltd., 2020), https://www.dimensiondata.com/en-gb/expertise/intelligent-customer-experience/customer-experience-benchmark-report-2020#form.

3. Ibid.

4. Daniel Goleman, Emotional Intelligence: Why It Can Matter More Than IQ (New York: Random House Publishing Group, 2005).

5. Clayton M. Christensen et al., Competing Against Luck: The Story of Innovation and Customer Choice, 1st edition (New York, NY: Harper Business, 2016).

6. Chris Woodford, "Technology Timeline," Explain That Stuff, March 18, 2021, http://www.explainthatstuff.com/timeline.html.

7. Alastair Baker, "How Were Steam Engines Used in Agriculture?," Bressingham Steam & Gardens (blog), August 31, 2014, https://www.bressingham.co.uk/blog/posts/2014/how-were-steam-engines-used-in-agriculture.aspx.

8. "Industrial Revolution - From Industry 1.0 to Industry 4.0," Desoutter Industrial Tools, accessed August 31, 2021, https://www.desouttertools.com/industry-4-0/news/503/industrial-revolution-from-industry-1-0-to-industry-4-0; "Fourth Industrial Revolution," in Wikipedia, The Free Encyclopedia, August 27, 2021, https://en.wikipedia.org/w/index.php?title=Fourth_Industrial_Revolution&oldid=1040901751.

9. John Louis Recchiuti, "America Moves to the City," Khan Academy, accessed August 31, 2021, https://www.khanacademy.org/humanities/us-history/the-gilded-age/gilded-age/a/america-moves-to-the-city.

10. Madison Horne, "Photos Reveal Shocking Conditions of Tenement Slums in Late 1800s," History, January 22, 2020, https://www.history.com/news/tenement-photos-jacob-riis-nyc-immigrants.

11. "Industrial Revolution: Steam Engine," Ducksters, accessed August 31, 2021, https://www.ducksters.com/history/us_1800s/steam_engine_industrial_revolution.php.

12. Freddie Wilkinson, "Industrialization, Labor, and Life," National Geographic, January 27, 2020, http://www.nationalgeographic.org/article/industrialization-labor-and-life/6th-grade/.

13. "Johari Window," in Wikipedia, The Free Encyclopedia, July 15, 2021, https://en.wikipedia.org/w/index.php?title=Johari_window&oldid=1033722333.

14. Werner Erhard, "The Eranos Foundation: 'A Breakthrough in Individual and Social Transformation,'" Werner Erhard, June 18, 2006, http://www.wernererhard.com/work_cont.html.

15. Trent Hamm, "If You Want Different Results, You Have to Try Different Approaches," The Simple Dollar (blog), April 8, 2020, https://www.thesimpledollar.com/make-money/if-you-want-different-results-you-have-to-try-different-approaches/.

16. Rob Markey et al., "The Loyalty Economy," Harvard Business Review, February 2020, https://hbr.org/2020/01/the-loyalty-economy.

17. Peter F. Drucker, Management: Tasks, Responsibilities, Practices (New York: Harper Business, 1993)..

18. "The Titans That Built America," The History Channel and Stephen David Entertainment, accessed August 31, 2021, https://www.history.com/shows/the-

titans-that-built-america.

19. Milton Friedman, "A Friedman Doctrine-- The Social Responsibility of Business Is to Increase Its Profits," The New York Times, September 13, 1970, https://www.nytimes.com/1970/09/13/archives/a-friedman-doctrine-the-social-responsibility-of-business-is-to.html.

20. "Purpose of a Corporation and How Companies Put It Into Action," Business Roundtable, August 2020, https://opportunity.businessroundtable.org/ourcommitment/.

21. Rob Markey, "Are You Undervaluing Your Customers?," Harvard Business Review, February 2020, https://hbr.org/2020/01/are-you-undervaluing-your-customers.

22. Undercover Boss, (CBS) https://www.cbs.com/shows/undercover_boss/.

23. Roger L. Martin, "The Age of Customer Capitalism," Harvard Business Review, February 2010, https://hbr.org/2010/01/the-age-of-customer-capitalism.

24. Roger L. Martin, When More Is Not Better: Overcoming America's Obsession with Economic Efficiency (Boston, Massachusetts: Harvard Business Review Press, 2020).

25. Katja Battarbee, Jane Fulton Suri, and Suzanne Gibbs Howard, "Empathy on the Edge: Scaling and Sustaining a Human-Centered Approach in the Evolving Practice of Design," IDEO, 2011, https://new-ideo-com.s3.amazonaws.com/assets/files/pdfs/news/Empathy_on_the_Edge.pdf.

26. "Personalization & Empathy in Customer Experience: Multinational Consumer Survey" (Genesys, June 2020), https://www.genesys.com/report/the-connected-customer-experience.

27. David Weinberger et al., The Cluetrain Manifesto, 1st edition (Cambridge, Mass.: Basic Books, 2000).

Chapter Two

1. iED Team, "The 4 Industrial Revolutions," Institute of Entrepreneurship Development (blog), June 30, 2019, https://ied.eu/project-updates/the-4-industrial-revolutions/.

2. "An Exponential Primer: Your Guide to Our Essential Concepts," Singularity University, accessed August 31, 2021, https://su.org/concepts/.

3. Bill Briggs, Nishita Henry, and Andy Main, "Tech Trends 2019: Beyond the Digital Frontier" (Deloitte Insights, 2019), https://www2.deloitte.com/content/dam/insights/us/articles/Tech-Trends-2019/DI_TechTrends2019.pdf.

4. Peter H. Diamandis, "5 AI Breakthroughs We'll Likely See in the Next 5 Years," Singularity Hub (blog), April 26, 2019, https://singularityhub.com/2019/04/26/5-ai-breakthroughs-well-likely-see-in-the-next-5-years/.

5. Klaus Schwab, The Fourth Industrial Revolution (New York: Currency, 2017).

6. George Westerman, Didier Bonnet, and Andrew McAfee, Leading Digital: Turning Technology into Business Transformation (Boston, Massachusetts: Harvard Business Review Press, 2014).

7. Ibid.

8. Charlene Li, The Disruption Mindset: Why Some Organizations Transform While Others Fail (Oakton, VA: IdeaPress Publishing, 2019).

9. Peter H. Diamandis and Steven Kotler, Abundance: The Future Is Better Than You Think (New York: Free Press, 2012); Peter H. Diamandis and Steven Kolter, The

Future Is Faster Than You Think: How Converging Technologies Are Transforming Business, Industries, and Our Lives (Simon & Schuster, 2020).

10. Steve Cichon, "Everything from 1991 Radio Shack Ad I Now Do with My Phone," Trending Buffalo (blog), January 14, 2014, http://www.trendingbuffalo.com/life/uncle-steves-buffalo/everything-from-1991-radio-shack-ad-now/.

11. Peter H. Diamandis and Steven Kotler, *Bold: How to Go Big, Create Wealth and Impact the World* (New York; NY: Simon & Schuster, 2016).

12. "Too Busy to Improve—Performance Management —Square Wheels" by Alan O'Rourke, CC BY 2.0 https://creativecommons.org/licenses/by/2.0, via Wikimedia Commons.

13. Chris H, "Rolls-Royce: Optimising Jet Engine Maintenance with Machine Learning," *Technology and Operations Management a Digital Initiative of Harvard Business School* (blog), November 13, 2018, https://digital.hbs.edu/platform-rctom/submission/rolls-royce-optimising-jet-engine-maintenance-with-machine-learning/.

14. Diamandis and Kotler, *Bold*.

15. Carla Tardi, "Moore's Law," *Investopedia* (blog), February 24, 2021, https://www.investopedia.com/terms/m/mooreslaw.asp.

16. Diamandis and Kotler, *Bold*.

17. Nicholas Mirzoeff, *How to See the World: An Introduction to Images, from Self-Portraits to Selfies, Maps to Movies, and More* (New York: Basic Books, 2016).

18. "InfoTrends' Study Shows Photography and Videography Industry Open to Change," Keypoint Intelligence, March 13, 2019, https://keypointintelligence.com/about-us/company-news/keypoint-intelligence-infotrends-study-shows-photography-and-videography-industry-open-to-change/.

19. Kevin R. Donley, "Digital Trends: Where's Your Camera?," *Multimediaman* (blog), August 30, 2016, https://multimediaman.blog/tag/digital-photography/.

20. Jeff Desjardins, "How Long Does It Take to Hit 50 Million Users?," *Visual Capitalist* (blog), June 8, 2018, https://www.visualcapitalist.com/how-long-does-it-take-to-hit-50-million-users/.

21. "Google Search Statistics," Internet Live Stats, accessed August 31, 2021, https://www.internetlivestats.com/google-search-statistics/.

22. Dave Evans, "The Internet of Things: How the Next Evolution of the Internet Is Changing Everything" (Cisco IBSG, April 2011), https://www.cisco.com/c/dam/en_us/about/ac79/docs/innov/IoT_IBSG_0411FINAL.pdf.

23. "IoT Trends to Expect in 2021," Krakul, December 18, 2020, https://krakul.eu/iot-trends-to-expect/.

24. Elizabeth Weise, "15,000 Robots Usher in Amazon's Cyber Monday," Krem2, December 2, 2014, https://www.krem.com/article/tech/15000-robots-usher-in-amazons-cyber-monday/293-157188459.

25. David Edwards, "Amazon Now Has 200,000 Robots Working in Its Warehouses," Robotics & Automation News, January 21, 2020, https://roboticsandautomationnews.com/2020/01/21/amazon-now-has-200000-robots-working-in-its-warehouses/28840/.

Chapter Three

1. "Television Delivers People," in *Wikipedia, The Free Encyclopedia*, August 29, 2021, https://en.wikipedia.org/w/index.php?title=Television_Delivers_People&oldid=1041182817.

2. Richard Serra and Carlota Fay Schoolman, *Television Delivers People (1973)*, YouTube Video (KunstSpektrum), 2011, https://www.youtube.com/watch?v=LvZYwaQlJsg.

3. Martha Mendoza, *Article: Internet users can get paid to surf the Web* (Associated Press Archive, 1999).

4. Usenet discussion message, Newsgroup, from Steve Atkins, December 1999 (Google Groups Search, Accessed 2017).

5. "You're Not the Customer; You're the Product," Quote Investigator, July 16, 2017, https://quoteinvestigator.com/2017/07/16/product/.

6. Claire Wolfe, *Little Brother Is Watching You: The Menace of Corporate America* (Port Townsend, Washington: Breakout Productions, 1996).

7. Tom Johnson, "You're Not the Customer, You're the Product," *Google Groups*, June 22, 2001, https://groups.google.com/g/rec.arts.tv.interactive/c/EY-nOSMlAPE/m/GtKHp6qQBiUJ?pli=1.

8. MetaFilter, "User-Driven Discontent," MetaFilter (weblog), August 26, 2010, http://bit.ly/93JYCJ.

9. Steffan Heuer and Pernille Tranberg, *Fake It! Guide to Digital Self-Defense.* (CreateSpace Independent Publishing Platform, 2013).

Chapter Four

1. Andrew Perrin, "Half of Americans Have Decided Not to Use A Product Or Service Because of Privacy Concerns," *PEW Research*, April 14, 2020, https://www.pewresearch.org/fact-tank/2020/04/14/half-of-americans-have-decided-not-to-use-a-product-or-service-because-of-privacy-concerns/.

2. "Personalization & Empathy in Customer Experience: Multinational Consumer Survey" (Genesys, June 2020), https://www.genesys.com/report/the-connected-customer-experience.

3. Seth Grimes, "Humanizing the Customer, via Neuromarketing," *Breakthrough Analysis* (blog), June 6, 2016, http://breakthroughanalysis.com/2016/06/06/neuromarketing-humanizing-the-customer/.

4. T.J. Keitt, "The US Customer Experience Index, 2021: How Brands Build Loyalty with the Quality of Their Experience," Forrester, June 1, 2021, https://www.forrester.com/report/The-US-Customer-Experience-Index-2021/RES165797.

5. Jake Sorofman, "Gartner Surveys Confirm Customer Experience Is the New Battlefield," *Gartner* (blog), October 23, 2014, https://blogs.gartner.com/jake-sorofman/gartner-surveys-confirm-customer-experience-new-battlefield/.

6. Satish Shankar and James Allen, "Keeping Up with Your Customers," *Bain & Company* (blog), September 3, 2006, https://www.bain.com/insights/keeping-up-with-your-customers/.

7. "The Role of Brand in Customer Experience," McorpCX, accessed August 31, 2021, https://www.mcorpcx.com/articles/the-role-of-brand-in-customer-experience.

8. B. Joseph Pine and James H. Gilmore, *The Experience Economy: Competing for Customer Time, Attention, and Money* (Boston, Massachusetts: Harvard Business Review Press, 2019).

9. Ibid.

10. Florian Stahl et al., "The Impact of Brand Equity on Customer Acquisition, Retention, and Profit Margin," *Journal of Marketing* 76, no. 4 (July 2012): 44–63, https://doi.org/10.1509/jm.10.0522.

11. Lynda Dugdale, "How David Thodey Put Customers First at Telstra," *INTHEBLACK* (blog), April 1, 2015, https://www.intheblack.com/articles/2015/04/01/the-rise-of-david-thodey-outgoing-telstra-ceo.

Chapter Five

1. Kristina Killgrove, "Meet the Worst Businessman of the 18th Century BC," *Forbes*, May 11, 2018, https://www.forbes.com/sites/kristinakillgrove/2018/05/11/meet-the-worst-businessman-of-the-18th-century/.

2. "Complaint tablet to Ea-Nasir 2020" by Zunkir is licensed by CC BY-SA 4.0, https://creativecommons.org/licenses/by-sa/4.0 via Wikimedia Commons.

3. "Muzak," in *Wikipedia, The Free Encyclopedia*, August 19, 2021, https://en.wikipedia.org/wiki/Muzak.

Chapter Six

1. Fred Reichheld, *The Ultimate Question: Driving Good Profits and True Growth*, (Boston, Massachusetts: Harvard Business School Press, 2006).

2. Ibid.

3. Howard Tiersky and Michelle McKenna, *Winning Digital Customers: The Antidote to Irrelevance* (San Antonio, TX: Cranberry Press, LLC, 2021).

4. Benjamin Snyder, "7 Insights from Legendary Investor Warren Buffett," *CNBC Make It*, May 1, 2017, https://www.cnbc.com/2017/05/01/7-insights-from-legendary-investor-warren-buffett.html.

5. Michael Redbord, "The State of Customer Service in 2019," *Hubspot* (blog), June 9, 2021, https://blog.hubspot.com/service/customer-service-2019.

6. "Edelman Trust Barometer Special Report: In Brands We Trust?" (Endelman, June 2019), https://www.edelman.com/research/trust-barometer-special-report-in-brands-we-trust.

7. "Consumer Intelligence Series: Protect.me," (PWC/CIScyber, 2017), https://www.fisglobal.com/-/media/fisglobal/worldpay/docs/insights/consumer-intelligence-series-protectme.pdf.

8. Reichheld, *The Ultimate Question*.

9. John Goodman, *Strategic Customer Service: Managing the Customer Experience to Increase Positive Word of Mouth, Build Loyalty, and Maximize Profits* (AMACOM, 2009).

10. Tom Puthiyamadam and José Reyes, "Experience Is Everything: Here's How to Get It Right" (PwC, 2018), https://www.pwc.com/us/en/zz-test/assets/pwc-consumer-intelligence-series-customer-experience.pdf#page=9.

11. Mark Taylor et al., "The Disconnected Customer: What Digital Customer Experience Leaders Teach Us about Reconnecting with Customers" (Capgemini Digital Transformation Institute, June 2017), https://www.capgemini.com/in-en/wp-content/uploads/sites/6/2017/08/the_disconnected_customer-what_digital_customer_experience_leaders_teach_us_about_reconnecting_with_customers.pdf.

Chapter Seven

1. Frederick Winslow Taylor, *The Principles of Scientific Management* (New York; London: Harper & Brothers, 1911).
2. Christoph Roser, "Where Lean Went Wrong – A Historical Perspective" *All About Lean* (blog), May 16, 2017, https://www.allaboutlean.com/where-lean-went-wrong/.
3. Thomas Davenport, "The Fad That Forgot People," *Fast Company*, October 31, 1995, https://www.fastcompany.com/26310/fad-forgot-people.
4. Veronica Krieg, "What Is the Cost of Employee Turnover in Your Contact Center?," *Sharpen* (blog), May 14, 2019, https://sharpencx.com/blog/what-is-the-cost-of-employee-turnover/.
5. William Hollingsworth Whyte, *The Organization Man* (New York: Simon and Schuster Inc., 1956).
6. Doc Childre and Deborah Rozman, *Transforming Stress: The HeartMath Solution for Relieving Worry, Fatigue, and Tension,* (Oakland, CA: New Harbinger Publications, March 2005).
7. David Whyte, *The Heart Aroused: Poetry and the Preservation of the Soul in Corporate America* (New York: Currency Doubleday, 1996).
8. Amy C. Edmondson, *The Fearless Organization: Creating Psychological Safety in the Workplace for Learning, Innovation, and Growth* (Hoboken: Wiley, 2018).
9. Brad Blanton, *Radical Honesty: How to Transform Your Life by Telling the Truth*, (Stanley, VA: Sparrowhawk Publications, March 2005).
10. Sarah Kerruish et al., *General Magic*, Documentary, 2019.
11. "General Magic," in *Wikipedia, The Free Encyclopedia*, May 27, 2021, https://en.wikipedia.org/w/index.php?title=General_Magic&oldid=1025411848.
12. Alexis C. Madrigal, "The iPhone Was Inevitable," *The Atlantic*, June 29, 2017, https://www.theatlantic.com/technology/archive/2017/06/the-iphone-was-inevitable/531963/.

Chapter Eight

1. B. Joseph Pine and James H. Gilmore, *The Experience Economy: Competing for Customer Time, Attention, and Money* (Boston, Massachusetts: Harvard Business Review Press, 2019).
2. Simon Dumont, "The Difference between UI and UX, According to Designer and Maze CEO, Jonathan Widawski," *Maze* (blog), July 17, 2021, https://maze.co/ui-vs-ux/.
3. Sarah Perez, "Creative Ways to Host a Virtual Party for Kids," (*Tech Crunch*, June 6, 2020), https://techcrunch.com/2020/04/06/creative-ways-to-host-a-virtual-birthday-party-for-kids/.

4. Addie Joseph, "The Coronavirus Pandemic Is Changing the Way People Celebrate Major Events and Holidays—Here's How They're Adapting," CNBC, April 17, 2020, https://www.cnbc.com/2020/04/18/coronavirus-pandemic-changes-the-way-people-celebrate-holidays.html.

5. "Personalization & Empathy in Customer Experience: Multinational Consumer Survey" (Genesys, June 2020), https://www.genesys.com/report/the-connected-customer-experience.

6. "Blindness and Vision Impairment," World Health Organization, February 26, 2021, https://www.who.int/news-room/fact-sheets/detail/blindness-and-visual-impairment.

7. Mark Wilson, "Starbucks Is about to Look a Lot Different—and COVID-19 Is Only Part of the Reason Why," Fast Company, June 10, 2020, https://www.fastcompany.com/90514230/starbucks-is-about-to-look-a-lot-different-and-covid-19-is-only-part-of-the-reason-why.

8. Danny Klein, "How COVID-19 Made Starbucks a Stronger Restaurant Chain," QSR Magazine, July 28, 2021, https://www.qsrmagazine.com/fast-food/how-covid-19-made-starbucks-stronger-restaurant-chain.

9. Ben Spicer, "Walmart Offering Free Virtual Summer Camp for Kids Using Star-Studded Cast," KSAT, July 15, 2020, https://www.ksat.com/news/local/2020/07/15/walmart-offering-free-virtual-summer-camp-for-kids-using-star-studded-cast/.

10. Kaila Mathis, "Walmart Wants to Salvage Summer With Drive-In Movie Theaters and Virtual Summer Camp," AdWeek (blog), July 6, 2020, https://www.adweek.com/brand-marketing/walmart-salvage-summer-drive-in-movie-theaters-virtual-summer-camp/.

11. "We're What's Next for Home Improvement Retail," Lowe's Innovation Labs, accessed September 1, 2021, https://www.lowesinnovationlabs.com.

12. Alison E. Berman, "Lowe's Joins Made In Space to Bring First Commercial Grade 3D Printer to Space," Singularity Hub (blog), October 30, 2015, https://singularityhub.com/2015/10/30/lowes-joins-made-in-space-to-bring-first-commercial-grade-3d-printer-to-space/.

13. "First Retailer on Orbit: Lowe's and Made In Space Send 3D Printer to Space Station," CollectSPACE, March 22, 2016, http://www.collectspace.com/news/news-032216a-lowes-madeinspace-3d-printer.html.

14. Liz Welch, "How Casper Became a $100 Million Company in Less Than Two Years," Inc. Magazine, February 25, 2016, https://www.inc.com/magazine/201603/liz-welch/casper-changing-mattress-industry.html.

15. "How Casper Uses AI to Create a Bot for Insomniacs," The Customer Collection, accessed September 1, 2021, https://www.thecustomercollection.com/practice/how-casper-uses-ai-to-create-a-bot-for-insomniacs.

16. Tanya Dua, "Casper's New Late-Night Low-Tech Chatbot Entertains Insomniacs," Digiday (blog), September 23, 2016, https://digiday.com/marketing/caspers-new-late-night-low-tech-chatbot-entertains-insomniacs/.

17. Joseph A. Schumpeter, Capitalism, Socialism, and Democracy (Rediscovered Books, 2014).

Chapter Nine

1. Kathryn Tyler, "Measuring Employee Engagement During a Crisis," *SHRM - RH Magazine,* November 30, 2020, https://www.shrm.org/hr-today/news/hr-magazine/winter2020/pages/measuring-employee-engagement-during-covid-19.aspx.

2. Alison DeNisco Rayome, "4 Ways IoT Can Improve the Customer Experience," TechRepublic, March 16, 2018, https://www.techrepublic.com/article/4-ways-iot-can-improve-the-customer-experience/.

3. Blake Morgan, "5 Customer Experience Lessons From USAA," Forbes.com, June 1, 2020, https://www.forbes.com/sites/blakemorgan/2020/06/01/5-customer-experience-lessons-from-usaa/?sh=25afc5b37e54.

Chapter Ten

1. Harvard Business Review Analytic Services, "The EI Advantage: Driving Innovation and Business Success through the Power of Emotional Intelligence," *Harvard Business Review* (research report), August 12, 2019, https://hbr.org/resources/pdfs/comm/fourseasons/TheEIAdvantage.pdf.

2. Marcus Buckingham and Curt Coffman, *First, Break All the Rules: What the World's Greatest Managers Do Differently* (Washington, D.C.: Gallup Press, 2016).

3. Kevin E. Kruse, *Employee Engagement 2.0: How to Motivate Your Team for High Performance,* 2nd edition (CreateSpace Independent Publishing Platform, 2012).

4. Reuters, "Wells Fargo CEO Ruffles Feathers with Comments about Diverse Talent," *NBC News,* September 22, 2020, https://www.nbcnews.com/news/nbcblk/wells-fargo-ceo-ruffles-feathers-comments-about-diverse-talent-n1240739.

5. Laura Sherbin and Ripa Rashid, "Diversity Doesn't Stick Without Inclusion," *Harvard Business Review,* February 1, 2017, https://hbr.org/2017/02/diversity-doesnt-stick-without-inclusion.

6. Scott E. Page, *Difference: How the Power of Diversity Creates Better Groups, Firms, Schools, and Societies* (Princeton, N.J.; Woodstock: Princeton University Press, 2008).

7. David Easley and Jon Kleinberg, *Networks, Crowds, and Markets: Reasoning about a Highly Connected World* (Cambridge: Cambridge University Press, 2010).

8. Lu Hong and Scott E. Page, "Groups of Diverse Problem Solvers Can Outperform Groups of High-Ability Problem Solvers," *PNAS - Proceedings of the National Academy of Sciences* 101, no. 46 (November 16, 2004): 16385–89, https://doi.org/10.1073/pnas.0403723101.

9. Alex "Sandy" Pentland, "Beyond the Echo Chamber," *Harvard Business Review,* November 2013, https://hbr.org/2013/11/beyond-the-echo-chamber.

10. Sylvia Ann Hewlett et al., "Innovation, Diversity and Market Growth" (New York: Coqual, September 2013).

11. Ibid.

12. Ibid.

13. Ibid.

14. David Rock and Heidi Grant, "Why Diverse Teams Are Smarter," *Harvard Business Review,* November 4, 2016, https://hbr.org/2016/11/why-diverse-teams-are-smarter.

15. Alison E. Berman, "The Motivating Power of a Massive Transformative Purpose," *Singularity Hub* (blog), November 8, 2016, https://singularityhub.com/2016/11/08/the-motivating-power-of-a-massive-transformative-purpose/.

16. Simon Sinek, *Start With Why: How Great Leaders Inspire Everyone to Take Action* (New York: Portfolio/Penguin, 2011).

17. Salim Ismail, "MTP: The Heartbeat of Every ExO," *Growth Institute* (blog), accessed September 1, 2021, https://blog.growthinstitute.com/exo/massive-transformative-purpose.

18. Salim Ismail et al., *Exponential Organizations: Why New Organizations Are Ten Times Better, Faster, and Cheaper than Yours (and What to Do about It)* (New York: Diversion, 2014).

19. Peter M. Senge, *The Fifth Discipline: The Art and Practice of The Learning Organization* (New York: Currency Doubleday, 2006).

20. Kim Armstrong, "'I Feel Your Pain': The Neuroscience of Empathy," *APS Observer* 31, no. 1 (December 29, 2017), https://www.psychologicalscience.org/observer/neuroscience-empathy.

21. London Image Institute, "How Much of Communication Is Nonverbal?," *London Image Institute* (blog), March 23, 2020, https://londonimageinstitute.com/how-much-of-communication-is-nonverbal/.

22. Shelly Fan, "This Is Where Empathy Lives in the Brain, and How It Works," *Singularity Hub* (blog), February 2, 2021, https://singularityhub.com/2021/02/02/this-is-where-empathy-lives-in-the-brain-and-how-it-works/.

23. Karla McLaren, *The Art of Empathy: A Complete Guide to Life's Most Essential Skill* (Boulder, Colorado: Sounds True, 2013).

24. Helen Riess M.D. and Liz Neporent, *The Empathy Effect: Seven Neuroscience-Based Keys for Transforming the Way We Live, Love, Work, and Connect Across Differences* (Boulder, Colorado: Sounds True, 2018), https://www.overdrive.com/search?q=11C8AC1C-C7E8-4B29-9819-631062BBEE86.

25. Shirzad Chamine, *Positive Intelligence: Why Only 20% of Teams and Individuals Achieve Their True Potential and How You Can Achieve Yours* (Austin, Texas: Greenleaf Book Group, 2012).

Chapter Eleven

1. Natalie Petouhoff PhD, Tamra Chandler, and Beth Montag-Schmaltz, "The Business Impact of Change Management," *Graziadio Business Review* 9, no. 3 (2006), https://gbr.pepperdine.edu/2010/08/the-business-impact-of-change-management/.

2. Ellyn J. Shook and Mark A. Knickrehm, "Reworking The Revolution: Are You Ready to Compete as Intelligent Technology Meets Human Ingenuity to Create the Future Workforce?" (Accenture Research, 2018), https://www.accenture.com/_acnmedia/PDF-69/Accenture-Reworking-the-Revolution-Jan-2018-POV.pdf.

3. Petouhoff PhD, Chandler, and Montag-Schmaltz, "The Business Impact."

4. Ibid.

5. Ibid.

6. Ibid.

7. Ibid., and Daniel T. Holt, Achilles A. Armenakis, Hubert S. Feild and Stanley G. Harris, "Readiness for Organizational Change: The Systematic Development of a Scale," Journal of Applied Behavioral Science, 2007 Vol. 43; 232, http://jab.sagepub.com/cgi/content/abstract/43/2/232, and Maria Vakola, "Multilevel Readiness to Organizational Change: A Conceptual Approach," Journal of Change Management, 2013 Vol. 13; 1, 96–109, https://citeseerx.ist.psu.edu/viewdoc/download?doi=10.1.1.1077.6350&rep=rep1&type=pdf.

8. Barbari Griesse, "The Influence of Age on Change Management," AVAAP (blog), July 7, 2020, https://avaap.com/2020/07/07/the-influence-of-age-on-change-management/.

Chapter Twelve

1. "John Boyd (Military Strategist)," in Wikipedia, The Free Encyclopedia, August 19, 2021, https://en.wikipedia.org/w/index.php?title=John_Boyd_(military_strategist)&oldid=1039565624.

2. W. Edwards Deming, The Essential Deming: Leadership Principles from the Father of Quality, ed. Joyce Orsini and Diana Deming Cahill, 1st edition (New York: McGraw-Hill Education, 2012).

3. David Weinberger et al., The Cluetrain Manifesto, 1st edition (Cambridge, Mass.: Basic Books, 2000).

4. Sons of Maxwell, United Breaks Guitars, YouTube Video, 2009, https://www.youtube.com/watch?v=5YGc4zOqozo.

5. Ravi Sawhney, "Broken Guitar Has United Playing the Blues to the Tune of $180 Million," Fast Company, July 30, 2009, https://www.fastcompany.com/1320152/broken-guitar-has-united-playing-blues-tune-180-million.

6. Bryan Adams, "This Avoidable Situation Is Costing US Businesses $11 Billion Every Year," INC., December 10, 2018, https://www.inc.com/bryan-adams/this-avoidable-situation-is-costing-us-businesses-11-billion-every-single-year.html.

7. Gabrielle Smith, "Employee Retention: The Real Cost of Losing an Employee," PeopleKeep (blog), September 17, 2021, https://www.peoplekeep.com/blog/employee-retention-the-real-cost-of-losing-an-employee.

8. "Watson Wyatt's WorkUSA Survey Identifies Steps to Keep Employees Engaged & Productive," KnowledgePay, 2009, https://knowledgepay.com/workusa0809/.

9. Shelly Kramer, "Business Success and the Role Employee Engagement Plays," Future of Work (blog), May 2, 2017, https://fowmedia.com/business-success-role-employee-engagement-plays/.

Closing Remarks

1. "What's Your Customer Effort Score?" Gartner, November 5, 2019, https://www.gartner.com/smarterwithgartner/unveiling-the-new-and-improved-customer-effort-score.

INDEX

Index